Every Which Way

CROCHET BORDERS

139 PATTERNS *for Customized Edgings*

Edie Eckman

Dedication

To Gwen Steege, for everything

The mission of Storey Publishing is to serve our customers by publishing practical information that encourages personal independence in harmony with the environment.

Edited by Gwen Steege
Art direction and book design by Jessica Armstrong
Text production by Liseann Karandisecky
Indexed by Eileen Clawson

Cover and interior photography by John Polak, except back cover, author photo by © Kelly Nuss Photography and pages 14, 162, and 170 by Mars Vilaubi
Patterns and diagrams by Karen Manthey
Glossary illustrations by Alison Kolesar

Storey Publishing
210 MASS MoCA Way
North Adams, MA 01247
storey.com

Printed in China by Toppan Leefung Printing Ltd.
10 9 8 7 6 5 4 3 2 1

Library of Congress Cataloging-in-Publication Data

Names: Eckman, Edie, author.
Title: Every which way crochet borders : 139 patterns for customized edgings / by Edie Eckman.
Description: North Adams, MA : Storey Publishing, 2017. | Includes index.
Identifiers: LCCN 2016036409 (print) | LCCN 2016036991 (ebook) | ISBN 9781612127408 (hardcover with concealed wire-o : alk. paper) | ISBN 9781612127415 (ebook)
Subjects: LCSH: Crocheting—Patterns. | Borders, Ornamental (Decorative arts)
Classification: LCC TT820 .E355 2017 (print) | LCC TT820 (ebook) | DDC 746.43/4—dc23
LC record available at https://lccn.loc.gov/2016036409

Contents

DESIGN CONCEPTS 1

Choices: Form Follows Function ⋆ Customizing Your
Borders ⋆ The Power of Swatching ⋆ Crocheted Border
Mechanics ⋆ Ending Rounds ⋆ About the Patterns

BORDER DESIGNS 31

*A collection of 139 borders, from narrow
and simple to wide and complex*

Going 'Round the Bend

You might think that with the 150 borders that appear in *Around the Corner Crochet Borders,* I would have used up all the border designs that I had floating around in my head, but apparently that was not the case. You might even say that I'm crazy about borders!

Here are 139 additional borders, each of them engineered to flow smoothly around the 90-degree corners that you'll find on blankets, sweaters, washcloths, and other items. No matter what your need — lacy, solid, textured, subtle, bold, narrow, medium, or wide — you'll find a border to fit it.

To encourage browsing, the borders are arranged on the following pages in no particular order. Browsing can pay off in a big way. You may think you want a ruffled edging, but when you see that textured border, you'll realize it's just the thing!

If you really have your mind made up, however, I've tagged each entry with attributes to help you quickly find what you are looking for. Use the lists beginning on page 204 to scan the borders categories: reversible, wide, medium, narrow, undulating, straight, motifs, open/lacy, layered, fringy, and textured.

Crocheted borders work on many types of fabric, including crocheted, knitted, and woven. You can add a crocheted border to non-woven fabric, such as felt or fleece, and you can make separate borders and sew or glue them onto other types of material.

As with *Around the Corner Crochet Borders,* I hope you'll use *Every Which Way Crochet Borders* as a starting point for discovering new techniques and for jump-starting your imagination.

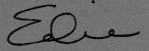

DESIGN CONCEPTS

Choosing a border design may seem overwhelming. After all, there are so many to choose from! Your choice will be determined by the project, your personal taste, and the taste of the person who will be using it. You may just go with your instincts when choosing a border, but if you want a more structured approach, you might keep in mind some of the following principles.

Choices: Form Follows Function

Simple, narrow borders may serve mostly functional tasks: hiding yarn ends, stabilizing edges, and serving as button and buttonhole bands. They may be the best choice to frame a throw or shawl or other item that is particularly busy, multicolored, or highly textured. In other words, for these projects, let the main fabric be the main act and the border be the supporting cast.

More decorative borders, on the other hand, may *be* the focal point of a design, or at least may serve to enhance and complement the main fabric. As a matter of fact, some borders are so versatile that they can be used for more than just borders! That fringy, dangly border that might not be the best choice for a much-used child's blankie might be perfect made into a necklace.

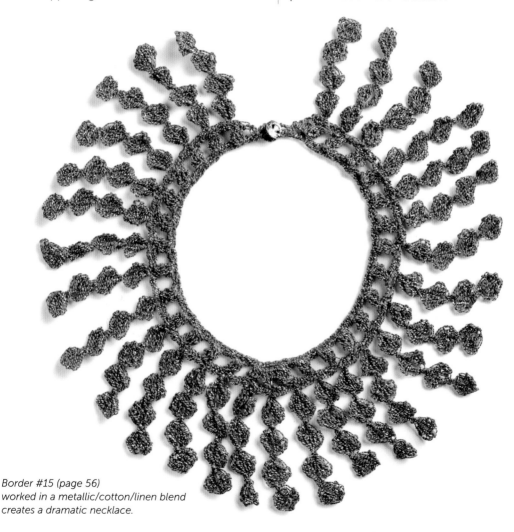

Border #15 (page 56)
worked in a metallic/cotton/linen blend
creates a dramatic necklace.

COMPLEMENT VS. CONTRAST

Consider choosing a border that picks up some aspect of the main fabric.

This border consists of granny squares and would look terrific on an afghan composed of granny stripes.

A very plain fabric may be enhanced by a fancy border, as demonstrated by this fan-based design on a shell-stitch fabric.

This example uses the same stitch pattern as the main fabric, but with reversed colors.

A crazy, multicolored fabric might need the settling influence of a solid-colored border.

A Matter of Scale

Pay attention to the scale of your border as it relates to whatever you are attaching it to. Avoid overwhelming a tiny project with a too-wide border, as seen in the photo at the left. (Unless, of course, that's the look you are going for!)

The Potential in Color

Colors play a very important part in design; a simple change of color can completely change the look of a border, as you can see in the examples on the facing page. A solid color used throughout can highlight the shape of the overall design, while a multicolor yarn may confuse and muddy that same shape. Using different solid colors in separate rounds can highlight individual stitches or groups of stitches. The order of the colors can matter; two colors may seem to go well in theory, but have unexpectedly unhappy results when placed next to each other. The color of the final round sets the tone of the entire border. You may need to play with color placement to ensure that the final round stands up to its role as both design anchor and focal point. And of course, we all have color preferences. Don't dismiss a border in the book based on color alone. You might love it in a different color!

This 7"/18 cm square washcloth is overwhelmed by its wide border, making the washcloth somewhat difficult to use for its intended purpose.

DESIGN CONCEPTS

WHAT A DIFFERENCE COLORS CAN MAKE

Border #8 (page 48) in the original solid (A), and in an entirely different solid color (B), worked in a multicolor (C), and worked with three different colors, on different rows (D)

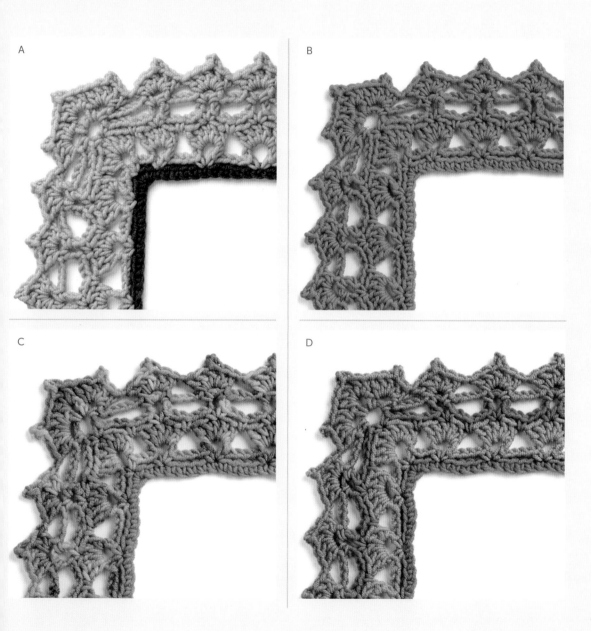

COLORS CALL ATTENTION TO STRUCTURE

Working in two colors highlights the construction of the border on the top (A), whereas working in one color simplifies the appearance and highlights the shape of the border on the bottom (B).

Color choices make the border on the top (C) appear to have three elements, while the one on the bottom (D) seems to have only two.

A

C

B

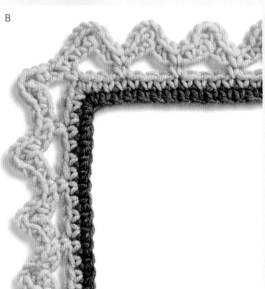

D

It's All About the Yarn

Beyond color choice — or perhaps before it — is yarn choice. Different fibers and yarn weights will make the same border look very different. When working on crocheted, knit, or woven fabrics, you will usually be using the same yarn that was used in the main fabric. This ensures that the weight and scale of the yarn works with the design. However, when this is not the case — either because the border is going on a non-yarn background or you are simply changing the yarn — you'll want to consider the scale of the border yarn and stitches and how they relate to the thing the border is attached to.

ABOVE: *The laceweight yarn border is much lighter and drapier than the heavy fabric that it is attached to.*

BELOW: *Border #16 (page 58) in laceweight mohair (A), in cotton thread (B), in smooth worsted wool (C), and in bulky alpaca (D)*

CROCHETED BORDERS
on Fine Fabric, Terry Cloth, and Knitwear

Two delicate antique batiste handkerchiefs with thread crochet trim; note that the border is crocheted directly onto the fabric (A); DK-weight linen border on a purchased terry cloth washcloth (B); DK-weight knitted shawl with a crocheted border in contrasting-color yarn (C).

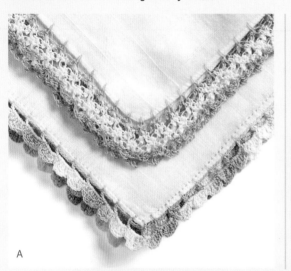

A

B

C

Customizing Your Borders

You have many options when it comes to customizing your border. Many borders have certain simple components in common. Examples of these elements can be found on pages 32–39. These elements may be an integral part of the design, or they may serve as a way to extend or deepen the border. They can be used on their own to subtly finish an edge. Often they may be combined with each other and with other elements to come up with new border combinations. Once you start thinking about individual components of a border, you'll see that it's fun to adapt or design your own. Here are some ways to get started.

Add Preliminary Rounds

Make a border wider or more complex by adding preliminary rounds of one simple border before working the final fancier rounds. Just remember that when you add preliminary rounds, you will be adding stitches at each corner and thus increasing the number of stitches on each side, so when it's time to start the final border, you may need to make adjustments to fit the stitch multiple needed. Furthermore, the added element may begin with a different multiple than that needed for the original border.

Add New Elements

Consider adding additional elements, such as reverse single crochet or picots. Here are examples of both.

REVERSE SINGLE CROCHET

Border #14 page 55 is the same as Border #13 page 54, but on Border #14 (B, below), Round 2 was worked into the back loops only, leaving free loops available to work a round of reverse single crochet. (For an illustration of reverse single crochet, see page 214.)

A

B

CASE STUDY: *Widening a Border*

To make Border #60 (page 113) wider, use Element G (page 35). Adding this element onto the base round adds 2 stitches to each side of the base round, but I need to end up with the called-for base round *after* adding the additional element. Here's how to think through the problem for the examples shown at right:

Original base round multiple on each side:
   Multiple of 4 + 3 + corners

Element G adds 2 stitches to each side, therefore:
   Multiple of 4 + (3 + 2) + corners = Multiple of 4 + 5 + corners

(Note that this is the same as: Multiple of 4 + 1 + corners)

This tells me that the number of stitches *after* adding the Element round is a multiple of 4 + 1 + corners. If this multiple worked for my chosen border (#60), then I can just work that border as written directly onto my Element round.
   Unfortunately, what I need is a multiple of 4 + 3 + corners, or 2 more stitches per side than I end up with after working the Element round. I have two choices:

• Fudge stitches (see Fudging Stitch Counts on page 23) as I work Round 1 of Border #60 onto the Element round, or

• Add 2 stitches per side by working another round of single crochet or another Element G (that is, another Element round) between the first Element and Round 1 of the border.

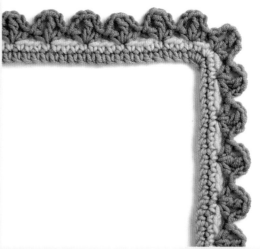

Original border #60

Same border (#60) with additional round(s) added, to match the original

PICOT REFINEMENTS

The oh-so-straight Border #5 (page 44) changes its shape with the addition of picots. Picots are often used to add tiny points to borders or to soften the line of a straight border. However, the appearance of the picot can change subtly, depending on the method used to create it. The generic instruction for picot is usually "ch 3, slip st in third chain from hook," but there are other ways of creating picots. If you aren't happy with the appearance of the picot created in that way, substitute one of these refinements, which are used throughout the book.

Variations A and B can be used in any circumstance a picot is called for, whether surrounded by chains, stitches, or a combination of both. Variations C and D can be used when there is a stitch immediately preceding the picot.

PICOT VARIATION A

Chain 3, slip stitch in third chain from hook.

PICOT VARIATION B

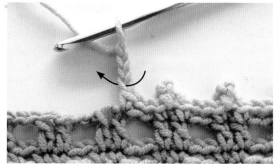

Chain 4, slip stitch in fourth chain from hook.

PICOT VARIATION C

Chain 3, slip stitch in stitch at base of chain.

PICOT VARIATION D

Chain 3, slip stitch in top of stitch below chain and in side of same stitch together.

When surrounded by chains, it would seem reasonable to place the picot in the center of a chain-space, as in "(chain 3, picot, chain 3)," but in reality this often visually sets the picot off-center (F, below). Instead, the instructions in this book often rely on a more visually appealing placement of the picot, as in "(ch 2, picot, ch 3)" (E, below).

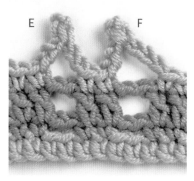

*Left (E): Ch 2, picot, ch 3.
Right (F): Ch 3, picot, ch 3.*

Combine Borders

Take elements from one or more borders and combine them. Since you'll have to engineer your way around the corners, you may find it helpful to see how the corner is handled on each round of your combined border and duplicate that as closely as possible. You may find it helpful to sketch the corners in advance on paper, using crochet symbols, a pencil, and an eraser. (You'll mostly likely need that eraser!)

Go 3-D

Add a layer of dimension by working back loop stitches on one or more rounds, then use the free loops in front to add another round of stitches to match or complement the other stitches in the border or use other post stitches or "working in the back bump" of stitches to add texture. For example, to make Border #13 (page 54) more dimensional, I worked Round 2 in back loop single crochet, then added a Round 4 to match Round 3. Border #21 (page 63) uses "back bump" single crochet to pop the tops of stitches to the front. (For an illustration of back bump, see page 210.)

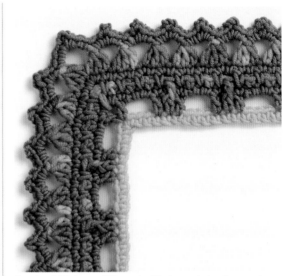

Border #20 (page 62) worked in its entirety, then a single crochet "base round," then Border #18 (page 60) worked in its entirety

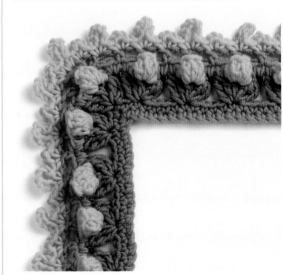

Rounds 1–4 of Border #28 (page 74), then Round 1 of Border #87 (page 154), adapting (fudging) a bit for stitch multiples, finished with Round 2 of Border #87 as written

FABDQs: (Frequently Asked Border Design Questions)

Years of teaching crochet and hanging out with crocheters have helped me develop responses to the questions I hear most often. This FAQ goes something like this:

Q *Can I use a different yarn from the yarn used in the main project?*

A Try it and see! If you don't like the results, rip it out and pick a different yarn.

Q *I want to use my own colors for this design. Which colors should I use?*

A It's your project. Try several colors and see which you like. If you don't like the results, try a different combination.

Q *Can I put a fancy border on my ripple-stitch afghan?*

A It's going to be tricky. The straight side edges aren't a problem, but the peaks and valleys of the rippled edges mean you'll have to do a good bit of experimentation to get any kind of fancy border to lie flat. Give it a try, but if it doesn't work out, you can always just stick to a simple edging and let the beautiful main fabric shine.

Q *What would happen if I . . .*

A Interesting idea! Try it and see. If you don't like the results, rip it out and try something else.

Are you getting the idea? You shouldn't be afraid to experiment with crochet. It's *so* easy to rip out a few (or many) stitches if you aren't happy with what's happening. Why are you crocheting, anyway? Isn't it partly to make something beautiful that is uniquely yours? You are the boss of your crochet, so act like it and tell it what to do. But, like a good boss, be willing to listen to what it's trying to tell you, and be willing to learn from it.

The Power of Swatching

Customizing your borders is where swatching comes in. "Swatch" is often an unwelcome concept, but many of the most skilled, talented, and creative designers and crocheters I know are committed serial swatchers. This is because a swatch serves so many useful purposes.

What is a swatch? It's a small piece of sample fabric made in the same yarn and with the same hook that you plan to use in your finished piece. It can reveal a lot besides your gauge. You can practice different stitches and color arrangements — as well as try out different borders to see which combinations are going to work best with your project — without the time and effort involved in doing a full-size sample.

It's best not to rip out your swatch, but to hang onto it at least until the project is finished. If you run short of yarn, you can always use the yarn from the swatch, but in the meantime, the swatch serves as a reference and reminder of what you are working on.

Border swatches can be worked on the swatch that you used for your main project. If you didn't swatch for the main project, or if the project is too small to need a swatch, you can always just put your border swatch around the corner or along the edge of the main project. You'll have to rip this one out before you work the final edging, of course, so be sure to take notes on what you decide to do. Once it's ripped out, you won't be able to refer to it again.

Crocheted Border Mechanics

The design of a border is important, but the execution of that border is equally important. Make sure that beautiful border is beautifully executed by understanding some of these best practices.

Working a Base Round/Row

Although it's tempting to start crocheting your fancy border directly onto the main fabric, it's a good idea to set a foundation by working a base round or row first. This base round will stabilize the edge and create a smooth surface on which to set your decorative stitches. It also sets up the stitch multiple for the first row of the border design and establishes corner stitches.

If possible, this base round should be worked in the same yarn or a similar yarn as the one used in the main fabric. If you can't use the same yarn, try to match the size and heft of the yarn to that of the main fabric. And if it's not being stitched directly onto a fabric, but is being attached by some other means, attempt to match the feel, drape, and scale of the border to the main project. The base round should serve as a happy transition between the main project and the border.

A round of single crochet usually works well as a base. Take care to work the base-round stitches evenly, in the same color as the main fabric whenever possible. The base round is usually worked with the right side of the fabric facing, but occasionally you may have trouble with your border tending to flip toward the front. If this happens, work the base round with the wrong side facing, then turn and work the border rounds with the right side facing.

The instructions in this book give a stitch count for the base round, assuming the base round is the

Base round on this swatch was worked with wrong side facing to ensure that border lies flat.

round immediately preceding the border design. The instructions don't indicate where to start the base round or how to work it; refer to the general directions that follow (pages 15–19). The base round can be seen in the photographed samples and is indicated by the light gray single crochet stitch symbols in each diagram.

CHOOSING COLOR FOR BASE ROUNDS

If you work a base round in a color that contrasts with the main piece, irregularities and skipped stitches may become obvious, especially when worked along a selvedge (see example A, below). Although the second round of stitches looks nice and even, a discerning eye may be unhappy with the unevenness of the first round.

In the swatch B, below, the base round was worked in the same color as the main piece, allowing the uneven stitches to blend in for a tidier appearance.

Placing Stitches in the Base Round

The specifics of stitch placement will vary based on the composition of your main fabric and the size and weight of the yarn and hook. Read on for suggested best practices for various border scenarios, but as always, use your judgment for best results!

WORKING INTO THE CROCHETED MAIN FABRIC

Determine the optimal spacing for the stitches, based on your personal gauge. Use the following as guidelines only:

- Make one single crochet in every single-crochet row-end.
- Make two single crochets per double-crochet row-end, three single crochets for every two double-crochet row-ends, or some other ratio that matches your single-crochet stitch gauge to your double-crochet row gauge.
- When working along a diagonal edge, you may have to work more stitches than you would for a straight edge. You'll have to play around until you find the right ratio for that particular angle.
- Concave (inward bending) curves will require a bit of decreasing to make a smooth base round, while convex (outward bending) curves require increases to lie flat.
- Sharply pointing edges such as you find in certain chevron- or ripple-stitch patterns require increases at the "peaks" and decreases at the "valleys" to lie flat.

Stop every few stitches and take a critical look at your work so far. If it doesn't look great, rip it out and try again. Get it right now, before you've added more rounds and it's too late!

WORKING A BORDER INTO CROCHETED FABRIC

On a piece that was worked in the round, all of the stitches will appear the same: insert the hook under both loops throughout.

On a piece that was worked back and forth in rows, insert the hook under both loops of the last row and under both loops of the foundation chain, if available (see A below).

A

When working into a foundation chain without two chain loops available because of the way the foundation was worked, insert under a single loop only (B).

B

Along the side edges (selvedges), insert the hook into row-end stitches rather than into the spaces between stitches (C).

C

WORKING INTO A KNITTED FABRIC

Experiment to find the optimal distance between stitches on the selvedges by using the following *as guidelines only*. You'll need to discover what works in your situation. Does it look terrific so far? If you can't answer yes, rip it out and try again.

- Two single crochets for every two or three stitches on horizontal edges.
- Two single crochets for every three stockinette stitch rows or three single crochets for every five stockinette stitch rows.
- One single crochet in every garter stitch ridge.
- For curves and diagonal lines, follow the same rules of thumb as for crocheted fabric, experimenting to get a flat edge.

On the bound-off edge, insert the hook under both loops of the bound-off stitches (D, below), skipping stitches or working single crochet 2 together as necessary to allow the edge to lie flat.

D

DESIGN CONCEPTS

On the cast-on edge, insert the hook under two strands of the cast-on stitch, if available, or under one strand, spacing stitches as for the bound-off edge (E, below).

E

On selvedges, insert the hook into the center of the edge stitch or into the space just beyond the edge stitch, taking care to make each stitch an equal distance in from the edge of the fabric (F, below). Try to match both the vertical distance "in" and the horizontal distance between stitches to the base-round stitches on the cast-on and bound-off edges.

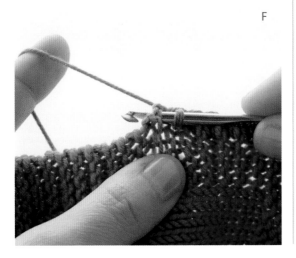

F

WORKING INTO NON-WOVEN FLEECE

Experimentation is key! Use small samples of your fleece to determine the best method before trying it on the main fabric. Because you'll be making holes in the fabric, it's harder to change your mind with fleece than it is with knitting or crochet, so swatching is key.

Space stitches equidistant from each other at an appropriate space for your gauge. Depending on the size of the hook and yarn, base-round stitches may be placed in one of the following ways:

Stitch directly into the fleece, using a crochet hook with a sharp point on the head. There are crochet hooks made especially for this purpose, but they may be too small for your yarn. If necessary, use a smaller hook to pierce the fabric and pull up a loop, then place the loop on the desired size hook to complete the stitch. You can use a small steel crochet hook, or the specially designed Edgit hook, which has an extra-sharp tip.

Because the small crochet hook may be too small to crochet with anything other than thread, you'll have to do a two-stage single crochet to accommodate the thickness of the yarn. Begin with a loop on the regular hook, pierce the fabric with the tiny hook, then carefully draw up a loop through the fabric with the small hook. Place that loop onto the larger hook and complete the stitch.

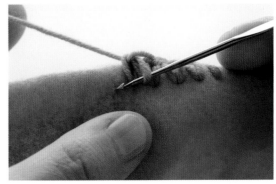

Using a small hook to pierce the fleece and draw the yarn through

Punch small holes in the fleece to allow the hook to pass through. *Note:* You may want to use a rotary cutter blade that punches evenly spaced holes in the fabric.

Using a rotary cutter to pierce holes in fleece

First work blanket stitch (see Glossary, page 210) or embroidered chain stitch (see page 211) into the fleece, and then use those stitches as a base for the crochet. If necessary for tidy stitching, space these stitches farther apart than the gauge of your single crochet stitches, then work two single crochets into some of the stitches at regular intervals.

Working single crochet into blanket stitch

Working single crochet into embroidered chain stitch

Whether you stitch directly into the fabric or into a blanket stitch or chain stitch, work far enough into the fabric to get a secure grip on the fabric, but not so far in that it becomes difficult to keep the fleece from shifting and gathering in toward the center.

WORKING INTO WOVEN FABRIC

As with non-woven fabric, experimentation is important. Use your swatch!

Edges must be finished in some way to prevent raveling. On lightweight commercial fabric, trim selvedges, then fold and press a narrow single or double hem along all edges and sew in place, then use one of the methods described above to add the base row. Alternately, you may be able to simply machine zigzag or serge the edges and then work over them; this would be the preferred method for heavier commercial fabric.

This fabric was hemmed first before single crochet was worked over the hem.

On handwovens, secure the weft with a machine-stitched zigzag or serged stitch. For lighter-weight fabric, you may want to turn this edge under to create a single or double hem before adding the border. However, it may be possible to simply work the first row over the machine-stitching, covering and enclosing the raw edge with crochet stitches. Handwoven selvedges may be left alone. However, keep in mind that if some edges are hemmed prior to adding the border, and others are not, there will be a difference in the way the sides feel: the unhemmed edge may feel insubstantial compared to the hemmed edge.

Once potential raveling has been addressed, place the first round/row of single crochet stitches directly into the fabric, or use embroidered chain stitch (see page 211) or blanket stitch (see page 210) to connect the base row to the fabric.

Working single crochet over a serged edge of handwoven fabric

TROUBLESHOOTING FABRIC FLATNESS

Despite careful attention to creating a smooth, flat base round, adding a border can sometimes cause the main fabric to ripple or become wavy. There are several things that can cause this:

- The first round wasn't truly flat; it had too many or too few stitches.

- The border itself isn't truly flat, so the ruffling or waviness of the border radiates back into the fabric.

- The border is too heavy and overwhelms the fabric it is attached to.

Sometimes this problem doesn't appear until two or three rounds into the border, at which time you might be unwilling to rip out what you've done! If you can't bear to go back and start over to fix the problem at its source, perhaps you can find a way to decrease stitches on the later rounds of the border to help mitigate the problem. If the border is too heavy, however, there is probably no solution other than going back and choosing a different yarn and/or design. If you can't fix it and you aren't willing to start over, chalk it up to Lessons Learned and move on.

Too many stitches around this swatch caused ruffling and wavy edges.

Handling the Corners on a Base Round

No matter what fabric you are edging, the goal is to create a base round that lies flat and is evenly spaced. But what happens when you reach a corner? Any type of corner requires extra stitches in order to lie flat. For a single-crochet base round, place 3 stitches in each corner stitch to go around a 90-degree corner. As you work, place a removable marker in the center stitch of these 3 single crochet stitches. The marker indicates the corner stitch, which will be referenced on the first round of the border. Until you are comfortable identifying corner stitches by sight, it's wise to continue using a marker in each corner stitch or space, moving it up each round as you work.

A marked corner stitch

What happens when your corner isn't a right angle? Any acute angle (one that is "pointier" than 90 degrees) will require more than 3 single crochets for the base. An obtuse angle (one that is less pointy than 90 degrees) will require fewer than 3 single crochets. This becomes a bit problematic when the "more than 3" or "less than 3" means that you end up with an even number of stitches in your corner,

because that means your base round doesn't have a true corner stitch. There are a couple of ways to handle this dilemma:

- Simply designate one of the corner stitches as *the* corner.
- If you need to put more than 3 single crochets in the corner, spread out the extra stitch(es) on each side of the corner. You may have 2 single crochets immediately preceding the corner, 3 single crochets *in* the corner, and 1 single crochet immediately after the corner, for a total of 4 "corner" stitches. The marker would go in the center of the 3-single crochet group.

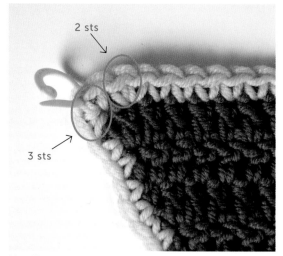

Handling an acute-angle corner

Stitch Multiples and
Why They Matter

Whether you are working in rounds on the perimeter of a project, or in back-and-forth rows, you want your design to be balanced, beginning and ending at the proper spot for the design. Where borders turn corners, you also want your corner treatment to actually land on the corner, so you must begin the round in the designated stitch as well (see Where to Begin the Round, page 22).

With each of the border patterns in the book, you'll find information on the stitch multiple needed, for example:

Base rnd, each side:
Multiple of x + y + corner stitches

You should read this as:

Base rnd, each side:
(Multiple of x) + y + corner stitches

Not as:

Base rnd, each side:
(Multiple of x + y) + corner stitches

IF YOU ARE WORKING IN THE ROUND WITH FOUR CORNERS, you'll do some simple math to determine the number of stitches needed on each side. Let's look at an example:

Border #86 (page 152) calls for a multiple of
8 + 7 + corner stitches

Begin by placing markers in each of the corner stitches. For each of the remaining sides, the number of base stitches along each side, not including those corner stitches, should be a multiple of 8 stitches, with a remainder of 7 stitches. Ideally, that would be one of the following numbers:

$(8 × 1) + 7 = 15$
$(8 × 2) + 7 = 23$
$(8 × 3) + 7 = 31$
and so on.

HOW DO YOU DETERMINE IF THE NUMBER OF STITCHES FITS THAT MULTIPLE? Let's say I have a blanket with a base round of 103 stitches on each short edge and 145 stitches on each long edge (plus my corner stitches). Take the number of stitches on one side, subtract the "plus" number, then divide by the multiple:

Short side:
103 stitches − 7 = 96
96 ÷ 8 = 12

Good! 103 is a multiple of 8 + 7, because my answer was a whole number.

Long side:
145 stitches − 7 = 138
138 ÷ 8 = 17.25

Oops! 17.25 is not a whole number, which means 145 is not a multiple of 8 + 7. We'll have to either change our base-round count on this side or do some fudging on the first round. More on fudging later (see Fudging Stitch Counts, page 23).

Let's rip out the base round and re-stitch it with either 143 or 151 stitches, as both of those are multiples of 8 + 7.

Where to Begin the Round

In order for each of the corners to land on the corner in the previous round, it's important not only to have the right stitch multiple, but also to begin the round in the right stitch. In the instructions for each pattern in the book, you'll see an indication of where the first stitch of Round 1 should go, counting from the corner stitch.

In the example below, you can see that the first stitch of Round 1 is made in the third stitch to the left of the corner stitch. Beginning and ending the round slightly away from the corner in this way makes the join less conspicuous.

Right-handed crocheters. The photo above right shows how to count stitches from right to left, which is the direction right-handed crocheters work. The marker is in the corner stitch; the stitch immediately to the left of the corner stitch is #1, the next stitch to the left is #2, and so on.

Left-handed crocheters. They live in a right-handed world, but work their crochet from left to right. Whenever a pattern instruction says "to right of" or "to left of," substitute the words "left" for "right"

RIGHT-HANDED COUNTING

LEFT-HANDED COUNTING

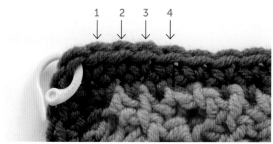

and "right" for "left." In the photo above, the marked stitch is the corner stitch; the stitch to the right of the corner stitch is #1, the next stitch to the right is #2, and so on.

EXAMPLE OF WHERE TO BEGIN ROUND 1

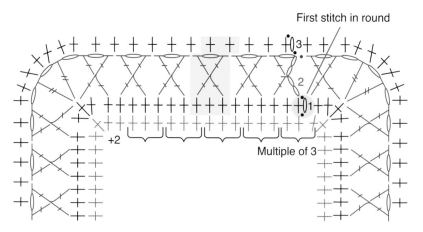

FUDGING STITCH COUNTS

If it's just too challenging to get exactly the right number of stitches in the base round, don't despair! It may be possible to do a little adjustment on Round 1 and have everything work out nicely. If you are just a few stitches too long or short for the multiple of your chosen border, take a look at the diagram for that border.

Are there skipped stitches in the first round? You might be able to skip 1 stitch more or less along the edge to end up with the correct number. If you have to do this more than once, space the adjustments evenly across the entire length. Keep in mind that it's easier to successfully fudge stitch counts across a longer length rather than a shorter one because there is more space in which to spread out the added or skipped stitches. Furthermore, patterns with longer stitch multiples may be harder to fit and fudge than those with shorter multiples.

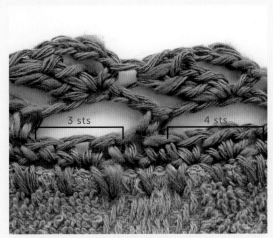

Fudging stitch counts on Round 1

Working in Rows

Since the main focus of this book is working in rounds and around 90-degree corners, all the border pattern text and photos assume that you are working in the round and that the right side of the work is facing you (with a few exceptions). However, there's no reason at all why you can't work them back and forth in rows and leave out the corners altogether. Each pattern in the book includes a diagram for making that design back and forth.

STITCH MULTIPLES IN ROWS

When working borders back and forth across a straight edge with no corners, you'll be putting the first stitch of Row 1 in the first stitch closest to the edge, but if you want it to end at a pleasing spot on the other edge, stitch multiples matter here, too. Beware: the plus number may not be the same as it is for the in-the-round version of the same border.

Take a look at the back-and-forth diagram for Border #120 on page 24: the multiple and "plus" number are indicated below the base row. Calculate the ideal number for your base row exactly as you did for the in-the-round version, omitting any concern about corner stitches (see Stitch Multiples and Why They Matter, page 21).

RIGHT AND WRONG SIDES

Note that when you are working back and forth, both the "right side" and "wrong side" of the stitches show alternately on the right side of your border. While a border worked this way won't look exactly like the photo of the crocheted border in the book, it's still correct. If you find you don't like the way the wrong side of the stitches looks, try working Row 1 as a wrong-side row, then continue to work back and forth. This will switch the right and wrong sides of the border and may provide you with a more pleasing design. Alternately, to maintain all rows as

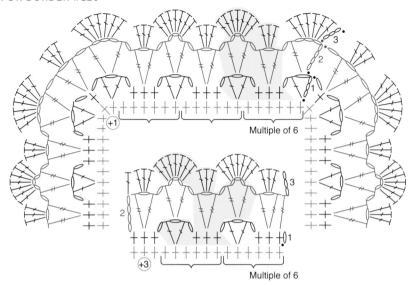

Note that the plus numbers (circled above) may be different depending on whether you work in rows or in rounds.

BORDER #88 WORKED IN ROUNDS

BORDER #88 WORKED IN ROWS

right-side rows, you may start every row with a new length of yarn, beginning on the right edge of the row (left edge for lefties). Some diagrams even call for this method; you'll be able to tell because the row numbers are on the side where the row begins. If there are two consecutive numbers on the same side of the diagram, work the rows without turning. The photos at left show the same border (#88) worked in the round and in rows.

Joining a New Yarn

Starting a new yarn at the beginning of a row or round can be done many different ways. It's good to become familiar with several of them; choose the one that will work best in each situation.

METHOD 1: BUILD-UP CHAIN (A.K.A. TURNING CHAIN)

Most crocheters are familiar with joining a new yarn with a slip stitch in the first stitch of the round or row, then chaining 1 to 4 stitches, depending on the height of the first stitch, to bring the hook up to the level of the first stitch of the next round or row.

When the first stitch of the round/row is single crochet, chain 1, then place the first single crochet in the same stitch as the beginning chain. The chain does not count as a stitch.

When the first stitch of the round/row is double crochet, chain 3 and count that chain 3 as a double crochet. Then, work the next stitch of the round/row in the next stitch, ignoring the stitch at the base of the chain, as the chain itself stands in place of the double crochet. The same holds true for half double crochet and treble crochet, which usually have build-up chains of 2 chain stitches and 4 chain stitches, respectively.

METHOD 2: STANDING STITCHES (A.K.A. CHAINLESS START)

This method goes by several different names. You may have seen it as "join with sc (or dc, and so on) in first stitch." The beauty of the standing-stitch method is that the stitch looks exactly like all the other stitches around it; there is not a wimpy little chain that stands out amidst its more robust brothers and sisters. Simply begin with a slip knot on the hook, then work the stitch into the designated stitch or space as normal. Photos at the right show the procedure for standing double crochet. For other stitches, the technique is similar, as described below.

For standing single crochet, beginning with a slip knot on the hook, insert hook into stitch or space indicated, yarnover and pull up a loop, yarnover and pull through 2 loops on the hook.

For standing half double crochet, beginning with a slip knot on the hook, yarnover, insert hook into stitch or space indicated, yarnover and pull up a loop, yarnover and pull through all 3 loops on the hook.

For standing treble crochet, beginning with a slip knot on the hook, yarnover two times, insert hook into stitch or space indicated, yarnover and pull up a loop, (yarnover and pull through 2 loops on the hook) three times.

STANDING DOUBLE CROCHET

1. Beginning with a slip knot on the hook, yarnover, insert hook into stitch or space indicated.

2. Yarnover and pull up a loop.

3. Yarnover and pull through 2 loops on the hook), two times.

But wait! There's a further refinement! If you don't like the knot left by the beginning slip knot, you can ignore the slip knot entirely and just start by looping the yarn over the hook. Just be sure to weave in that end carefully.

Ending Rounds

Most rounds end with a slip stitch in the first stitch to close the round, leaving the hook in position ready to begin the next round on top of the first stitch of the previous round. Sometimes, however, the round ends with a chain stitch or two, then a single, half double, or double crochet into the first stitch. This method places the hook somewhere to the right of the beginning of the previous round, ready to begin the next round.

A slip stitch closes most rounds.

Shown above in two photos, a double crochet join can take the place of a chain-3/slip stitch join. This positions the hook 3 stitches to the right in preparation to begin the next round.

A single crochet can be used in place of a chain-1/slip stitch join. This positions the hook 1 stitch to the right in preparation to begin the next round.

DESIGN CONCEPTS

TAPESTRY NEEDLE JOIN *(a.k.a. Invisible Join)*

If you prefer, use a tapestry needle join to make the join as tidy as possible, especially on the final round.

If the instructions say to end the round with a "chain, slip st to join," you may want to use the following method instead:

1. Complete the round, omitting the final chain and join. Cut the yarn, leaving a tail. Pull tail through the final stitch, then thread the tail onto a blunt-tip tapestry needle. Insert the needle from back to front under both loops at the top of the first stitch of the round and pull through.

2. Insert the needle from front to back into the top of the last stitch of the round, in the same spot where the tail came from. Pull yarn through. This creates a sewn chain in place of the omitted chain.

3. The joined stitch may be a bit loose. Adjust the tension of the final stitch to create a seamless line across the top of the stitches.

If the instructions say to end the round with a stitch followed by a "slip st to join":

1. Complete the round, omitting the final join. Cut the yarn, leaving a tail. Pull tail through the final stitch, then thread the tail onto a blunt-tip tapestry needle. Insert the needle from back to front under both loops at the top of the second stitch of the round and pull through.

2. Insert the needle from front to back into the top of the last stitch of the round, in the same spot where the tail came from. Pull yarn through tightly. The duplicate stitch you just made should sit gently on top of the first stitch of the round.

3. Adjust the tension of the final stitch to create a seamless line across the top of the stitches.

About the Patterns

Each of the patterns in this book is presented as both text and a diagram worked in the round from the right side. If you prefer to work the borders back-and-forth in rows without corners, simply use the back-and-forth diagram provided. If you are new to reading diagrams, don't worry. There's plenty of support both here in the book and online to help you through any difficulties (see Appendix, page 198).

Most of the instructions are written as if you are going to make the border with a single yarn color and want to minimize tails to weave in. In other words, the end of the round usually flows into the beginning of the next round with a slip stitch or other joining stitch (see page 26), followed by a build-up chain to start the next round (see page 24).

Some borders really beg for multiple colors, however, while others just look better if you fasten off and begin the new round fresh, even if you are using a single color. Those patterns are written with instructions for fastening off between 2 or more rounds. Joining the new yarn is usually done with a standing stitch (see page 25), my all-time favorite technique for beginning a new yarn at the beginning of a round or row. See the examples at right.

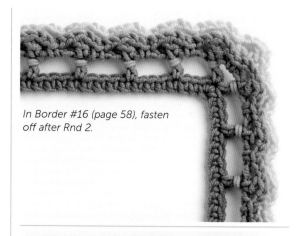

In Border #16 (page 58), fasten off after Rnd 2.

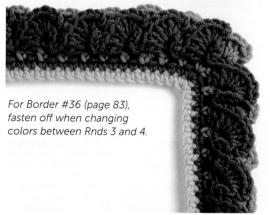

For Border #36 (page 83), fasten off when changing colors between Rnds 3 and 4.

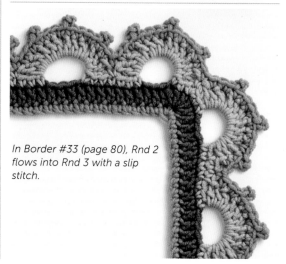

In Border #33 (page 80), Rnd 2 flows into Rnd 3 with a slip stitch.

Reading the Patterns

If you are unfamiliar with reading crochet instructions or crochet diagrams, refer to pages 198–203, which cover everything you need to know about reading patterns and diagrams in general.

Each written pattern instruction includes a repeated group of stitches that is worked across the edge as many times as needed; these instructions are usually indicated in brackets, as in the following example:

Border #20

Rnd 1: Ch 3 (counts as dc), dc in next 2 sts, *ch 3, skip 3 sts, [dc in next 3 sts, ch 3, skip 3 sts] to corner st, 3 dc in corner st; rep from * around, ending last rep ch 2, skip 3 sts, join with sc to top of ch-3.

In the diagrams, the repeated unit is shaded in yellow. If you are comparing the repeated stitches in the text to the shaded section in the diagram, you may find that they do not correspond exactly. This happens because the repeated section of stitches

A NOTE TO UK CROCHETERS

American and British crocheters use different terminology for the same stitches, which can cause massive confusion if you aren't aware of the difference! Luckily, the symbols in the diagrams remain the same on both sides of the Atlantic, as they represent the way the stitch is made, not what it is named. In this book, we are using United States terminology throughout, so "translate" the instructions to your own crochet language as necessary:

US Term	UK Term
Slip stitch	Slip stitch
Single crochet	Double crochet
Half double crochet	Half treble crochet
Double crochet	Treble crochet
Treble/triple crochet	Double treble crochet
Double treble crochet	Treble treble crochet

REPEATED SECTION HIGHLIGHTED IN YELLOW

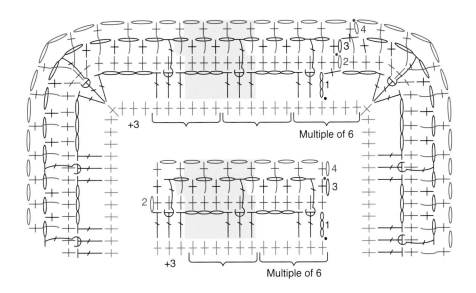

in the written pattern is optimized for readability in words, while the repeated stitches in the diagram are visually optimized. If this is confusing for you, just be consistent and follow either the text or the diagram throughout a project.

The instructions within the brackets direct you to work the repeated section "to corner stitch," "to corner space," "to 1 stitch before corner stitch," or some other location just before the corner. They might even direct you to work the bracketed instructions "across," placing a portion of the last bracketed instruction in the corner stitch. The instructions immediately following the bracket include the special treatment needed for the corner to lie flat.

Since the corner treatments are important, it is essential that you understand where the corner is. Don't hesitate to use stitch markers to keep track of your corners (see photos, page 20). As you become more experienced, you'll be able to identify corners without the aid of markers. The photos give examples of each of these situations.

QUICK-START GUIDE

If you just can't wait to get started, here are the things you must know:

- Work a single crochet foundation into your fabric to serve as a foundation for the border. When possible, crochet this base in the same color as your main fabric.

- Make sure that the base round has the appropriate number of stitches along each edge (that is, the correct multiple for the pattern, and accommodation for the corners), as indicated in the instructions.

- Begin Round 1 in the base-round stitch indicated. This will ensure that you reach the corner stitches at the right point.

- If you are working back and forth in rows, use the alternate diagrams.

BORDER
DESIGNS

We begin with elemental borders, the simplest borders imaginable. Narrow and simple, they can stand on their own, but they can also be combined with other elements and with wider borders to create new edgings. See if you can discover other elements on your own! The borders that follow them vary in style, width, and function, and are arranged in no particular order. Keep in mind that these borders are not shown to scale. Some of the larger borders have been reduced in size to fit on the page; some of the narrower ones have been enlarged. Refer to their attributes to get a sense of relative border size. Above all, have fun exploring new ways to embellish your work!

Base rnd: Any multiple.

Begin in any st.

■ Standing sc in first st, sc in each st around, placing 2 or 3 sc in each corner st, join with slip st to first st.

Narrow

Straight

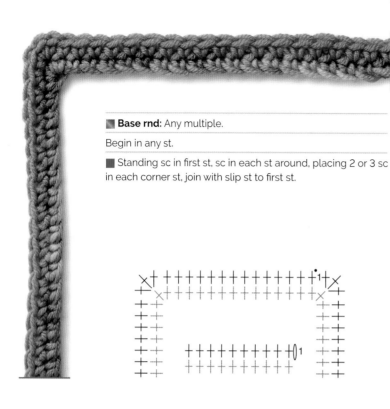

ELEMENT

B

Base rnd: Any multiple.

Begin in any st.

■ Working from left to right (right to left for lefties) with RS facing, standing sc in first st, reverse sc in each st around, placing 2 reverse sc in each corner st, join with slip st to first sc. (For reverse single crochet, see page 214.)

Narrow

Straight

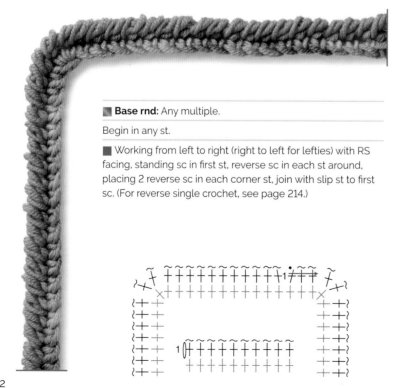

ELEMENT C

Narrow
Undulating

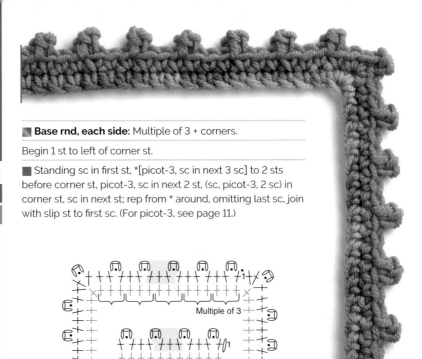

◼ **Base rnd, each side:** Multiple of 3 + corners.

Begin 1 st to left of corner st.

◼ Standing sc in first st, *[picot-3, sc in next 3 sc] to 2 sts before corner st, picot-3, sc in next 2 st, (sc, picot-3, 2 sc) in corner st, sc in next st; rep from * around, omitting last sc, join with slip st to first sc. (For picot-3, see page 11.)

ELEMENT D

Narrow
Undulating

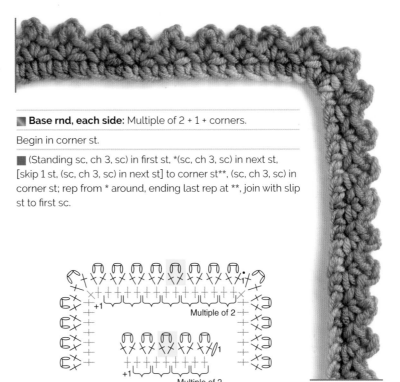

◼ **Base rnd, each side:** Multiple of 2 + 1 + corners.

Begin in corner st.

◼ (Standing sc, ch 3, sc) in first st, *(sc, ch 3, sc) in next st, [skip 1 st, (sc, ch 3, sc) in next st] to corner st**, (sc, ch 3, sc) in corner st; rep from * around, ending last rep at **, join with slip st to first sc.

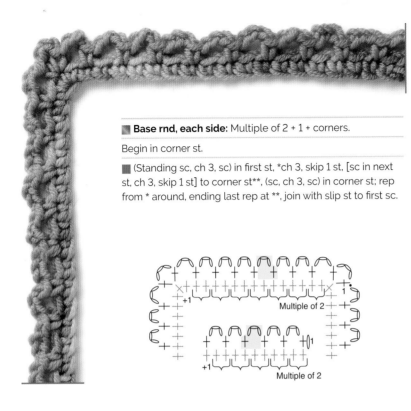

ELEMENT

E

Base rnd, each side: Multiple of 2 + 1 + corners.

Begin in corner st.

(Standing sc, ch 3, sc) in first st, *ch 3, skip 1 st, [sc in next st, ch 3, skip 1 st] to corner st**, (sc, ch 3, sc) in corner st; rep from * around, ending last rep at **, join with slip st to first sc.

Narrow

Undulating

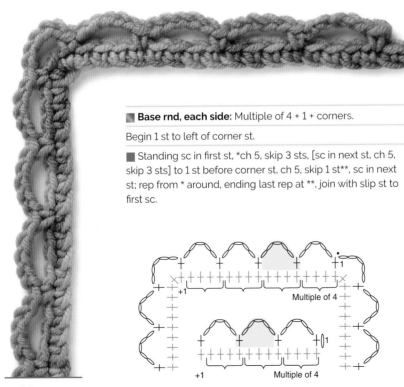

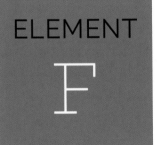

ELEMENT

F

Base rnd, each side: Multiple of 4 + 1 + corners.

Begin 1 st to left of corner st.

Standing sc in first st, *ch 5, skip 3 sts, [sc in next st, ch 5, skip 3 sts] to 1 st before corner st, ch 5, skip 1 st**, sc in next st; rep from * around, ending last rep at **, join with slip st to first sc.

Narrow

Undulating

ELEMENT G

Narrow
Straight

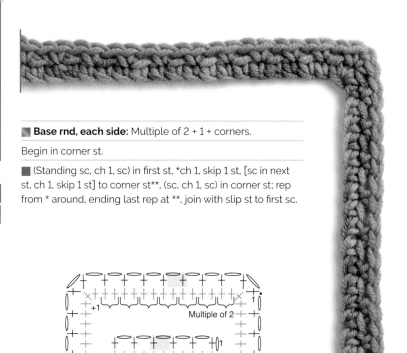

■ **Base rnd, each side:** Multiple of 2 + 1 + corners.

Begin in corner st.

■ (Standing sc, ch 1, sc) in first st, *ch 1, skip 1 st, [sc in next st, ch 1, skip 1 st] to corner st**, (sc, ch 1, sc) in corner st; rep from * around, ending last rep at **, join with slip st to first sc.

ELEMENT H

Narrow
Straight

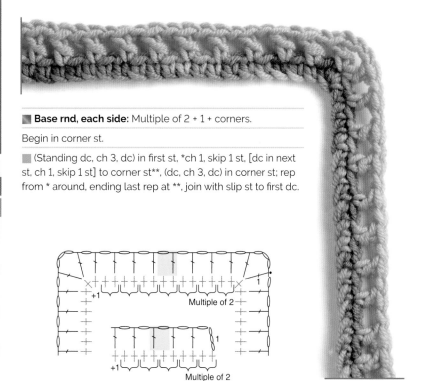

■ **Base rnd, each side:** Multiple of 2 + 1 + corners.

Begin in corner st.

■ (Standing dc, ch 3, dc) in first st, *ch 1, skip 1 st, [dc in next st, ch 1, skip 1 st] to corner st**, (dc, ch 3, dc) in corner st; rep from * around, ending last rep at **, join with slip st to first dc.

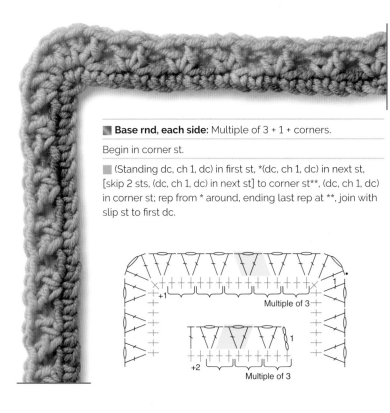

■ **Base rnd, each side:** Multiple of 3 + 1 + corners.

Begin in corner st.

■ (Standing dc, ch 1, dc) in first st, *(dc, ch 1, dc) in next st, [skip 2 sts, (dc, ch 1, dc) in next st] to corner st**, (dc, ch 1, dc) in corner st; rep from * around, ending last rep at **, join with slip st to first dc.

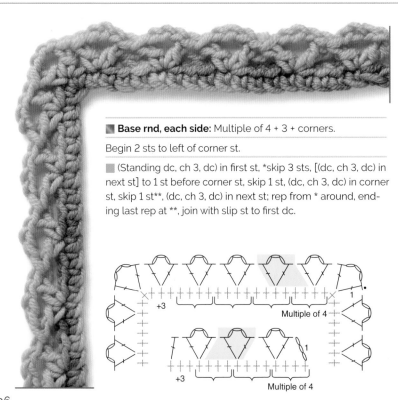

■ **Base rnd, each side:** Multiple of 4 + 3 + corners.

Begin 2 sts to left of corner st.

■ (Standing dc, ch 3, dc) in first st, *skip 3 sts, [(dc, ch 3, dc) in next st] to 1 st before corner st, skip 1 st, (dc, ch 3, dc) in corner st, skip 1 st**, (dc, ch 3, dc) in next st; rep from * around, ending last rep at **, join with slip st to first dc.

ELEMENT K

Narrow

Undulating

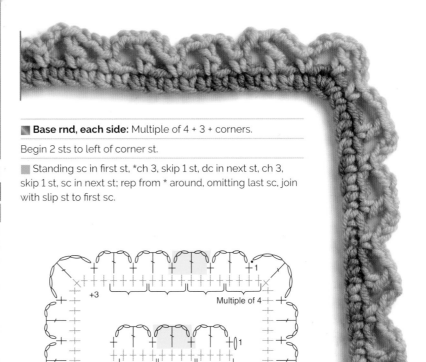

Base rnd, each side: Multiple of 4 + 3 + corners.

Begin 2 sts to left of corner st.

Standing sc in first st, *ch 3, skip 1 st, dc in next st, ch 3, skip 1 st, sc in next st; rep from * around, omitting last sc, join with slip st to first sc.

ELEMENT L

Narrow

Undulating

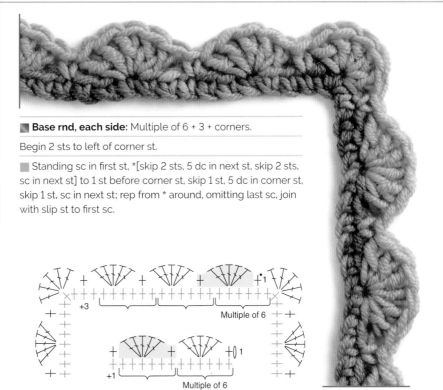

Base rnd, each side: Multiple of 6 + 3 + corners.

Begin 2 sts to left of corner st.

Standing sc in first st, *[skip 2 sts, 5 dc in next st, skip 2 sts, sc in next st] to 1 st before corner st, skip 1 st, 5 dc in corner st, skip 1 st, sc in next st; rep from * around, omitting last sc, join with slip st to first sc.

◣ **Base rnd, each side:** Multiple of 3 + 2 + corners.

Begin 2 sts to left of corner st.

▨ Beginning with slip knot on hook, *Flat X-st across to 1 st before corner st, ch 1, Corner Flat X-st, ch 1; rep from * around, join with slip st to first st. Fasten off.

Stitches & Notes

Corner Flat X-st (Corner Flat X-stitch): Yarnover two times, insert hook into st before corner st and pull up a loop, yarnover and pull through 2 loops, yarnover, skip corner st, insert hook into next st, yarnover and pull up a loop, (yarnover and pull through 2 loops) four times, ch 3, dc under 2 loops where two legs of this st join.

Flat X-st (Flat X-stitch): Yarnover two times, insert hook into next st or space indicated and pull up a loop, yarnover and pull through 2 loops, yarnover, skip 1 st, insert hook into next st or space, yarnover and pull up a loop, (yarnover and pull through 2 loops) four times, ch 1, dc under 2 loops where two legs of this st join. (For an illustration of Flat X-stitch, see page 211.)

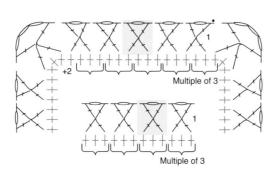

Multiple of 3

Narrow

Straight

Open/Lacy

ELEMENT

N

Stitches & Notes

Puff st (puff stitch):
(Yarnover, insert hook and pull up a loop) three times in st or space indicated, yarnover and pull through all 7 loops on hook. (For an illustration of puff stitch, see page 214.)

Base rnd, each side: Multiple of 2 + 1 + corners.

Begin 2 sts to left of corner st.

Beginning with slip knot on hook, puff st in first st, ch 1, skip 1 st, *[puff st in next st, ch 1, skip 1 st] to corner st, (puff st, ch 1) three times in corner st, skip 1 st; rep from * around, join with slip st to first puff st.

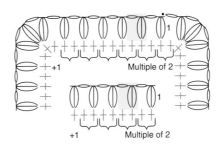

Narrow

Straight

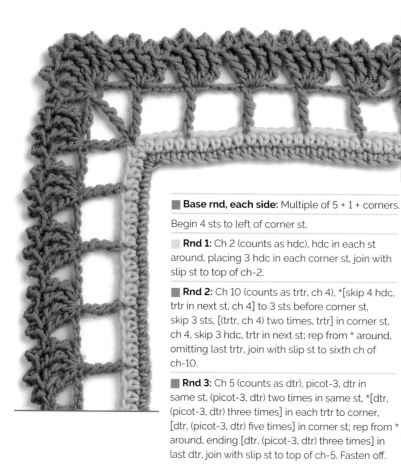

Base rnd, each side: Multiple of 5 + 1 + corners.
Begin 4 sts to left of corner st.

Rnd 1: Ch 2 (counts as hdc), hdc in each st around, placing 3 hdc in each corner st, join with slip st to top of ch-2.

Rnd 2: Ch 10 (counts as trtr, ch 4), *[skip 4 hdc, trtr in next st, ch 4] to 3 sts before corner st, skip 3 sts, [(trtr, ch 4) two times, trtr] in corner st, ch 4, skip 3 hdc, trtr in next st; rep from * around, omitting last trtr, join with slip st to sixth ch of ch-10.

Rnd 3: Ch 5 (counts as dtr), picot-3, dtr in same st, (picot-3, dtr) two times in same st, *[dtr, (picot-3, dtr) three times] in each trtr to corner, [dtr, (picot-3, dtr) five times] in corner st; rep from * around, ending [dtr, (picot-3, dtr) three times] in last dtr, join with slip st to top of ch-5. Fasten off.

Stitches & Notes

Dtr (double treble crochet): Yarnover three times, insert hook into st or space indicated, yarnover and pull up a loop, (yarnover and pull through 2 loops on hook) four times.

Picot-3: Ch 3, slip st in third chain from hook.

Trtr (triple treble crochet): Yarnover four times, insert hook into st or space indicated, yarnover and pull up a loop, (yarnover and pull through 2 loops) five times.

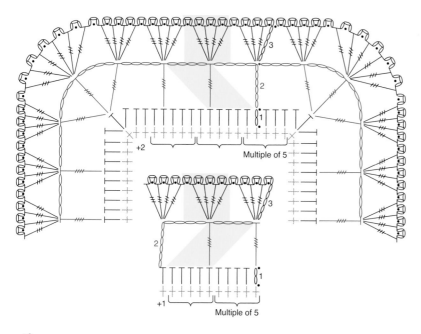

Reversible
Wide
Undulating
Open/Lacy
Fringy

#2

Stitches & Notes

This is a great fringe because it doesn't unravel, making it a good choice for yarns that don't usually hold up well for fringe. However, it does take a bit of experimentation to find the right combination of (1) length of loop and (2) number of twists. Be sure to work a swatch first.

To keep the loops a consistent size, cut a template out of cardboard and use it to help size the original long loop; twist that loop the same number of times for each fringe. (For an illustration of twisted fringe, see page 212.)

The loops for the fringe shown in this DK-weight yarn were drawn up to 6½"/16.5 cm and twisted 20 times, for a final length of 2½"/6.5 cm.

Note: *You may find it easier to twist the loop with your forefinger: remove the hook from the loop and use your forefinger to make the twists, then replace the loop on the hook and continue.*

Reversible

Wide

Fringy

■ **Base rnd, each side:** Any multiple.

Begin 1 st to left of corner st.

▨ **Rnd 1 and** ■ **Rnd 2:** Ch 1, sc in each sc around, placing 3 sc in each corner st, join with slip st to first sc.

■ **Rnd 3:** Ch 1, slip st in first st, *pull up loop on hook to two-and-a-half times the desired length of fringe, rotate hook counterclockwise (or clockwise, but be consistent) 15 to 30 times (or more or less, depending on the length of your loop and the attributes of your yarn), bring hook back toward the border and allow loop to twist back upon itself, slip st in same st, slip st in next st; rep from * around, omitting last slip st. Fasten off.

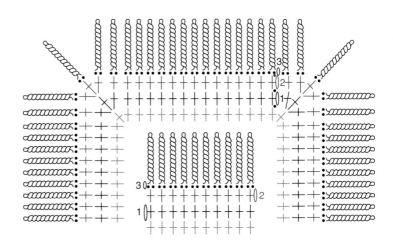

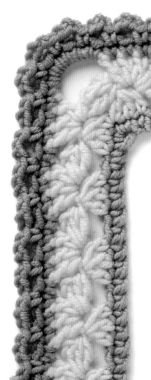

#3

■ **Base rnd, each side:** Multiple of 4 + 1 + corners.

Begin in corner st.

■ **Rnd 1:** Ch 2 (counts as partial dc), dc2tog over next 2 sts, *[ch 3, 2-dc cluster in third ch from hook, skip 1 st, dc3tog over next 3 sts] to corner, placing last leg of dc3tog in corner st, ch 4, 2-tr cluster in fourth ch from hook**, dc3tog over same corner, st and next 2 sts; rep from * around, ending last rep at **, join with slip st to first st.

■ **Rnd 2:** Ch 3 (counts as dc), 2 dc in same st, *[ch 1, 3 dc in next dc3tog] to corner cluster, ch 5**, 3 dc in next dc3tog; rep from * around, ending last rep at **, join with slip st to top of ch-3.

■ **Rnd 3:** Ch 1, sc in each dc and ch-1 space and 7 sc in each ch-5 corner space around, join with slip st to first sc.

■ **Rnd 4:** Ch 1, sc in first sc, *ch 3, skip 1 sc, sc in next sc; rep from * around, omitting last sc, join with slip st to first sc. Fasten off.

Stitches & Notes

2-dc Cluster: Yarnover, insert hook into st or space indicated and pull up a loop, yarnover and pull through 2 loops, yarnover, insert hook into same st or space and pull up a loop, yarnover and pull through 2 loops, yarnover and pull through all 3 loops on hook.

2-tr Cluster: *Yarnover two times, insert hook into stitch or space indicated and pull up a loop, (yarnover and pull through 2 loops) two times; rep from * once, yarnover and pull through all 3 loops on hook.

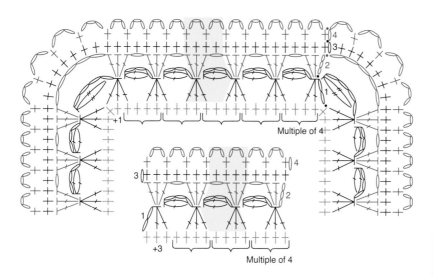

Reversible
Medium
Straight

#4

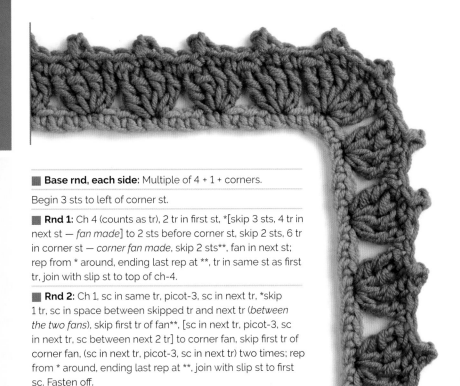

Stitches & Notes

Picot-3: Ch 3, slip st in third chain from hook.

Base rnd, each side: Multiple of 4 + 1 + corners.

Begin 3 sts to left of corner st.

Rnd 1: Ch 4 (counts as tr), 2 tr in first st, *[skip 3 sts, 4 tr in next st — *fan made*] to 2 sts before corner st, skip 2 sts, 6 tr in corner st — *corner fan made*, skip 2 sts**, fan in next st; rep from * around, ending last rep at **, tr in same st as first tr, join with slip st to top of ch-4.

Rnd 2: Ch 1, sc in same tr, picot-3, sc in next tr, *skip 1 tr, sc in space between skipped tr and next tr (*between the two fans*), skip first tr of fan**, [sc in next tr, picot-3, sc in next tr, sc between next 2 tr] to corner fan, skip first tr of corner fan, (sc in next tr, picot-3, sc in next tr) two times; rep from * around, ending last rep at **, join with slip st to first sc. Fasten off.

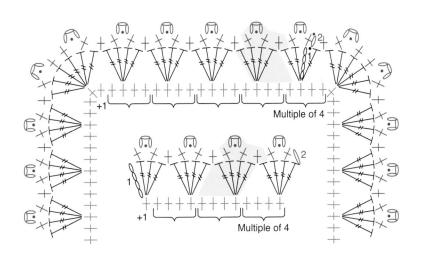

Reversible

Narrow

Undulating

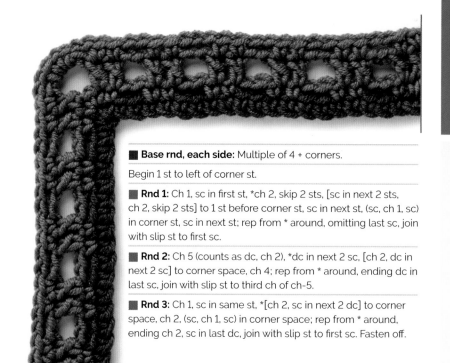

#5

■ **Base rnd, each side:** Multiple of 4 + corners.

Begin 1 st to left of corner st.

■ **Rnd 1:** Ch 1, sc in first st, *ch 2, skip 2 sts, [sc in next 2 sts, ch 2, skip 2 sts] to 1 st before corner st, sc in next st, (sc, ch 1, sc) in corner st, sc in next st; rep from * around, omitting last sc, join with slip st to first sc.

■ **Rnd 2:** Ch 5 (counts as dc, ch 2), *dc in next 2 sc, [ch 2, dc in next 2 sc] to corner space, ch 4; rep from * around, ending dc in last sc, join with slip st to third ch of ch-5.

■ **Rnd 3:** Ch 1, sc in same st, *[ch 2, sc in next 2 dc] to corner space, ch 2, (sc, ch 1, sc) in corner space; rep from * around, ending ch 2, sc in last dc, join with slip st to first sc. Fasten off.

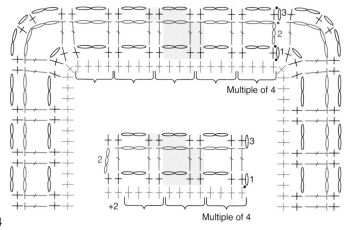

Reversible

Narrow

Straight

Open/Lacy

Textured

#6

Stitches & Notes

This pattern shows up best when the colors in Rnds 1 and 2 contrast strongly.

Picot-3: Ch 3, slip st in third chain from hook.

Puff st (puff stitch): (Yarnover, insert hook and pull up a loop) three times in st or space indicated, yarnover and pull through all 7 loops on hook. (For an illustration of puff stitch, see page 214.)

Tight picot-3: Ch 3, slip st in third ch from hook and in st at bottom of ch together. (For an illustration of tight picot-3, see page 214.)

Narrow

Undulating

Layered

Textured

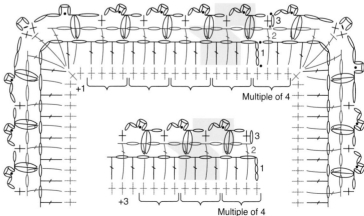

■ **Base rnd, each side:** Multiple of 4 + 1 + corners.

Begin 4 sts to left of corner st.

■ **Rnd 1:** Ch 4 (counts as dc, ch 1), *skip 1 st, [dc in next st, ch 1, skip 1 st**] to corner st, (dc, ch 3, dc) in corner st, ch 1; rep from * around, ending last rep at** join with slip st to third ch of ch-4. Fasten off.

Note: All Rnd-2 stitches are worked into the base rnd, holding the Rnd-1 sts alternately to the front and back of the current stitches.

■ **Rnd 2:** Working in front of Rnd-1 sts, standing dc in last skipped st of base rnd, *ch 1, working behind Rnd-1 sts, dc in next skipped st, ch 1; [working in front of Rnd-1 sts, dc in next skipped st, ch 1, working behind Rnd-1 sts, dc in next skipped st, ch 1] to corner; working in front of Rnd-1 corner ch, dc in corner base-rnd st; working over same Rnd-1 corner ch, dc in same corner base-rnd st; working in front of same Rnd-1 corner ch, dc in same corner base-rnd st; rep from * around, ending ch 1, working behind Rnd-1 sts, dc in next skipped st, ch 1, join with slip st to first sc.

Note: Rnd-3 puff stitches are worked into the ch-1 spaces from Rnd 1, keeping the Rnd-2 sts to the back throughout, and skipping the dc behind the puff st.

■ **Rnd 3:** Ch 1, sc in same st, ch 1, *puff st in next Rnd-1 space, picot-3, ch 2**, [sc in next Rnd-2 dc, ch 1, puff st in next Rnd-1 space, picot-3, ch 2] to dc before corner dc, skip 1 dc, (sc, tight picot-3, sc) in corner dc, ch 2, skip 1 dc; rep from * around, ending last rep at **, join with slip st to first sc. Fasten off.

45

Stitches & Notes

The optimal length of fringe varies according to the yarn, project, and personal taste. Before cutting batches of fringe, experiment with different lengths to determine the best length for your project. Although the picture shows fringes worked in every other chain space, you could put them in every chain space for a fuller fringe.

■ **Base rnd, each side:** Multiple of 4 + 3 + corners.

Begin 1 st to left of corner st.

■ **Rnd 1:** Ch 1, sc in each st around, placing 3 sc in each corner st, join with slip st to first sc.

■ **Rnd 2:** Ch 1, sc in first sc, *ch 1, skip 1 sc, [sc in next sc, ch 1, skip 1 sc] to corner sc, (sc, ch 1, sc) in corner sc; rep from * around, ending ch 1, skip 1 sc, join with slip st to first sc.

■ **Rnd 3:** Ch 1, sc in each sc and ch-1 space around, placing 3 sc in each corner space, join with slip st to first sc. Fasten off.

■ ■ ■ **Fringe:** Cut one strand of each color yarn for each fringe, following the instructions for braided fringe on page 213. Referring to the stitch diagram on the facing page, attach braided fringe in locations shown, or as desired. Trim fringe.

Reversible
Wide
Straight
Fringy

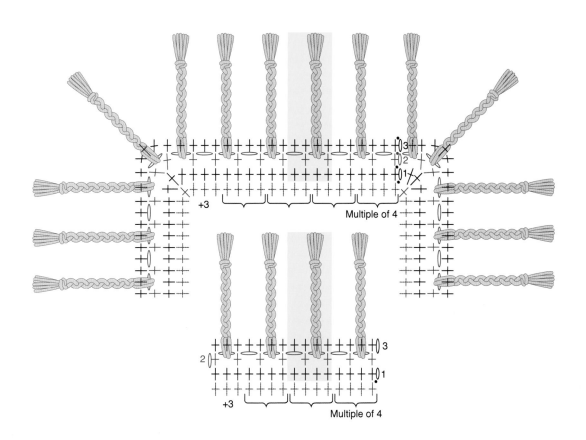

+3

Multiple of 4

+3

Multiple of 4

#8

Stitches & Notes

Picot-3: Ch 3, slip st in third chain from hook.

■ **Base rnd, each side:** Multiple of 5 + corners.

Begin 3 sts to left of corner st.

▓ **Rnd 1:** Ch 1, sc in first st, *[ch 4, skip 4 sts, (sc, ch 5, sc) in next st] to 2 sts before corner st, ch 3, skip 2 sts, (sc, ch 5, sc) in corner st, ch 3, skip 2 sts**, (sc, ch 5, sc) in next st; rep from * around, ending last rep at **, sc in same st as beginning sc, ch 2, join with dc to first sc.

▓ **Rnd 2:** Ch 3 (counts as dc), 2 dc in space formed by joining dc, ch 1, *[5 dc in next ch-5 space, ch 1] to corner, 7 dc in corner ch-5 space, ch 1; rep from * around, ending last rep 2 dc in same space as beginning, join with slip st to first dc.

▓ **Rnd 3:** Ch 1, sc first st, ch 2, skip 2 dc, sc in next space, *[ch 2, skip 2 dc**, (sc, ch 5, sc) in next dc, ch 2, skip 2 dc, sc in next space] to 3 dc before corner st, ch 3, skip 3 dc, (sc, ch 5, sc) in corner dc, ch 3, skip 3 dc, sc in next space; rep from * around, ending last rep at **, sc in same st as beginning st, ch 2, join with dc to first sc.

▓ **Rnd 4:** Ch 1, sc in first st, *[ch 4, (sc, ch 3, sc) in next ch-5 space] across to corner space, ch 5, [sc, (ch 3, sc) three times] in corner space — *corner group made*, ch 5**, (sc, ch 3, sc) in next ch-5 space; rep from * around, ending last rep at **, sc in same space as first sc, join with dc to first sc.

▓ **Rnd 5:** Ch 3 (counts as dc), (dc, picot-3, 3 dc) in space formed by joining dc, ch 1, *(2 dc, picot-3, 3 dc, ch 1) in each ch-3 space to corner group, (2 dc, picot-3, 3 dc) in next ch-3 space, (2 dc, picot-3, 2 dc) in corner space, (2 dc, picot-3, 3 dc) in next ch-3 space, ch 1; rep from * around, join with slip st to top of ch-3. Fasten off.

Reversible

Wide

Undulating

Open/Lacy

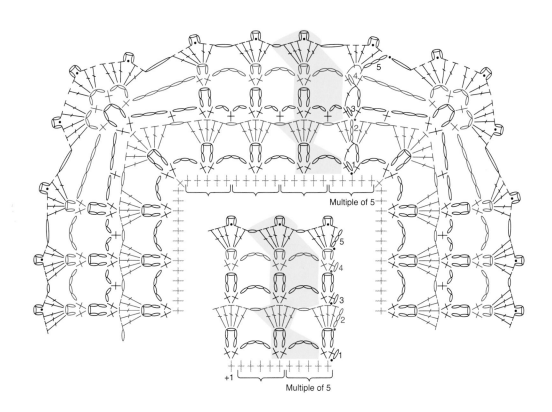

Multiple of 5

+1

Multiple of 5

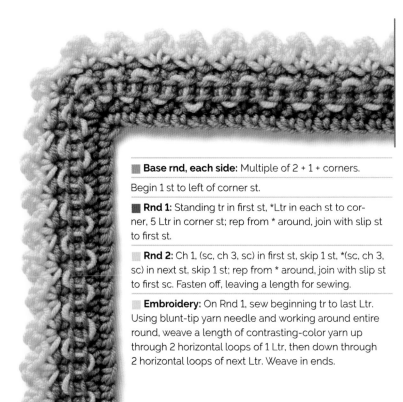

#9

Base rnd, each side: Multiple of 2 + 1 + corners.

Begin 1 st to left of corner st.

Rnd 1: Standing tr in first st, *Ltr in each st to corner, 5 Ltr in corner st; rep from * around, join with slip st to first st.

Rnd 2: Ch 1, (sc, ch 3, sc) in first st, skip 1 st, *(sc, ch 3, sc) in next st, skip 1 st; rep from * around, join with slip st to first sc. Fasten off, leaving a length for sewing.

Embroidery: On Rnd 1, sew beginning tr to last Ltr. Using blunt-tip yarn needle and working around entire round, weave a length of contrasting-color yarn up through 2 horizontal loops of 1 Ltr, then down through 2 horizontal loops of next Ltr. Weave in ends.

Stitches & Notes

Linked trebles create a solid border that resembles afghan stitch. Embroider under the horizontal bars of the stitches as shown here, or leave them unadorned: crocheter's choice. This is an example of how changing the final round transforms the border from a no-nonsense straight border into a frilly edging.

Ltr (linked treble crochet): Insert hook into horizontal loop in middle front of the stitch just made, yarnover and pull up a loop, insert hook in next horizontal loop on front of same st, yarnover and pull up a loop, insert hook in next stitch of round/row, yarnover and pull up a loop, (yarnover and pull through 2 loops on hook) three times.

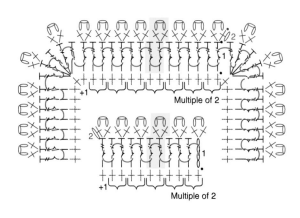

Multiple of 2

Multiple of 2

Medium

Undulating

Textured

#10

Base rnd, each side: Any multiple.

Begin 1 st to left of corner st.

Rnd 1: Ch 1, sc in each st around, placing 3 st in each corner st, join with slip st to first sc.

Rnd 2: Ch 4 (counts as tr), tr in each sc around, placing 5 tr in each corner st, join with slip st to top of ch-4.

Rnd 3: Rep Rnd 1.

Rnd 4: Ch 1, reverse sc in each sc around, join with slip st in first reverse sc. Fasten off. (For an illustration of reverse single crochet, see page 214.)

Embroidery: Work loose backstitch around the Rnd 2 posts, as follows: Thread a blunt-tip yarn needle with a length of yarn. Working around the treble posts, bring needle from back to front between beginning chain and next treble, pull through to RS, leaving a tail for weaving in. Insert needle from front to back in space between 2 previous sts (the next space to the right), then from back to front in next free space between sts to the left (between the second and third sts) and pull yarn thorough, wrapping stitches loosely. Continue to work "backward one space, forward two spaces" around. Insert needle above previous embroidery on each stitch.

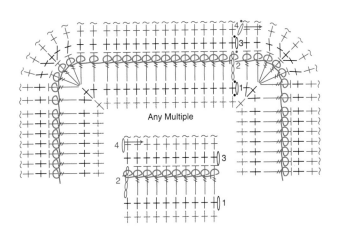

Any Multiple

Medium

Straight

51

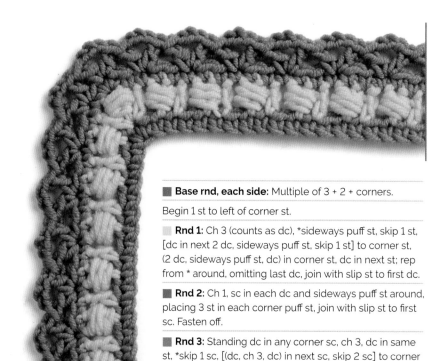

#11

■ **Base rnd, each side:** Multiple of 3 + 2 + corners.

Begin 1 st to left of corner st.

■ **Rnd 1:** Ch 3 (counts as dc), *sideways puff st, skip 1 st, [dc in next 2 dc, sideways puff st, skip 1 st] to corner st, (2 dc, sideways puff st, dc) in corner st, dc in next st; rep from * around, omitting last dc, join with slip st to first dc.

■ **Rnd 2:** Ch 1, sc in each dc and sideways puff st around, placing 3 st in each corner puff st, join with slip st to first sc. Fasten off.

■ **Rnd 3:** Standing dc in any corner sc, ch 3, dc in same st, *skip 1 sc, [(dc, ch 3, dc) in next sc, skip 2 sc] to corner st**, (dc, ch 3, dc) in corner sc; rep from * around, ending last rep at **, join with slip st to first dc. Fasten off.

Stitches & Notes

Sideways puff st (sideways puff stitch): (Yarnover, insert hook around post of dc just made, yarnover and pull up a loop) three times, yarnover and pull through all 7 loops on hook.

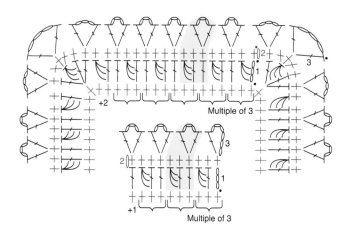

Reversible

Medium

#12

Stitches & Notes

Y-st (Y-stitch): Make 1 tr, then dc around post of tr just made.

■ **Base rnd, each side:** Multiple of 2 + 1 + corners.

Begin 2 sts to left of corner st.

■ **Rnd 1:** Beginning with slip knot on hook, Y-st in first st, *skip 1 st, [Y-st in next st, skip 1 st] to corner st, 3 Y-sts in corner st; rep from * around, ending skip 1 st, join with slip st to first tr. Fasten off.

■ **Rnd 2:** Beginning with slip knot on hook, Y-st in space between last Y-st made and first Y-st of Rnd 1, *[Y-st in space before next Y-st] to corner Y-st, Y-st in center of corner st (between the tr and dc of corner Y-st); rep from * around, join with slip st to first tr.

■ **Rnd 3:** Ch 1, (sc, ch 3, sc) in center of each Y-st around, join with slip st to first sc. Fasten off.

Reversible

Medium

Undulating

Open/Lacy

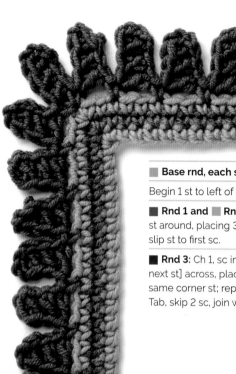

#13

Base rnd, each side: Multiple of 3 + 1 + corners.

Begin 1 st to left of corner st.

Rnd 1 and Rnd 2: Ch 1, sc in first st, sc in each st around, placing 3 sc in each corner st, join with slip st to first sc.

Rnd 3: Ch 1, sc in first st, *[Tab, skip 2 sc, sc in next st] across, placing last sc in corner st, Tab, sc in same corner st; rep from * around, ending last rep Tab, skip 2 sc, join with slip st to first sc. Fasten off.

Stitches & Notes

Tab: Ch 6, dc in back bump of fourth ch from hook, dc in back bump of next 2 ch. (For an illustration of back bump, see page 210.)

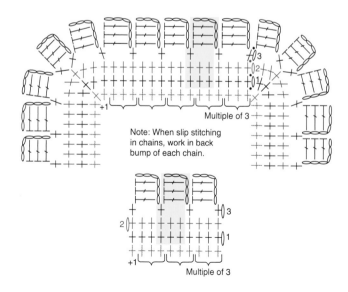

Multiple of 3

Note: When slip stitching in chains, work in back bump of each chain.

Multiple of 3

Reversible

Medium

Undulating

Fringy

#14

Stitches & Notes

Changing Border #13's (facing page) Rnd 2 to back loop single crochet leaves the front loops available for a round of reverse single crochet, adding another dimension to the border.

BLsc (back loop single crochet): Single crochet into the back loop only.

Reverse sc (reverse single crochet): Single crochet from left-to-right (right-to-left for lefties), as follows: with RS facing and keeping hook pointing to the left (to the right for lefties), insert hook into st indicated and pull up a loop, yarnover and pull through 2 loops. (For an illustration of reverse single crochet, see page 214.)

Tab: Ch 6, dc in back bump of fourth ch from hook, dc in back bump of next 2 ch. (For an illustration of working in the back bump, see page 210.)

- Medium
- Undulating
- Fringy
- Textured

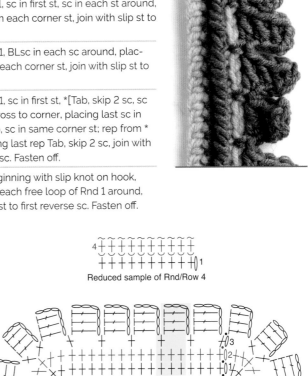

Base rnd, each side: Multiple of 3 + 1 + corners.

Begin 1 st to left of corner st.

Rnd 1: Ch 1, sc in first st, sc in each st around, placing 3 sc in each corner st, join with slip st to first sc.

Rnd 2: Ch 1, BLsc in each sc around, placing 3 BLsc in each corner st, join with slip st to first sc.

Rnd 3: Ch 1, sc in first st, *[Tab, skip 2 sc, sc in next st] across to corner, placing last sc in corner st, Tab, sc in same corner st; rep from * around, ending last rep Tab, skip 2 sc, join with slip st to first sc. Fasten off.

Rnd 4: Beginning with slip knot on hook, reverse sc in each free loop of Rnd 1 around, join with slip st to first reverse sc. Fasten off.

Reduced sample of Rnd/Row 4

Multiple of 3

Note: When slip stitching in chains, work in back bump of each chain.

Multiple of 3

55

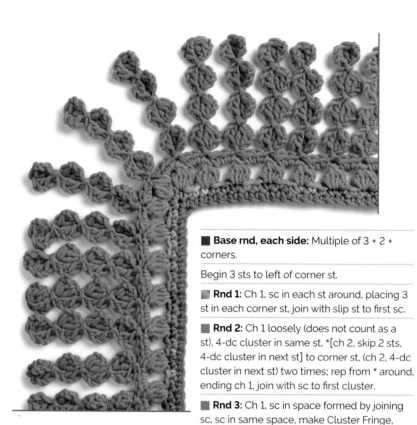

#15

Stitches & Notes

Adapt the length of the Cluster Fringe to complement the size of your project: shorter fringe for a small project or longer fringe for a large project.

4-dc Cluster (4 double crochet cluster): Yarnover, insert hook into st or space indicated and pull up a loop, yarnover and pull through 2 loops, (yarnover, insert hook into same st or space and pull up a loop, yarnover and pull through 2 loops) three times, yarnover and pull through all 5 loops on hook.

Cluster Fringe: (Ch 4, 2 partial dc in third ch from hook, yarnover and pull through all 3 loops on hook) four times; turn to continue working back along long piece just made; [ch 3, dc in third ch from hook, slip st over ch-1 at base of next cluster] four times.

■ **Base rnd, each side:** Multiple of 3 + 2 + corners.

Begin 3 sts to left of corner st.

■ **Rnd 1:** Ch 1, sc in each st around, placing 3 st in each corner st, join with slip st to first sc.

■ **Rnd 2:** Ch 1 loosely (does not count as a st), 4-dc cluster in same st, *[ch 2, skip 2 sts, 4-dc cluster in next st] to corner st, (ch 2, 4-dc cluster in next st) two times; rep from * around, ending ch 1, join with sc to first cluster.

■ **Rnd 3:** Ch 1, sc in space formed by joining sc, sc in same space, make Cluster Fringe, *3 sc in next ch-2 space, make Cluster Fringe; rep from * around, ending last rep sc in same space as first sc, join with slip st to first sc. Fasten off.

Reversible

Wide

Fringy

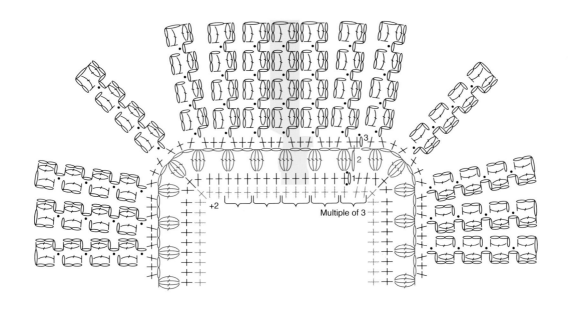

+3
+2
+1
+2 Multiple of 3 +

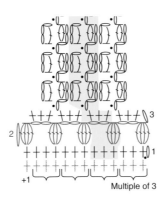

3
2
1
+1 Multiple of 3

#16

Base rnd, each side: Multiple of 4 + 3 + corners.

Begin 4 sts to left of corner st.

Rnd 1: Ch 6 (counts as dc, ch 3), *skip 3 sts, [dc in next st, ch 3, skip 3 sts] to corner st, (dc, ch 3, dc) in corner st**, ch 3; rep from * around, ending last rep at **, ch 1, join with hdc to third ch of ch-6.

Rnd 2: Ch 1, sc in space formed by joining hdc, ch 2, dc in top of ch-3, *[ch 2, sc in next ch-3 space, ch 2, dc in next dc] to corner space, ch 3, sc in corner space, ch 3, dc in next dc; rep from * around, ending ch 2, join with slip st to first sc. Fasten off.

Note: Rnd 3 sts are worked around posts of Rnd-1 sts throughout.

Rnd 3: Standing BPdc around beginning ch-3 of Rnd 1, *[ch 3, BPdc in next Rnd-1 dc] to corner, ch 5, BPdc in next Rnd-1 dc; rep from * around, ending ch 1, join with hdc to first BPdc.

Rnd 4: Ch 1, sc in space formed by joining hdc, ch 2, dc in top of next BPdc, *[ch 2, sc in next ch-3 space, ch 2, dc in next BPdc] to corner, ch 2, (sc, ch 2, dc, ch 2, sc) in corner space, ch 2, dc in next BPdc; rep from * around, ending ch 2, join with slip st to first sc. Fasten off.

Stitches & Notes

BPdc (back post double crochet): Yarnover, insert hook from back to front to back around post of st, yarnover and pull up a loop, (yarnover and pull through 2 loops) two times.

Standing BPdc (standing back post double crochet): Beginning with slip knot on hook, yarnover, insert hook from back to front to back around post of st, yarnover and pull up a loop, (yarnover and pull through 2 loops) two times.

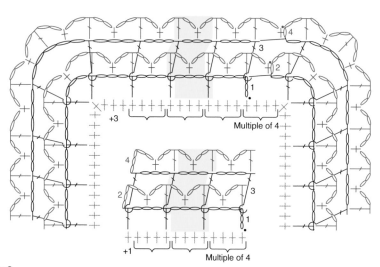

Narrow

Undulating

Layered

Textured

#17

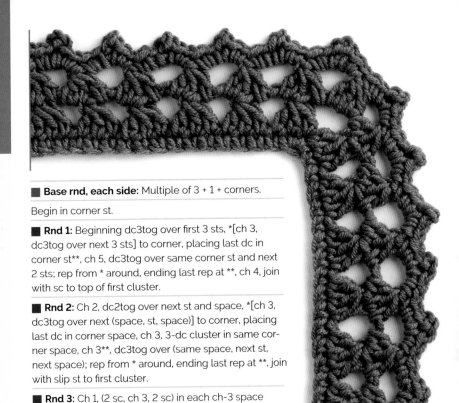

Stitches & Notes

3-dc Cluster (3 double crochet cluster):
Yarnover, insert hook into st or space indicated and pull up a loop, yarnover and pull through 2 loops, (yarnover, insert hook into same st or space and pull up a loop, yarnover and pull through 2 loops) two times, yarnover and pull through all 4 loops on hook.

Beginning dc3tog (beginning double crochet 3 together):
With slip knot on hook, yarnover, insert hook into first st or space and pull up a loop, yarnover and pull through 2 loops, (yarnover, insert hook into next st or space indicated and pull up a loop, yarnover and pull through 2 loops) two times, yarnover and pull through all 4 loops on hook.

Reversible
Medium
Undulating
Open/Lacy

■ **Base rnd, each side:** Multiple of 3 + 1 + corners.

Begin in corner st.

■ **Rnd 1:** Beginning dc3tog over first 3 sts, *[ch 3, dc3tog over next 3 sts] to corner, placing last dc in corner st**, ch 5, dc3tog over same corner st and next 2 sts; rep from * around, ending last rep at **, ch 4, join with sc to top of first cluster.

■ **Rnd 2:** Ch 2, dc2tog over next st and space, *[ch 3, dc3tog over next (space, st, space)] to corner, placing last dc in corner space, ch 3, 3-dc cluster in same corner space, ch 3**, dc3tog over (same space, next st, next space); rep from * around, ending last rep at **, join with slip st to first cluster.

■ **Rnd 3:** Ch 1, (2 sc, ch 3, 2 sc) in each ch-3 space around, join with slip st to first sc. Fasten off.

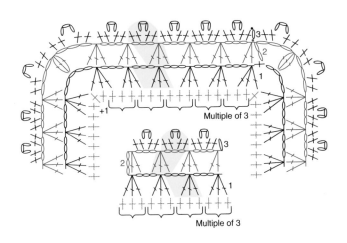

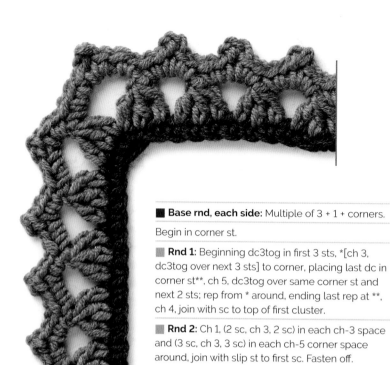

#18

Stitches & Notes

Border #18 mimics Border #17 (page 59), simply leaving out the middle round and adapting the final round to fit.

Picot-4: Ch 4, slip st in third chain from hook.

■ **Base rnd, each side:** Multiple of 3 + 1 + corners. Begin in corner st.

▨ **Rnd 1:** Beginning dc3tog in first 3 sts, *[ch 3, dc3tog over next 3 sts] to corner, placing last dc in corner st**, ch 5, dc3tog over same corner st and next 2 sts; rep from * around, ending last rep at **, ch 4, join with sc to top of first cluster.

▨ **Rnd 2:** Ch 1, (2 sc, ch 3, 2 sc) in each ch-3 space and (3 sc, ch 3, 3 sc) in each ch-5 corner space around, join with slip st to first sc. Fasten off.

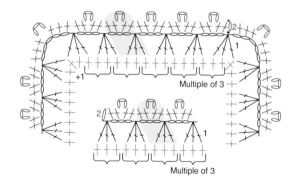

Multiple of 3

Multiple of 3

Reversible

Narrow

Undulating

Open/Lacy

#19

Stitches & Notes

Rnds 1 and 2 of this border are the same as for those in Border #17 (page 59). The final round differs, however; this slight change turns the gently scalloped edge into a much more angular one.

Picot-4: Ch 4, slip st in third chain from hook.

■ **Base rnd, each side:** Multiple of 3 + 1 + corners.

Begin in corner st.

■ **Rnd 1:** Beginning dc3tog in first 3 sts, *[ch 3, dc3tog over next 3 sts] to corner, placing last dc in corner st**, ch 5, dc3tog over same corner st and next 2 sts; rep from * around, ending last rep at **, ch 4, join with sc to top of first cluster.

■ **Rnd 2:** Ch 2, dc2tog over next st and space, *[ch 3, dc3tog over next (space, st, space)] to corner, placing last dc in corner space, ch 3, 3-dc cluster in same corner space, ch 3**, dc3tog over (same space, next st, next space); rep from * around, ending last rep at **, join with slip st to first cluster.

■ **Rnd 3:** Ch 1, (3 sc, picot-4) in each ch-3 space around, join with slip st to first sc. Fasten off.

Reversible

Medium

Undulating

Open/Lacy

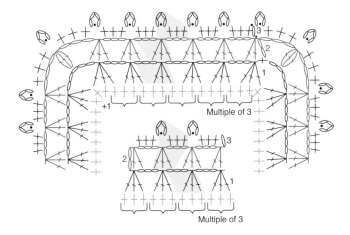

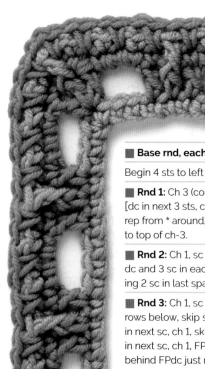

Base rnd, each side: Multiple of 6 + 3 + corners.

Begin 4 sts to left of corner.

■ **Rnd 1:** Ch 3 (counts as dc), dc in next 2 sts, *ch 3, skip 3 sts, [dc in next 3 sts, ch 3, skip 3 sts] to corner st 3 dc in corner st; rep from * around, ending last rep ch 2, skip 3 sts, join with sc to top of ch-3.

■ **Rnd 2:** Ch 1, sc in space formed by joining sc, sc in each dc and 3 sc in each ch-3 space and corner st around, ending 2 sc in last space, join with slip st to first sc.

■ **Rnd 3:** Ch 1, sc in first sc, *ch 1, skip 1 st, [FPdc in next st 2 rows below, skip st behind FPdc just made, ch 1, skip 1 sc, (sc in next sc, ch 1, skip 1 st) two times] to 1 st before corner st, sc in next sc, ch 1, FPdc in next corner dc 2 rows below, skip st behind FPdc just made, ch 1, (sc in next sc, ch 1, skip 1 sc**) two times, sc in next sc; rep from * around, ending last rep at **, sc in next sc, join with sc to first sc.

Note: When working scs in the row below, work over the ch-1 spaces from Rnd 3.

■ **Rnd 4:** Ch 1, sc in sc 2 rows below, *ch 1, skip 1 sc, [sc in next sc 2 rows below, ch 1, skip 1 sc**] to space before corner st, ch 1, sc in next corner sc 2 rows below, ch 2, sc in same corner sc 2 rows below; rep from * around, ending last rep at **, join with slip st to first sc. Fasten off.

#20

Stitches & Notes

FPdc (front post double crochet): Yarnover, insert hook from front to back to front around post of st indicated, yarnover and pull up a loop, (yarnover and pull through 2 loops) two times.

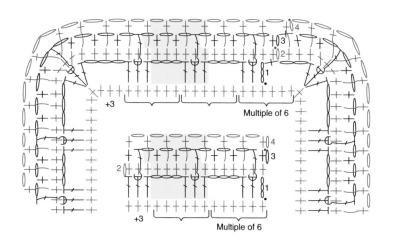

Medium

Straight

Textured

#21

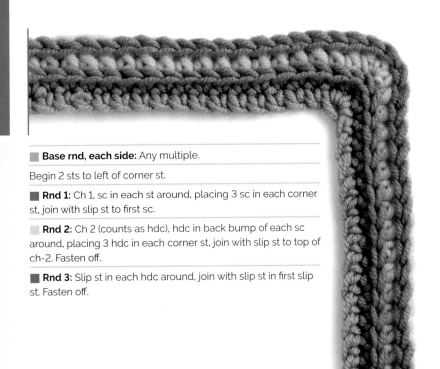

Stitches & Notes

For an illustration of how to work in the back bump, see page 210.

▨ **Base rnd, each side:** Any multiple.

Begin 2 sts to left of corner st.

▨ **Rnd 1:** Ch 1, sc in each st around, placing 3 sc in each corner st, join with slip st to first sc.

▨ **Rnd 2:** Ch 2 (counts as hdc), hdc in back bump of each sc around, placing 3 hdc in each corner st, join with slip st to top of ch-2. Fasten off.

▨ **Rnd 3:** Slip st in each hdc around, join with slip st in first slip st. Fasten off.

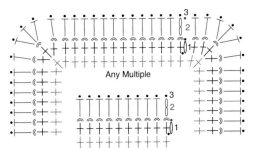

Any Multiple

Narrow

Straight

Textured

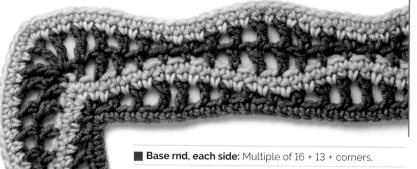

Base rnd, each side: Multiple of 16 + 13 + corners.

Begin 2 sts to left of corner st.

Rnd 1: Ch 2 (counts as hdc), *[ch 1, skip 1 st, dc in next st, (ch 1, skip 1 dc, tr in next st) two times, ch 1, skip 1 st, dc in next st, ch 1, skip 1 st, hdc in next st**, (ch 1, skip 1 st, sc in next st) two times, ch 1, skip 1 st, hdc in next st] to 1 st before corner ending at **; ch 1, skip 1 st, (sc, ch 1, sc) in corner st, ch 1, skip 1 st, hdc in next st; rep from * around, omitting last hdc, join with slip st to first hdc.

Rnd 2: Ch 1, sc in each st and ch-1 space around, placing 3 sc in each corner space, join with slip st to first sc.

Rnd 3: Ch 1, sc in each st around, placing 3 sc in each corner st, join with slip st to first sc.

Rnd 4: Ch 4 (counts as dc and ch 1 here and throughout), *[skip 1 sc, hdc in next sc, (ch 1, skip 1 sc, sc in next sc) two times, ch 1, skip 1 sc, hdc in next sc, ch 1, skip 1 sc, dc in next sc**, (ch 1, skip 1 sc, tr in next sc) two times, ch 1, skip 1 sc, dc in next sc, ch 1] to 4 sts before corner st, ending at **, ch 1, skip 1 sc, tr in next sc, ch 1, skip 1 sc, dc in next sc, ch 1, sc in corner st, ch 1, dc in next sc, ch 1, skip 1 sc, tr in next sc, ch 1, skip 1 sc,***, dc in next sc, ch 1; rep from * around, ending last rep at ***, join with slip st to third ch of ch-4.

Rnd 5: Ch 4, *[hdc in next hdc, (ch 1, sc in next sc) two times, ch 1, hdc in next hdc, ch 1, dc in next dc**, (ch 1, tr in next tr) two times, ch 1, dc in next dc, ch 1] to tr before corner st, ending at **, ch 1, dc in next tr, ch 1, tr in next dc, ch 1, (tr, ch 1) three times in corner sc, tr in next dc, ch 1, dc in next tr, ch 1***, dc in next dc, ch 1; rep from * around, ending last rep at ***, join with slip st to third ch of ch-4.

Rnd 6: Ch 1, sc in each st and ch-1 space around, placing 3 sc in each corner tr, join with slip st to first sc.

Rnd 7: Ch 1, sc in each sc around, join with slip st to first sc. Fasten off.

Reversible

Wide

Undulating

Open/Lacy

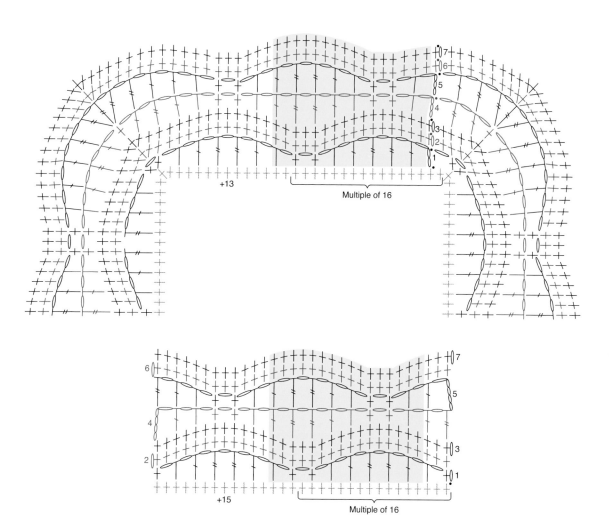

+13

Multiple of 16

+15

Multiple of 16

Base rnd, each side: Multiple of 6 + 3 + corners. Begin 5 sts to left of corner st.

■ **Rnd 1:** Ch 3 (counts as dc), dc in each st around, placing 5 dc in each corner st, join with slip st to top of ch-3.

▨ **Rnd 2:** Ch 1, reverse sc in front loop of each dc around, placing 2 reverse sc in front loop of each corner st, join with slip st to first st. (For an illustration of reverse single crochet, see page 214.)

■ **Rnd 3:** Ch 1, BLsc in each Rnd-1 dc around, placing 3 BLsc in each corner st, join with slip st to first sc.

■ **Rnd 4:** Ch 1, sc in first sc, *[fsc Arch, skip 5 sc, sc in next sc] to 1 st before corner st, fsc Arch, skip 3 sc, sc in next sc; rep from * around, ending fsc Arch, skip 5 sc, join with slip st to first sc. Fasten off.

Note: Rnd-5 sts are worked into the center sc of each of the skipped 5-sc groups of Rnd 3, keeping Rnd-4 sts to the back.

■ **Rnd 5:** Standing sc in any corner st of Rnd 3, *fsc Arch, skip 4 sts, sc in next skipped sc (at center of 5 skipped sts), [fsc Arch, skip 5 sts, sc in next skipped sc] to 4 sts before corner st, fsc Arch, skip 4 sts, sc in corner sc; rep from * around, omitting last sc, join with slip st to first sc. Fasten off.

#23

Stitches & Notes

BLsc (back loop single crochet): Single crochet into the back loop only.

Fsc Arch (foundation single crochet arch): Insert hook into same st, yarnover and pull up a loop, yarnover and pull through 1 loop — *1 chain made.* Yarnover and pull through 2 loops — *1 fsc made,* * Insert hook under 2 loops of ch at base of previous fsc, yarnover and pull up a loop, yarnover and pull through 1 loop, yarnover and pull through 2 loops; rep from * three times, ch 3, fsc in ch at base of previous fsc, fsc 4. (For illustrations of foundation single crochet arch, see page 212.)

Wide

Undulating

Layered

Textured

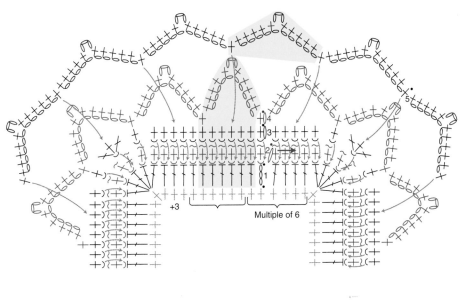

+3

Multiple of 6

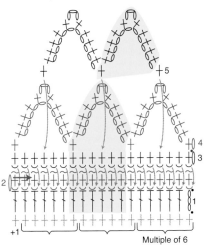

+1

Multiple of 6

#24

Base rnd, each side: Multiple of 12 + 5 + corners.

Begin 2 sts to left of corner st.

Rnd 1: Ch 4 (counts as dc here and ch 1), *skip 1 st, [dc in next st, ch 1, skip 1 st] to corner st, (dc, ch 3, dc) in corner st, ch 1; rep from * around, skip 1 st, join with slip st to third ch of ch-4.

Rnd 2: Ch 1, sc in each sc and ch-1 space around, placing 3 sc in each corner space, join with slip st to first sc. Fasten off.

Fan

Row 1: Standing dc in desired st, ch 5, dc in same st, turn.

Row 2: Ch 3 (counts as dc), 5 dc in ch-5 space, turn. You now have 6 dc.

Row 3: Ch 5 (counts as dc, ch 2 here and throughout), (dc in next dc, ch 2) four times, dc in top of turning-ch, turn.

Row 4: Ch 5, dc in first space, ch 2, (dc, ch 2) two times in each ch-space across, ending with (dc, ch 2, dc) in last space, turn. You now have 9 ch-2 spaces and 10 dc.

Row 5: Ch 1, (sc, ch 3, sc) in each space across. Fasten off.

Stitches & Notes

There are so many ways to do this one! Each of these fans is worked separately, making it easy to change colors and adjust spacing to your preferences.

If you prefer, put a fan in each corner, space them farther apart, or join the outside corner of each fan to the previous fan as you go.

Reversible

Wide

Straight

Motifs

Fringy

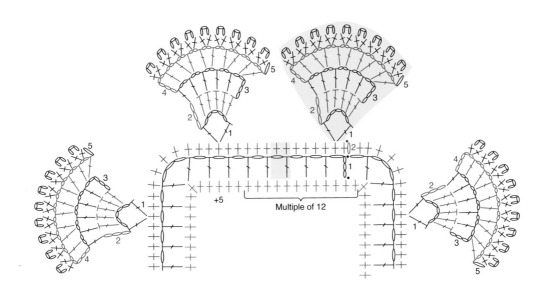

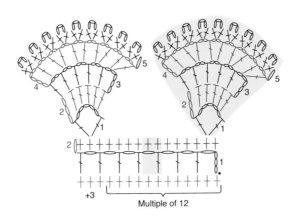

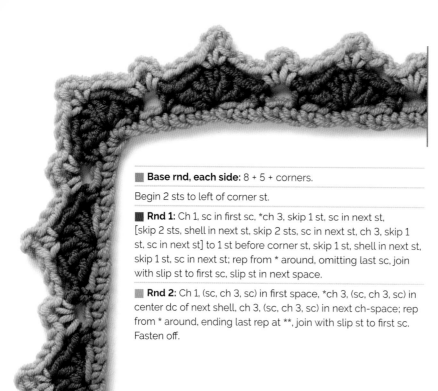

#25

Base rnd, each side: 8 + 5 + corners.

Begin 2 sts to left of corner st.

Rnd 1: Ch 1, sc in first sc, *ch 3, skip 1 st, sc in next st, [skip 2 sts, shell in next st, skip 2 sts, sc in next st, ch 3, skip 1 st, sc in next st] to 1 st before corner st, skip 1 st, shell in next st, skip 1 st, sc in next st; rep from * around, omitting last sc, join with slip st to first sc, slip st in next space.

Rnd 2: Ch 1, (sc, ch 3, sc) in first space, *ch 3, (sc, ch 3, sc) in center dc of next shell, ch 3, (sc, ch 3, sc) in next ch-space; rep from * around, ending last rep at **, join with slip st to first sc. Fasten off.

Stitches & Notes

Shell: 5 dc in st or space indicated.

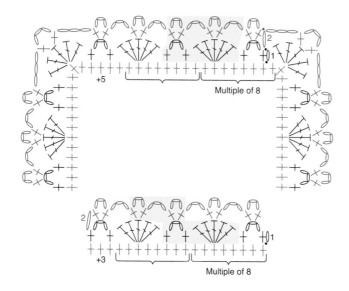

Reversible

Narrow

Undulating

#26

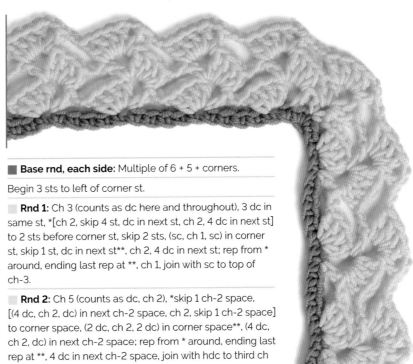

■ **Base rnd, each side:** Multiple of 6 + 5 + corners.

Begin 3 sts to left of corner st.

▨ **Rnd 1:** Ch 3 (counts as dc here and throughout), 3 dc in same st, *[ch 2, skip 4 st, dc in next st, ch 2, 4 dc in next st] to 2 sts before corner st, skip 2 sts, (sc, ch 1, sc) in corner st, skip 1 st, dc in next st**, ch 2, 4 dc in next st; rep from * around, ending last rep at **, ch 1, join with sc to top of ch-3.

▨ **Rnd 2:** Ch 5 (counts as dc, ch 2), *skip 1 ch-2 space, [(4 dc, ch 2, dc) in next ch-2 space, ch 2, skip 1 ch-2 space] to corner space, (2 dc, ch 2, 2 dc) in corner space**, (4 dc, ch 2, dc) in next ch-2 space; rep from * around, ending last rep at **, 4 dc in next ch-2 space, join with hdc to third ch of ch-5.

▨ **Rnd 3:** Ch 5 (counts as dc, ch 2), 4 dc in same space formed by joining hdc, *ch 2, skip 1 ch-2 space, [(dc, ch 2, 4 dc) in next ch-2 space, ch 2, skip 1 ch-2 space] to corner space, (dc, ch 2, 4 dc) in corner space, ch 2**, (dc, ch 2, 4 dc) in next ch-2 space; rep from * around, join with slip st to third ch of ch-5. Fasten off.

Reversible

Medium

Undulating

Open/Lacy

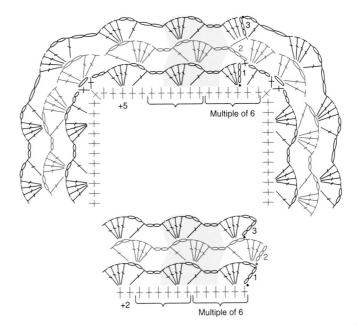

#27

Stitches & Notes

Here's an example of how simple textured stitches can combine to make an interesting border. Because there is no true corner stitch or space here, it is helpful to use markers at each of the corners in this border.

Crossed dcs: Skip 1 st, dc in next st, dc in skipped st working behind dc just made.

■ **Base rnd, each side:** Multiple of 2 + corners. Begin 3 sts to left of corner st.

▧ **Rnd 1:** Ch 3 (counts as dc here and throughout), dc in next st to the right (left for lefties) working behind dc just made, *make crossed dcs across, placing first leg of last crossed dc in corner st, 2 dc in same corner st, place marker in second of these 2 sts to mark corner st, crossed dc in next st and in corner st; rep from * around, join with slip st to top of ch-3.

■ **Rnd 2:** Ch 1, *sc in each dc to corner st, 2 sc in marked st, move marker to first of these 2 sts; 2 sts in next st; rep from * around, ending last repeat sc in last 2 dc, join with slip st to first sc.

▨ **Rnd 3:** Ch 1, sc in first st, *[tr in next st, sc in next st] to marked sc, (tr, sc) in next 2 sts and move marker to second of these 4 sts; rep from * around, ending last repeat tr in next st, sc in next st, tr in next st, join with slip st to first sc.

■ **Rnd 4:** Ch 1, *sc in each st to marked st, 2 sc in next 2 sts and move marker to second of these 4 sts; rep from * around, ending last rep sc in each st to end of rnd, join with slip st to first sc.

▧ **Rnd 5:** Ch 3, dc in next st to the right (left for lefties) working behind ch just made, *make crossed dcs to 2 sts before marked st, (ch 1, crossed dcs over next 2 sts) three times; rep from * around, ending crossed dcs in last 2 sts, join with slip st to top of ch-3.

■ **Rnd 6:** Ch 1, sc in each dc and ch-1 space around, placing 2 sc in ch-1 spaces if needed to allow edge to lie flat, join with slip st to first sc. Fasten off.

Reversible
Wide
Straight
Textured

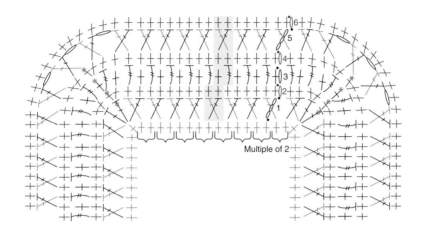

Multiple of 2

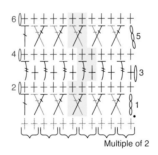

Multiple of 2

#28

Base rnd, each side: Multiple of 5 + 3 + corners.

Begin 2 sts to left of corner st.

Rnd 1: Ch 1, sc in each sc around, placing 3 sc in each corner st, join with slip st to first sc.

Rnd 2: Ch 4 (counts as dc and ch 1), 2-tr cluster in same st, *ch 1, [skip 4 sc, Cluster Shell in next st, ch 1] to 2 sts before corner st, skip 2 sc, Cluster Shell in corner st, ch 1, skip 2 sc**, Cluster Shell in next st; rep from * around ending last rep at **, 2-tr cluster in same st as first st, join with sc to third ch of ch-4.

Rnd 3: Ch 1, sc in space formed by joining sc, *ch 1, popcorn in next dc, ch 1, sc in next ch-1 space, ch 3, skip (cluster, ch-1 space, cluster), sc in next ch-1 space; rep from * around, omitting last sc, join with slip st to first sc. Fasten off.

Note: Rnd 4 sts are worked into the clusters and ch-1 spaces of Rnd 2, working over and enclosing the chains of Rnd 3.

Rnd 4: Standing sc in first Rnd-2 cluster after any corner, *sc in next ch-1 space, sc in next cluster, [ch 3 keeping popcorn to the front, sc in next (cluster, ch-1 space, cluster)] to corner, ch 5 keeping popcorn to the front **, sc in next cluster; rep from * around, ending last rep at **, join with slip st to first sc. Fasten off.

Rnd 5: Standing sc in first ch-3 space after any corner, (3 dc, sc) in same space, *skip 1 sc, sc in next sc**, [(sc, 3 dc, sc) in next space, skip 1 sc, sc in next sc] to corner space, (sc, 5 dc, sc) in corner space; rep from * around, ending last rep at **, join with slip st to first sc. Fasten off.

Stitches & Notes

2-tr Cluster: *Yarnover two times, insert hook into stitch or space indicated and pull up a loop, (yarnover and pull through 2 loops) two times; rep from * once, yarnover and pull through all 3 loops on hook.

Cluster Shell: (2-tr Cluster, ch 1, dc, ch 1, 2-tr Cluster) in one st.

Popcorn: 5 dc in st or space indicated, drop loop from hook, insert hook from front to back through top of first of these 5 dc, place loop on hook, and pull through st, ch 1 to close.

Medium

Undulating

Textured

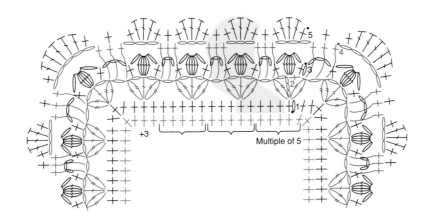

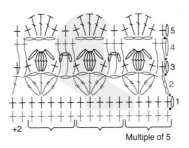

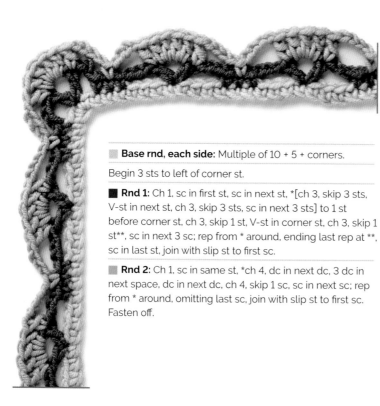

#29

Base rnd, each side: Multiple of 10 + 5 + corners.

Begin 3 sts to left of corner st.

Rnd 1: Ch 1, sc in first st, sc in next st, *[ch 3, skip 3 sts, V-st in next st, ch 3, skip 3 sts, sc in next 3 sts] to 1 st before corner st, ch 3, skip 1 st, V-st in corner st, ch 3, skip 1 st**, sc in next 3 sc; rep from * around, ending last rep at **, sc in last st, join with slip st to first sc.

Rnd 2: Ch 1, sc in same st, *ch 4, dc in next dc, 3 dc in next space, dc in next dc, ch 4, skip 1 sc, sc in next sc; rep from * around, omitting last sc, join with slip st to first sc. Fasten off.

Stitches & Notes

V-st (V-stitch): (Dc, ch 2, dc) in st or space indicated.

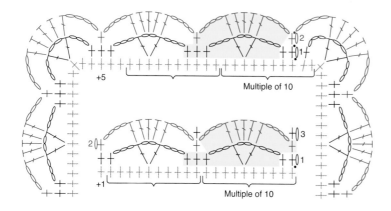

Reversible

Medium

Undulating

Open/Lacy

#30

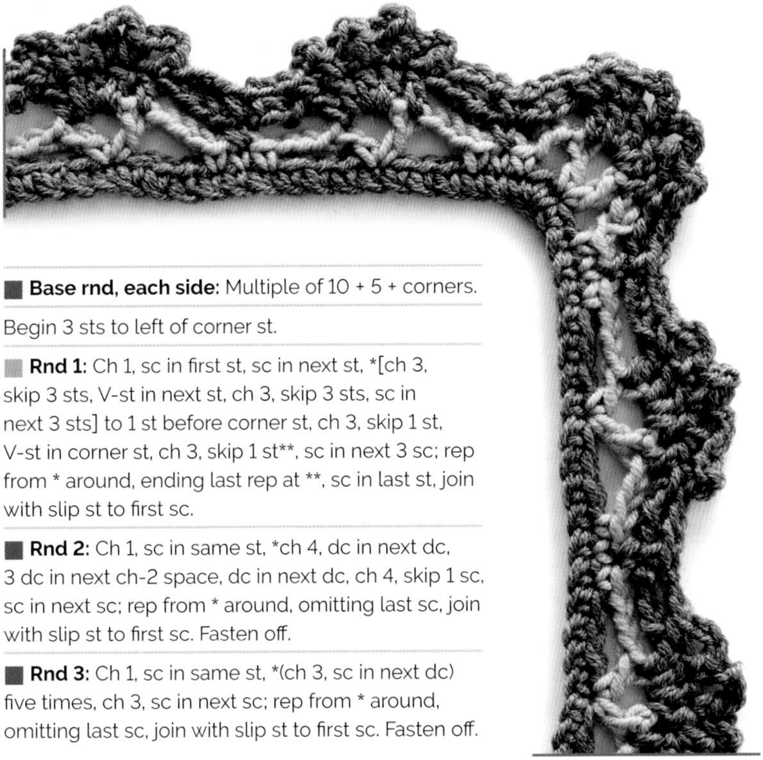

Stitches & Notes

Adding a third round to Border #29 (facing page) adds a bit of flair to otherwise smooth curves.

V-st (V-stitch): (Dc, ch 2, dc) in st or space indicated.

Base rnd, each side: Multiple of 10 + 5 + corners.

Begin 3 sts to left of corner st.

Rnd 1: Ch 1, sc in first st, sc in next st, *[ch 3, skip 3 sts, V-st in next st, ch 3, skip 3 sts, sc in next 3 sts] to 1 st before corner st, ch 3, skip 1 st, V-st in corner st, ch 3, skip 1 st**, sc in next 3 sc; rep from * around, ending last rep at **, sc in last st, join with slip st to first sc.

Rnd 2: Ch 1, sc in same st, *ch 4, dc in next dc, 3 dc in next ch-2 space, dc in next dc, ch 4, skip 1 sc, sc in next sc; rep from * around, omitting last sc, join with slip st to first sc. Fasten off.

Rnd 3: Ch 1, sc in same st, *(ch 3, sc in next dc) five times, ch 3, sc in next sc; rep from * around, omitting last sc, join with slip st to first sc. Fasten off.

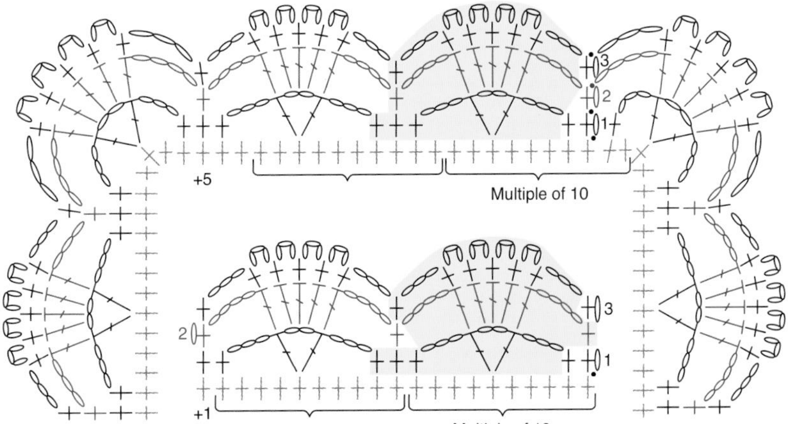

Reversible

Medium

Undulating

Open/Lacy

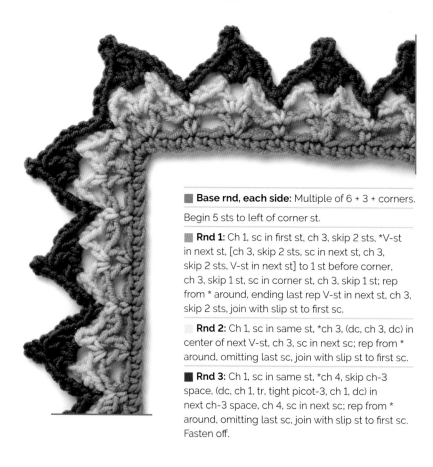

#31

Base rnd, each side: Multiple of 6 + 3 + corners. Begin 5 sts to left of corner st.

Rnd 1: Ch 1, sc in first st, ch 3, skip 2 sts, *V-st in next st, [ch 3, skip 2 sts, sc in next st, ch 3, skip 2 sts, V-st in next st] to 1 st before corner, ch 3, skip 1 st, sc in corner st, ch 3, skip 1 st; rep from * around, ending last rep V-st in next st, ch 3, skip 2 sts, join with slip st to first sc.

Rnd 2: Ch 1, sc in same st, *ch 3, (dc, ch 3, dc) in center of next V-st, ch 3, sc in next sc; rep from * around, omitting last sc, join with slip st to first sc.

Rnd 3: Ch 1, sc in same st, *ch 4, skip ch-3 space, (dc, ch 1, tr, tight picot-3, ch 1, dc) in next ch-3 space, ch 4, sc in next sc; rep from * around, omitting last sc, join with slip st to first sc. Fasten off.

Stitches & Notes

Tight picot-3: Ch 3, slip st in third ch from hook and in st at bottom of ch together. (For an illustration of tight picot-3, see page 214.)

V-st (V-stitch): (Dc, ch 1, dc) in st or space indicated.

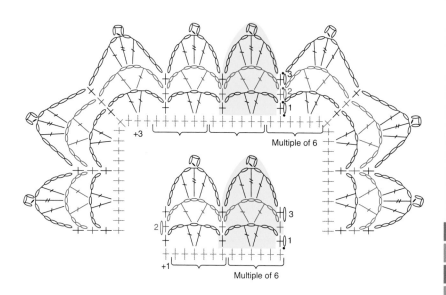

Reversible

Medium

Undulating

Open/Lacy

#32

Stitches & Notes

The first two rounds of Border #32 are the same as Border #31 (facing page), but the third round is more solid and substantial.

Picot-3: Ch 3, slip st in third chain from hook.

V-st (V-stitch): (Dc, ch 1, dc) in st or space indicated.

■ **Base rnd, each side:** Multiple of 6 + 3 + corners.

Begin 5 sts to left of corner st.

■ **Rnd 1:** Ch 1, sc in first st, ch 3, skip 2 sts, *V-st in next st, [ch 3, skip 2 sts, sc in next st, ch 3, skip 2 sts, V-st in next st] to 1 st before corner, ch 3, skip 1 st, sc in corner st, ch 3, skip 1 st; rep from * around, ending last rep V-st in next st, ch 3, skip 2 sts, join with slip st to first sc.

■ **Rnd 2:** Ch 1, sc in same st, *ch 3, (dc, ch 3, dc) in center of next V-st, ch 3, sc in next sc; rep from * around, omitting last sc, join with slip st to first sc.

■ **Rnd 3:** Ch 1, sc in same st, *ch 3, skip ch-3 space, (3 dc, picot-3, 3 dc) in next ch-3 space, ch 3, sc in next sc; rep from * around, omitting last sc, join with slip st to first sc. Fasten off.

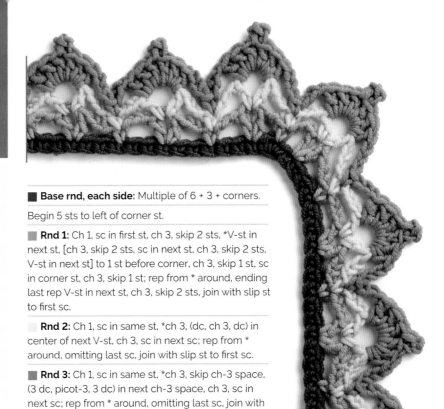

Reversible

Medium

Undulating

Open/Lacy

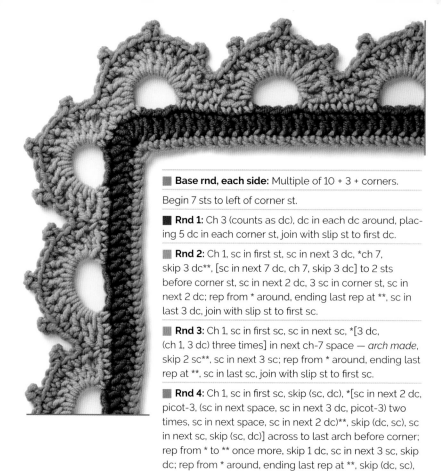

■ **Base rnd, each side:** Multiple of 10 + 3 + corners.

Begin 7 sts to left of corner st.

■ **Rnd 1:** Ch 3 (counts as dc), dc in each dc around, placing 5 dc in each corner st, join with slip st to first dc.

■ **Rnd 2:** Ch 1, sc in first st, sc in next 3 dc, *ch 7, skip 3 dc**, [sc in next 7 dc, ch 7, skip 3 dc] to 2 sts before corner st, sc in next 2 dc, 3 sc in corner st, sc in next 2 dc; rep from * around, ending last rep at **, sc in last 3 dc, join with slip st to first sc.

■ **Rnd 3:** Ch 1, sc in first sc, sc in next sc, *[3 dc, (ch 1, 3 dc) three times] in next ch-7 space — *arch made*, skip 2 sc**, sc in next 3 sc; rep from * around, ending last rep at **, sc in last sc, join with slip st to first sc.

■ **Rnd 4:** Ch 1, sc in first sc, skip (sc, dc), *[sc in next 2 dc, picot-3, (sc in next space, sc in next 3 dc, picot-3) two times, sc in next space, sc in next 2 dc)**, skip (dc, sc), sc in next sc, skip (sc, dc)] across to last arch before corner; rep from * to ** once more, skip 1 dc, sc in next 3 sc, skip dc; rep from * around, ending last rep at **, skip (dc, sc), join with slip st to first sc. Fasten off.

#33

Stitches & Notes

Picot-3: Ch 3, slip st in third chain from hook.

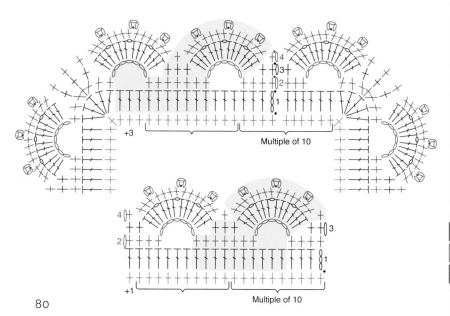

Reversible

Wide

Undulating

#34

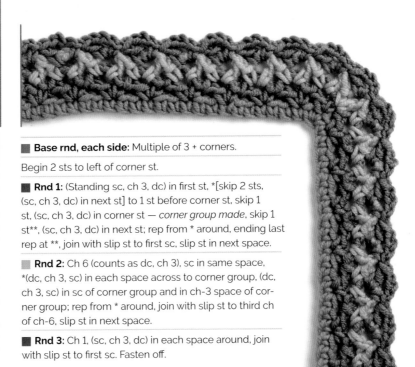

■ **Base rnd, each side:** Multiple of 3 + corners.

Begin 2 sts to left of corner st.

■ **Rnd 1:** (Standing sc, ch 3, dc) in first st, *[skip 2 sts, (sc, ch 3, dc) in next st] to 1 st before corner st, skip 1 st, (sc, ch 3, dc) in corner st — *corner group made*, skip 1 st**, (sc, ch 3, dc) in next st; rep from * around, ending last rep at **, join with slip st to first sc, slip st in next space.

■ **Rnd 2:** Ch 6 (counts as dc, ch 3), sc in same space, *(dc, ch 3, sc) in each space across to corner group, (dc, ch 3, sc) in sc of corner group and in ch-3 space of corner group; rep from * around, join with slip st to third ch of ch-6, slip st in next space.

■ **Rnd 3:** Ch 1, (sc, ch 3, dc) in each space around, join with slip st to first sc. Fasten off.

Reversible

Medium

Undulating

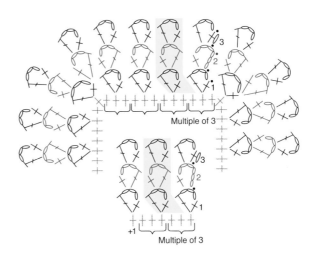

Stitches & Notes

The half double crochet mesh that serves as the base for the fringe offers many possibilities for the placement of the fringe. This border requires some sampling on your part to determine the optimal length and placement for the fringe. Customize the border by using fewer (or more) base rounds/rows, longer or shorter fringe, or more or less dense fringe.

Base rnd, each side: Multiple of 4 + 1 + corners.

Begin 2 sts to left of corner st.

Rnd 1: Ch 3 (counts as hdc and ch 1 here and throughout), *skip 1 st, [hdc in next st, ch 1, skip 1 st] to corner st, (hdc, ch 2, hdc) in corner st, ch 1; rep from * around, ending skip 1 st, join with slip st to second ch of ch-3.

Rnd 2: Ch 3, *[hdc in next hdc, ch 1**] to corner space, (hdc, ch 2, hdc, ch 1) in corner space; rep from * around, ending last rep at **, join with slip st to second ch of ch-3. Fasten off.

Fringe: Cut 3 lengths of yarn for each fringe, determining the optimal fringe length for your project. (Fringe shown was cut in 8"/20.5 cm lengths.) Referring to stitch diagram, attach fringe in locations marked, or as desired. Trim fringe.

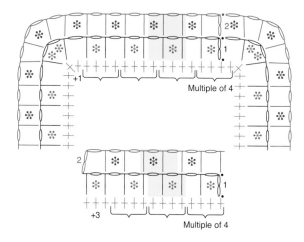

Reversible

Wide

Straight

Fringy

#36

■ **Base rnd, each side:** Multiple of 8 + 3 + corners.

Begin 1 st to left of corner st.

■ **Rnd 1:** Ch 1, sc in each st around, placing 3 sc in each corner st, join with slip st to first sc.

■ **Rnd 2:** Ch 1, sc in first sc, *ch 1, skip 1 st, [sc in next st, ch 1, skip 1 st] to corner st, (sc, ch 1, sc) in corner st; rep from * around, ending ch 1, skip 1 st, join with slip st to first sc, slip st in next space.

■ **Rnd 3:** Ch 1, sc in same space, *ch 3, dc in next space, ch 3, 7 dc around post of dc just made, sc in next space; rep from * around, omitting last sc, join with slip st to first sc. Fasten off.

Note: Rnd 4 is worked into Rnd-2 spaces, working behind the petals of Rnd 3; place each st to the left of the st made in Rnd 3.

■ **Rnd 4:** Standing sc in first space to the left (right for lefties) of corner space, *ch 3, dc in next space, ch 3, 7 dc around post of dc just made, sc in next space; rep from * around, omitting last sc, join with slip st to first sc. Fasten off.

Medium

Undulating

Layered

Textured

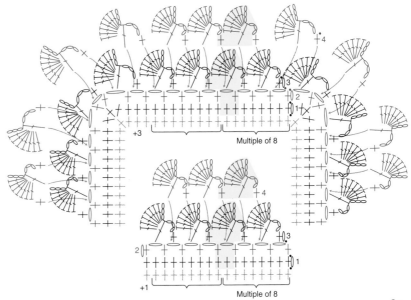

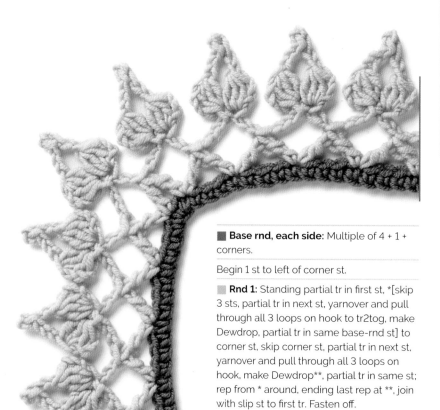

Stitches & Notes

3-dc Cluster (three double crochet cluster): Yarnover, insert hook into st or space indicated and pull up a loop, yarnover and pull through 2 loops, (yarnover, insert hook into same st or space and pull up a loop, yarnover and pull through 2 loops) two times, yarnover and pull through all 4 loops on hook.

Dewdrop: Ch 7, 3-dc cluster in fourth ch from hook, ch 2, picot-3, ch 7, 3-dc cluster in fourth ch from hook, slip st in top of first cluster, ch 3.

Partial tr (partial treble crochet): Yarnover two times, insert hook into st or space indicated and pull up a loop, (yarnover and pull through 2 loops on hook) two times.

Picot-3: Ch 3, slip st in third chain from hook.

Standing partial tr (partial treble crochet): Beginning with slip knot on hook, work partial tr.

■ **Base rnd, each side:** Multiple of 4 + 1 + corners.

Begin 1 st to left of corner st.

■ **Rnd 1:** Standing partial tr in first st, *[skip 3 sts, partial tr in next st, yarnover and pull through all 3 loops on hook to tr2tog, make Dewdrop, partial tr in same base-rnd st] to corner st, skip corner st, partial tr in next st, yarnover and pull through all 3 loops on hook, make Dewdrop**, partial tr in same st; rep from * around, ending last rep at **, join with slip st to first tr. Fasten off.

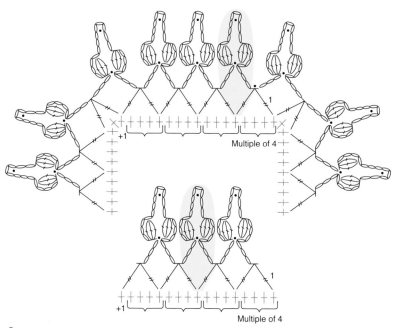

- Reversible
- Wide
- Open/Lacy
- Fringy

#38

■ **Base rnd, each side:** Multiple of 6 + 5 + corners.

Begin 3 sts to left of corner st.

■ **Rnd 1:** Ch 1, sc in first st, *ch 3, skip 2 sts, sc in next st; rep from * around, omitting last sc, join with slip st to first sc. Fasten off.

Note: Rnds 2 and 3 are worked into base-round sts, working alternately in front of and behind existing sts.

■ **Rnd 2:** Standing sc in first skipped st in front of Rnd-1 sts, *ch 3, skip next (skipped st, sc), sc in next st *behind* the Rnd-1 sts, ch 3, skip next (skipped st, sc)**, sc in next st *in front of* Rnd-1 sts; rep from * around working ch 4 instead of ch 3 at corners, ending last repeat at **, join with slip st in first sc *in front of* Rnd-1 sts. Fasten off.

■ **Rnd 3:** Standing sc in first free skipped st *behind* existing sts, *ch 4, sc in next free skipped st *in front of* existing sts, ch 4**, sc in next free skipped st *behind* existing sts; rep from * around, ending last repeat at **, join with slip st in first sc *behind* Rnd-1 sts. Fasten off.

Reversible

Narrow

Straight

Layered

Textured

#39

Base rnd, each side: Multiple of 3 + 1 + corners.

Begin 1 st to left of corner st.

Rnd 1: Ch 1, sc in first sc, *[ch 1, bullion coil, ch 2, skip 2 sc, sc in next sc] to corner st, ch 1, bullion coil, skip corner st, sc in next st; rep from * around, omitting last sc, join with slip st to first sc.

Stitches & Notes

For best results on this border, use a crochet hook with a long shank and without a thumb rest. Take your time, and use your fingers to pull the wraps over the loop on the hook, rather than trying to pull the loop through the wraps. If the bullion coils are too heavy for your yarn, try wrapping fewer times, or using a picot in place of every other bullion.

Bullion Coil: (Yarnover) 12 times, yarnover and pull through all 13 loops on hook, ch 1 to close, pulling chain tightly to fold coil. (For an illustration of bullion coil, see page 211.)

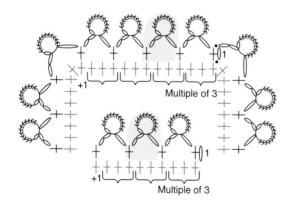

Multiple of 3

Multiple of 3

Reversible

Narrow

Undulating

Motifs

Fringy

#40

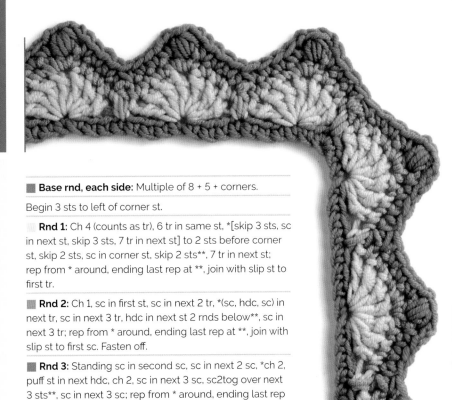

Stitches & Notes

Puff st (puff stitch):
(Yarnover, insert hook
and pull up a loop) three
times in st or space
indicated, yarnover
and pull through all 7
loops on hook. (For an
illustration of puff stitch,
see page 214.)

Sc2tog over 3 sts: Insert
hook into next st and pull
up a loop, skip 1 st, insert
hook into next st and pull
up a loop, yarnover and
pull through all 3 loops
on hook.

■ **Base rnd, each side:** Multiple of 8 + 5 + corners.

Begin 3 sts to left of corner st.

▨ **Rnd 1:** Ch 4 (counts as tr), 6 tr in same st, *[skip 3 sts, sc
in next st, skip 3 sts, 7 tr in next st] to 2 sts before corner
st, skip 2 sts, sc in corner st, skip 2 sts**, 7 tr in next st;
rep from * around, ending last rep at **, join with slip st to
first tr.

▨ **Rnd 2:** Ch 1, sc in first st, sc in next 2 tr, *(sc, hdc, sc) in
next tr, sc in next 3 tr, hdc in next st 2 rnds below**, sc in
next 3 tr; rep from * around, ending last rep at **, join with
slip st to first sc. Fasten off.

▨ **Rnd 3:** Standing sc in second sc, sc in next 2 sc, *ch 2,
puff st in next hdc, ch 2, sc in next 3 sc, sc2tog over next
3 sts**, sc in next 3 sc; rep from * around, ending last rep
at **, join with slip st to first sc. Fasten off.

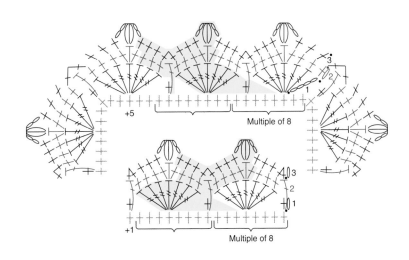

Reversible

Medium

Undulating

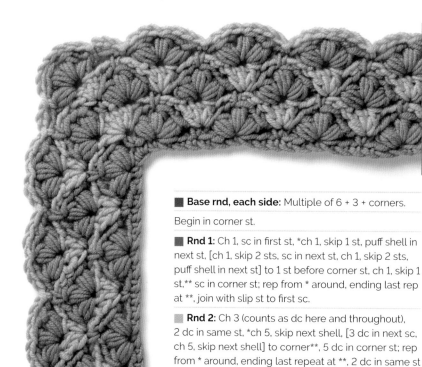

Base rnd, each side: Multiple of 6 + 3 + corners.

Begin in corner st.

■ **Rnd 1:** Ch 1, sc in first st, *ch 1, skip 1 st, puff shell in next st, [ch 1, skip 2 sts, sc in next st, ch 1, skip 2 sts, puff shell in next st] to 1 st before corner st, ch 1, skip 1 st,** sc in corner st; rep from * around, ending last rep at **, join with slip st to first sc.

■ **Rnd 2:** Ch 3 (counts as dc here and throughout), 2 dc in same st, *ch 5, skip next shell, [3 dc in next sc, ch 5, skip next shell] to corner**, 5 dc in corner st; rep from * around, ending last repeat at **, 2 dc in same st as beginning ch, join with slip st to top of ch-3.

■ **Rnd 3:** Ch 1, sc in same st, *[ch 1, skip 1 dc, puff shell in next dc, ch 1; working over ch-5 loop, sc in center puff st of next shell in rnd below] to 2 sts before corner st, ch 1, puff shell in next dc, ch 1, skip 1 dc, sc in corner dc; rep from * around, omitting last sc, join with slip st to first sc.

■ **Rnd 4:** Ch 3, dc in same st, *ch 5, skip next shell, [3 dc in next sc, ch 5, skip next shell] to corner**, 3 dc in corner sc; rep from * around, ending last repeat at **, dc in same st as beginning ch, join with slip st to top of ch-3.

■ **Rnd 5:** Ch 1 loosely (does not count as st), * [(puff st, ch 2) three times, puff st] in corner st — *corner shell made*, ch 1, sc in center puff of next shell in rnd below, [ch 1, skip 1 dc, puff shell in next dc, ch 1, sc in center puff of next shell in rnd below] to 1 st before corner st, ch 1, skip 1 dc; rep from * around, join with slip st to first puff st.

■ **Rnd 6:** *Ch 3, slip st in center ch-2 space of corner shell, ch 3, slip st in last puff of corner shell, ch 3, slip st in next sc, [ch 3, slip st in center puff of next shell, ch 3, slip st in next sc] to corner shell, ch 3, slip st in first puff of corner shell; rep from * around, ending last rep slip st in first slip st. Fasten off.

Stitches & Notes

Puff st (puff stitch): (Yarnover, insert hook and pull up a loop) three times in st or space indicated, yarnover and pull through all 7 loops on hook. (For an illustration of puff stitch, see page 214.)

Puff shell: [Puff st, (ch 2, puff st) two times] in st indicated.

Reversible

Wide

Undulating

Textured

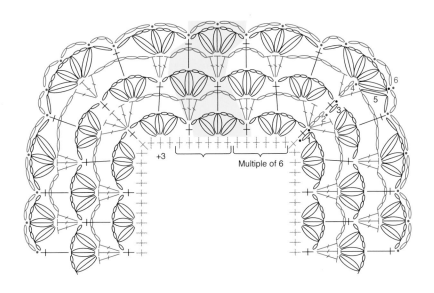

+3

Multiple of 6

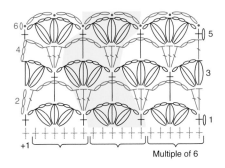

+1

Multiple of 6

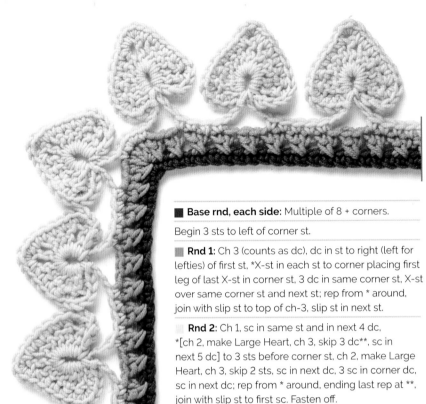

Stitches & Notes

X-st (X-stitch): *Worked over 2 sts and counts as 2 sts.* Skip 1 st, dc in next st, working over dc just made, dc in last skipped st.

■ **Base rnd, each side:** Multiple of 8 + corners.

Begin 3 sts to left of corner st.

■ **Rnd 1:** Ch 3 (counts as dc), dc in st to right (left for lefties) of first st, *X-st in each st to corner placing first leg of last X-st in corner st, 3 dc in same corner st, X-st over same corner st and next st; rep from * around, join with slip st to top of ch-3, slip st in next st.

▒ **Rnd 2:** Ch 1, sc in same st and in next 4 dc, *[ch 2, make Large Heart, ch 3, skip 3 dc** sc in next 5 dc] to 3 sts before corner st, ch 2, make Large Heart, ch 3, skip 2 sts, sc in next dc, 3 sc in corner dc, sc in next dc; rep from * around, ending last rep at **, join with slip st to first sc. Fasten off.

Large Heart

Ch 5, slip st in 5th ch from hook to form a ring, turn.

▒ **Row 1:** Ch 3 (counts as dc), (2 tr, 3 dc, ch 1, tr, ch 1, 3 dc, 2 tr, ch 3, slip st) in ring, turn.

▒ **Row 2:** Sc in next 3 ch, 3 sc in next tr, sc in next (4 sts, space), 3 sc in next tr, sc in next (space, 4 sts), 3 sc in next tr, sc in next 3 ch, slip st in ring.

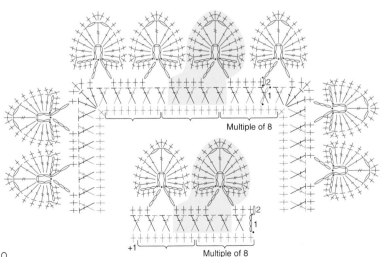

Reversible

Wide

Undulating

Motifs

Fringy

#43

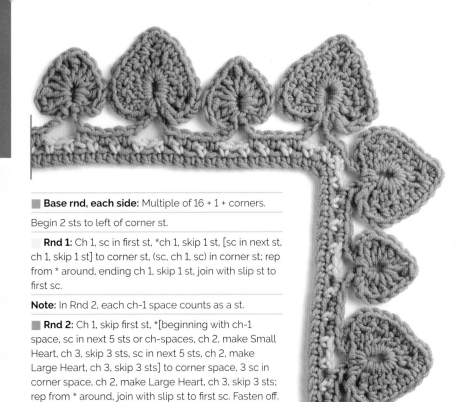

Stitches & Notes

This version shows alternating small and large hearts. How many other ways can you think of to adapt heart dangles?

Base rnd, each side: Multiple of 16 + 1 + corners.

Begin 2 sts to left of corner st.

Rnd 1: Ch 1, sc in first st, *ch 1, skip 1 st, [sc in next st, ch 1, skip 1 st] to corner st, (sc, ch 1, sc) in corner st; rep from * around, ending ch 1, skip 1 st, join with slip st to first sc.

Note: In Rnd 2, each ch-1 space counts as a st.

Rnd 2: Ch 1, skip first st, *[beginning with ch-1 space, sc in next 5 sts or ch-spaces, ch 2, make Small Heart, ch 3, skip 3 sts, sc in next 5 sts, ch 2, make Large Heart, ch 3, skip 3 sts] to corner space, 3 sc in corner space, ch 2, make Large Heart, ch 3, skip 3 sts; rep from * around, join with slip st to first sc. Fasten off.

Large Heart

For instructions, see facing page.

Small Heart

Make as for Large Heart through Rnd 1. Fasten off.

Reversible

Wide

Undulating

Motifs

Fringy

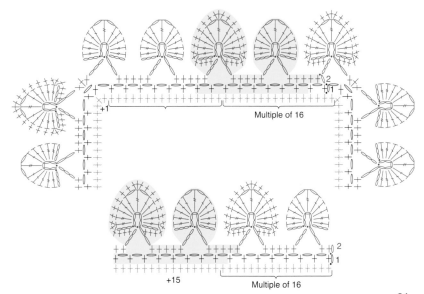

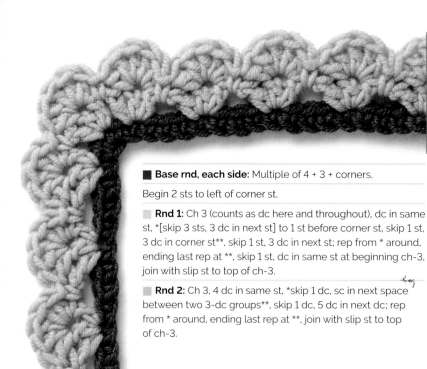

■ **Base rnd, each side:** Multiple of 4 + 3 + corners.

Begin 2 sts to left of corner st.

▦ **Rnd 1:** Ch 3 (counts as dc here and throughout), dc in same st, *[skip 3 sts, 3 dc in next st] to 1 st before corner st, skip 1 st, 3 dc in corner st**, skip 1 st, 3 dc in next st; rep from * around, ending last rep at **, skip 1 st, dc in same st at beginning ch-3, join with slip st to top of ch-3.

▧ **Rnd 2:** Ch 3, 4 dc in same st, *skip 1 dc, sc in next space between two 3-dc groups**, skip 1 dc, 5 dc in next dc; rep from * around, ending last rep at **, join with slip st to top of ch-3.

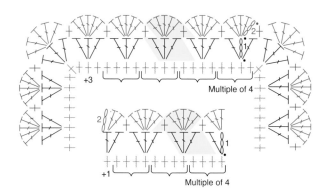

Reversible

Narrow

Undulating

#45

Stitches & Notes

A few simple changes to Border #44 (facing page) turn this into a new border.

Dtr (double treble crochet): Yarnover three times, insert hook into st or space indicated, yarnover and pull up a loop, (yarnover and pull through 2 loops) four times.

■ **Base rnd, each side:** Multiple of 4 + 3 + corners.

Begin 2 sts to left of corner st.

■ **Rnd 1:** Ch 5 (counts as dtr), dc in same st, *[skip 3 sts, (dc, dtr, dc) in next st] to 1 st before corner st, skip 1 st, (dc, dtr, dc) in corner st**, skip 1 st, (dc, dtr, dc) in next st; rep from * around, ending last rep at **, skip 1 st, dc in same st at beginning ch-3, join with slip st to top of ch-3.

■ **Rnd 2:** Ch 3 (counts as dc), dc in same st, *ch 1, skip 1 dc, sc in next space between two 3-st groups, ch 1, skip 1 dc**, 3 dc in next dtr; rep from * around, ending last rep at **, dc in same st as beginning ch-3, join with slip st to top of ch-3. Fasten off.

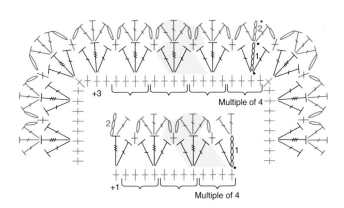

Narrow

Undulating

Textured

#46

Base rnd, each side: Multiple of 8 + 3 + corners.

Begin in corner st.

Rnd 1: Standing tr in first st, *Triple Cluster, Sideways Cluster, [partial tr in same base-rnd st, skip 3 sts, partial tr in next st, yarnover and pull through all 3 loops on hook to tr2tog, Triple Cluster, Sideways Cluster] to corner placing last cluster of Triple Cluster in corner st, (tr, ch 4, tr) in corner st; rep from * around, omitting last tr, join with slip st to top ch-4 — *flower bases complete.*

Rnd 2: Ch 1, sc in first st, *ch 4, 3-tr cluster in top of Triple Cluster, ch 4, [3 partial tr in same st, skip 1 cluster, partial tr in top of next tr2tog, yarnover and pull through all 5 loops on hook, ch 4, partial tr in same st, 3 partial tr in top of next Triple Cluster, yarnover and pull through all 5 loops on hook, ch 4] to last flower base before corner, 3-tr Cluster in same st, (ch 4, sc in next tr) two times; rep from * around, omitting last sc, join with slip st to first sc.

Rnd 3: Ch 1, sc in first sc, sc in each st and 4 sc in each ch-space around, join with slip st to first sc. Fasten off.

Stitches & Notes

3-tr Cluster (3 treble crochet cluster): Yarnover two times, insert hook into st or space indicated and pull up a loop, (yarnover and pull through 2 loops on hook) two times, [yarnover two times, insert hook into same st or space and pull up a loop, (yarnover and pull through 2 loops on hook) two times] two times, yarnover and pull through all 4 loops on hook.

Partial tr (partial treble crochet): Yarnover two times, insert hook into st or space indicated and pull up a loop, (yarnover and pull through 2 loops) two times.

Sideways Cluster: Ch 4, 2 partial tr in fourth ch from hook, yarnover and pull through all 3 loops on hook.

Triple Cluster: Ch 4, 2 partial tr in fourth ch from hook, 3 partial tr in same base-rnd st, skip 3 sts, 3 partial tr in next st, yarnover and pull through all 9 loops on hook, ch 1.

Reversible

Wide

Undulating

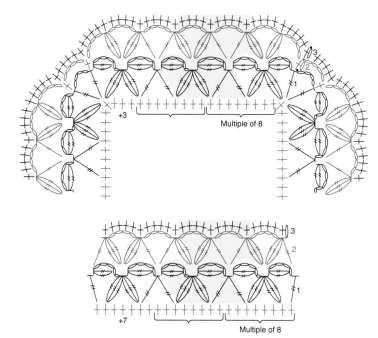

Multiple of 8

+3

+7

Multiple of 8

#47

Stitches & Notes

Picot-3: Ch 3, slip st in third ch from hook.

Picot-4: Ch 4, slip st in third ch from hook.

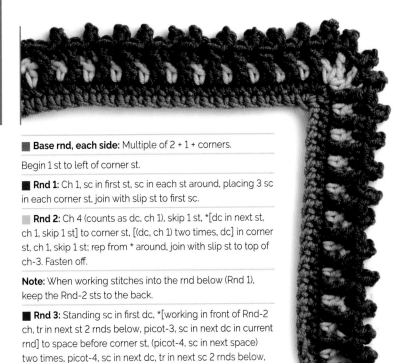

■ **Base rnd, each side:** Multiple of 2 + 1 + corners.

Begin 1 st to left of corner st.

■ **Rnd 1:** Ch 1, sc in first st, sc in each st around, placing 3 sc in each corner st, join with slip st to first sc.

■ **Rnd 2:** Ch 4 (counts as dc, ch 1), skip 1 st, *[dc in next st, ch 1, skip 1 st] to corner st, [(dc, ch 1) two times, dc] in corner st, ch 1, skip 1 st; rep from * around, join with slip st to top of ch-3. Fasten off.

Note: When working stitches into the rnd below (Rnd 1), keep the Rnd-2 sts to the back.

■ **Rnd 3:** Standing sc in first dc, *[working in front of Rnd-2 ch, tr in next st 2 rnds below, picot-3, sc in next dc in current rnd] to space before corner st, (picot-4, sc in next space) two times, picot-4, sc in next dc, tr in next sc 2 rnds below, picot-3, sc in next dc in current rnd; rep from * around, omitting last sc, join with slip st to first sc. Fasten off.

Reversible

Medium

Undulating

Textured

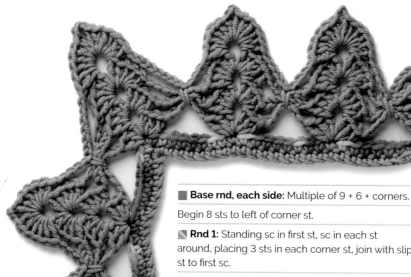

#48

■ **Base rnd, each side:** Multiple of 9 + 6 + corners.

Begin 8 sts to left of corner st.

◣ **Rnd 1:** Standing sc in first st, sc in each st around, placing 3 sts in each corner st, join with slip st to first sc.

■ **Rnd 2:** Ch 5 (counts as dc, ch 2 here and throughout), 3 dc in same st, *[ch 6, skip 8 sc, (3 dc, ch 2, 3 dc) in next st] to 8 sts before corner st, ch 7, skip 8 sc, (3 dc, ch 2, 3 dc) in corner st, ch 7, skip 8 sc, (3 dc, ch 2, 3 dc) in next st; rep from * around, ending ch 7, skip 8 sc, 2 dc in same st as first dc of rnd, join with slip st to third ch of ch-5, slip st in next space.

■ **Rnd 3:** Ch 6 (counts as dc, ch 3), 4 dc in same space, *[ch 6, skip next ch-space, (4 dc, ch 2, 4 dc) in next space] to space before corner space, ch 8, skip next ch-space, (4 dc, ch 2, 4 dc) in corner space, ch 8, skip next ch-space**, (4 dc, ch 2, 4 dc) in next space; rep from * around, ending last repeat at **, 3 dc in same space as first dcs of rnd, join with slip st to third ch of ch-5, slip st in next space.

■ **Rnd 4:** Ch 5, 5 dc in same space, *[ch 6, skip next ch-space, (5 dc, ch 2, 5 dc) in next space] to space before corner space, ch 8, skip next ch-space, (5 dc, ch 3, 5 dc) in corner space, ch 8, skip next ch-space**, (5 dc, ch 2, 5 dc) in next space; rep from * around, ending last rep at **, 4 dc in same space as first dcs of rnd, join with slip st to third ch of ch-5, slip st in next space.

Note: All Rnd-5 scs are worked into the spaces made in Rnd 2, working over the 2 chain loops from Rnds 3 and 4.

■ **Rnd 5:** Ch 6 (counts as dc, ch 3), 6 dc in same st, *[ch 4, sc in next ch-space 3 rnds below, ch 4, (6 dc, ch 3, 6 dc) in next space] to space before corner space, ch 4, sc in next ch-space 3 rnds below, ch 8, (6 dc, ch 3, 6 dc) in corner space, ch 8, sc in next ch-space 3 rnds below, ch 4**, (6 dc, ch 3, 6 dc) in next space; rep from * around, ending last rep at **, 5 dc in same st as first dcs of rnd, join with slip st to third ch of ch-5. Fasten off.

Reversible

Wide

Undulating

Motifs

Open/Lacy

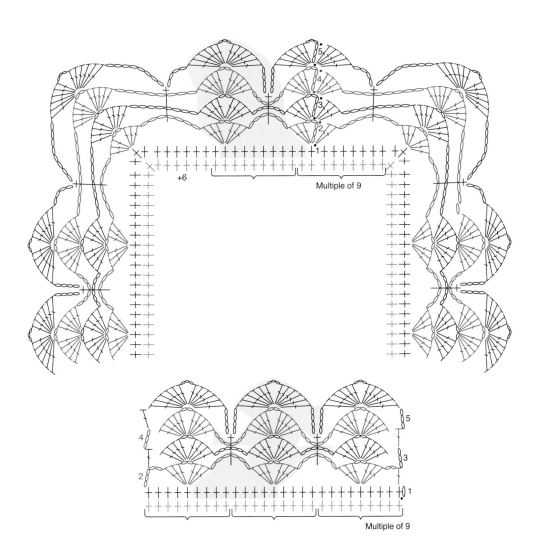

+6

Multiple of 9

Multiple of 9

#49

Base rnd, each side: Multiple of 2 + 1 + corners.

Begin 1 st to left of corner st.

Rnd 1: Ch 2 (counts as hdc), *[picot-3, skip 1 st, hdc in next st] to corner st, picot-3, (hdc, picot-3, hdc) in corner st, picot-3**, hdc in next st; rep from * around, ending last rep at **, join with slip st to first hdc.

Rnd 2: Ch 1, (sc, ch 4, sc) in first picot, *(sc, ch 4, sc) in each picot around; join with slip st to first sc.

Note: Allow Rnd-2 ch-4s to pop to the right side as you work Rnd 3.

Rnd 3: Ch 1, sc in first sc, *[picot-3, sc in next 2 sc] across, placing last sc in sc before corner ch-4 space, (picot-3, sc in same sc and in next sc) two times; repeat from * around, ending last rep picot-3, sc in next sc, join with slip st to first sc. Fasten off.

Stitches & Notes

Picot-3: Ch 3, slip st in third chain from hook.

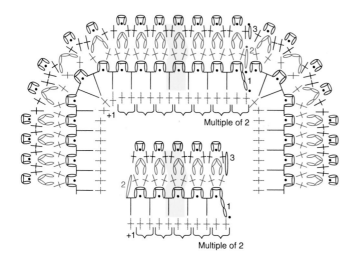

Multiple of 2

Multiple of 2

Medium

Undulating

Layered

Textured

#50

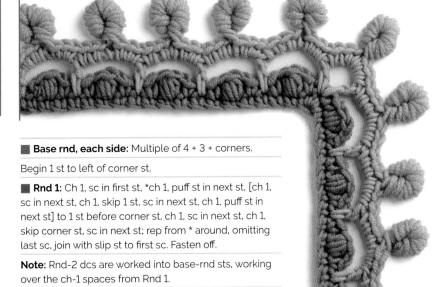

Stitches & Notes

For best results on this border, use a crochet hook with a long shank and without a thumb rest. Take your time, and use your fingers to pull the wraps over the loop on the hook, rather than trying to pull the loop through the wraps. If the bullion coils are too heavy for your yarn, try wrapping fewer times, or using a picot in place of every other bullion.

Bullion Coil: Yarnover 19 times, yarnover and pull through all 20 loops on hook, ch 1 to close, pulling chain tightly to fold coil. (For an illustration of bullion coil, see page 211.)

Puff st (puff stitch): (Yarnover, insert hook into st or space indicated, yarnover and pull up a loop) three times in same st or space, yarnover and pull through all 7 loops on hook. (For an illustration of puff stitch, see page 214.)

- Medium
- Undulating
- Open/Lacy
- Layered
- Textured

■ Base rnd, each side: Multiple of 4 + 3 + corners.

Begin 1 st to left of corner st.

■ Rnd 1: Ch 1, sc in first st, *ch 1, puff st in next st, [ch 1, sc in next st, ch 1, skip 1 st, sc in next st, ch 1, puff st in next st] to 1 st before corner st, ch 1, sc in next st, ch 1, skip corner st, sc in next st; rep from * around, omitting last sc, join with slip st to first sc. Fasten off.

Note: Rnd-2 dcs are worked into base-rnd sts, working over the ch-1 spaces from Rnd 1.

■ Rnd 2: Standing dc in any base-rnd corner st, ch 3, *[dc in next skipped st of base rnd, ch 3]** to corner, (dc, ch 3) two times in corner st; rep from * around, ending last rep at **, dc in same corner st as first dc, ch 3, join with slip st to first dc, slip st in next ch-3 space.

■ Rnd 3: Ch 1, (3 sc, bullion coil, 3 sc) in each ch-3 space around, join with slip st to first sc. Fasten off.

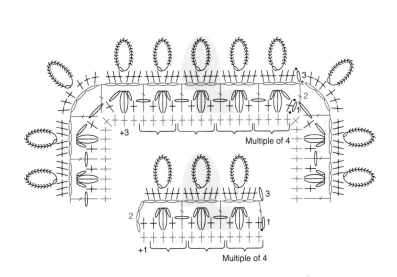

Stitches & Notes

The construction of this border is interesting and unusual. Rnd 1 is straightforward; Rnd 2 is a separate piece that serves as the foundation for the rondels that will be worked in Rnds 3 and 4. Rnd 3 is worked in a join-as-you-go method to Rnd 1. Rnds 2–4 should be worked in the same color.

Don't try to think ahead or guess what's going on, but take your time to follow the written instructions step-by-step, and you'll do fine!

Flat join: Drop loop from hook, insert hook from front to back through st or space indicated, place loop back on hook and pull through to front.

■ **Base rnd, each side:** Multiple of 8 + 7 + corners.

Begin in any st.

■ **Rnd 1:** Standing sc in first sc, sc in each sc around, placing 3 sc in each corner st, join with slip st to first sc. Fasten off.

To plan for Rnd 2, follow these steps:

Place marker in ninth st after any corner st.

Calculate the number of repeats you'll need to work in the next rnd, as follows:

For each side, after Rnd 1:

[(Number of sts on side, excluding corner sts – 1) ÷ 8] + 1 = number of repeats for one side

Total the numbers of repeats for all sides – 1 = X

X is the number you'll need to plug in on Rnd 2. See Example on facing page.

▨ **Rnd 2:** Ch 6, dc in third ch from hook, [ch 10, dc in third ch from hook] X times, ch 4, join with slip st to first ch, being careful not to twist. You now have a long skinny circular chain with X + 1 "rings."

▨ **Rnd 3:** 4 dc in next ring; holding main fabric (Rnd 1) so that the right side is facing and is above the current rnd, flat join to marked st, *[3 dc in same ring, skip 2 ch, slip st in next ch, ch 1, skip 1 ch, slip st in next ch, 4 dc in next ring**, skip 7 Rnd-1 sts, flat join in next st] to corner st, rep from * to ** once, skip corner st, flat join in next st; rep from * around, ending last rep with 3 dc in last ring, skip 2 ch, slip st in next ch, ch 1, skip 1 ch, join with slip st in first dc, turn.

▨ **Rnd 4:** Ch 1, (sc, ch 1, sc) over both ch-spaces of Rnd 2 and Rnd 3 together, slip st in next ch of Rnd 3, *7 dc in next ring to complete rondel, [skip 2 ch, slip st in next ch**, sc over both ch-spaces of Rnd 2 and Rnd 3 together, slip st in next ch, 7 dc in next ring] to corner, skip 2 ch, slip st in same ch as Rnd-3 slip st, (sc, ch 1, sc) over both corner ch-spaces of Rnd 2 and Rnd 3 together; rep from * around, ending last rep at **, join with slip st to first sc. Fasten off.

Wide

Undulating

Rnd 5: Standing sc in last sc of previous rnd, ch 5, sc in next sc, ch 1, skip corner ch-1 space, sc in next sc, *[ch 5, sc in center dc of next rondel, ch 5**, sc in next sc] to corner space, ch 1, sc in next sc; rep from * around, ending last rep at **, join with slip st to first sc. Fasten off.

Rnd 6: Standing sc in last sc of previous rnd, *9 tr in corner ch-1 space, skip 1 sc, sc in next sc, [7 tr in next sc, sc in next sc] across; rep from * around, omitting last sc, join with slip st to first sc. Fasten off.

EXAMPLE,
Round 2 Preparation

After working Round 1, two sides have 73 sts each and two sides have 89 sts each, not including corner sts.

$$[(73 - 1) \div 8] + 1 = 10 \text{ repeats per side}$$

$$[(89 - 1) \div 8] + 1 = 12 \text{ repeats per side}$$

$$(10 \times 2) + (12 \times 2) = 44 \text{ total number of repeats for all sides}$$

$$44 - 1 = 43; 43 = X$$

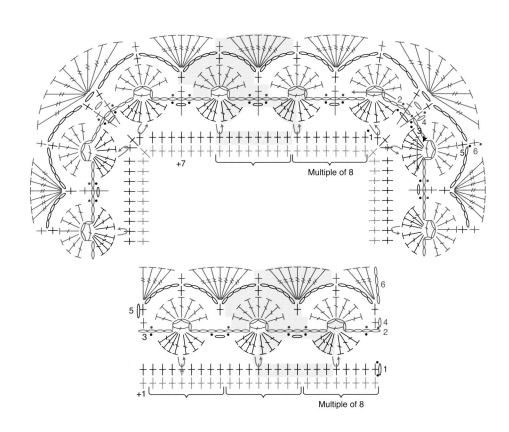

#52

Base rnd, each side: Multiple of 8 + 7 + corners.

Begin in any stitch.

Work Rnds 1–4 of Border #51 (page 101).

Stitches & Notes

For a different look, simplify Border #51 by leaving off a couple of rounds.

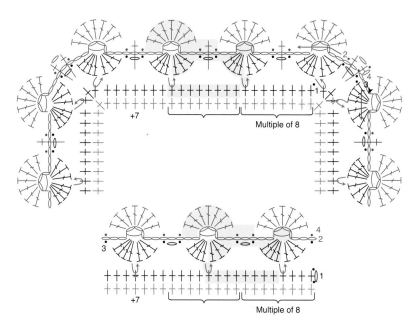

Reversible

Medium

Undulating

#53

Stitches & Notes

Left unblocked, this border makes a gentle ruffle after Rnd 4. However, after blocking, the arches draw out and lie flat. Crocheter's choice.

Picot-3: Ch 3, slip st in third chain from hook.

■ **Base rnd, each side:** Multiple of 6 + 5 + corners.

Begin 6 sts to left of corner st.

■ **Rnd 1:** Ch 1, sc in first st, *ch 3, picot-3, ch 4, skip 5 sts**, [sc in next st, ch 3, picot-3, ch 4, skip 5 sts] to corner st, sc in corner st; rep from * around, ending last rep at **, join with slip st to first sc.

■ **Rnd 2:** Ch 1, sc in same st, *ch 9, skip next ch-space**, [sc in next sc, ch 9, skip next ch-space] to corner st, (sc, ch 1, sc) in corner st; rep from * around, ending last rep at **, join with slip st to first sc.

■ **Rnd 3:** Ch 1, sc in same st, *ch 9, skip next ch-space**, [sc in next sc, ch 9, skip next ch-space] to sc before corner space, sc in next sc, ch 5, sc in next sc; rep from * around, ending last rep at **, join with slip st to first sc.

Note: When working into Rnd-2 ch-spaces, work over the chain-loops from Rnds 2 and 3.

■ **Rnd 4:** Ch 1, sc in same st, [ch 5, working over Rnd 3 ch-space, (sc, picot-3 sc) in Rnd 2 ch-space, ch 5, sc in next sc], around, omitting last sc, join with slip st to first sc. Fasten off.

Reversible

Medium

Undulating

Open/Lacy

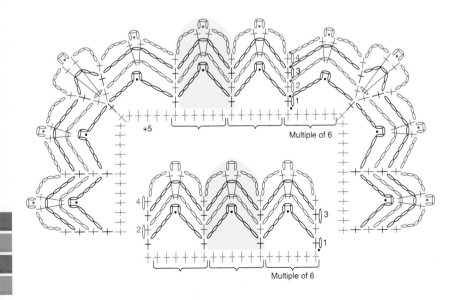

#54

Stitches & Notes

This is an easily adjustable border. It's a simple matter to increase or decrease the intervals between the chain loops, or to make the chain loops longer, as desired. The knots do add weight, so before committing to the design as written, crochet a sample for several inches/cm to ensure that you have the optimal proportions for your project.

■ **Base rnd, each side:** Multiple of 8 + corners.

Begin 2 sts to left of corner st.

■ **Rnd 1:** Ch 1, sc in each sc around, placing 3 sc in each corner st, join with slip st to first sc.

■ **Rnd 2:** Ch 1, sc in first sc, sc in next 7 sc, *[ch 28, sc in next 8 sc] to 1 st before corner st, ch 28, sc in next st, 3 sc in corner st, sc in next st; rep from * around, ending last rep ch 28, join with slip st to first sc.

■ **Rnd 3:** Ch 1, sc in first sc, sc in next 7 sc, *ch 26, [skip 28 ch, sc in next 8 sc, ch 26] to 2 sts before corner st, sc in next 2 sc, 3 sc in corner sc, sc in next 2 sc; rep from * around, ending last rep ch 26, skip 28 ch, join with slip st to first sc.

■ **Rnd 4:** Ch 1, sc in first sc, sc in next 7 sc, *ch 28, [skip 26 ch, sc in next 8 sc, ch 28] to 3 sts before corner st, sc in next 3 sc, 3 sc in corner st, sc in next 3 sc; rep from * around, ending last rep ch 28, skip 26 ch, join with slip st to first sc. Fasten off.

Tie each trio of chains into an overhand knot at base. Do not pull too tight.

Wide

Straight

Fringy

Textured

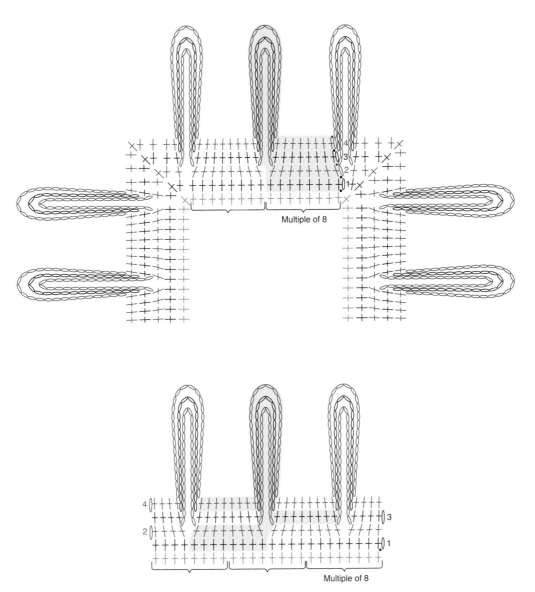

Multiple of 8

Multiple of 8

#55

■ **Base rnd, each side:** Multiple of 6 + 3 + corners.

Begin 2 sts to left of corner st.

■ **Rnd 1:** Ch 1, sc in first st, *[skip 2 sts, shell in next st, skip 2 sts, sc in next st] to 1 st before corner st, skip 1 st, shell in corner st, skip 1 st, sc in next st; rep from * around, omitting last sc, join with slip st to first sc. Fasten off.

■ **Rnd 2:** Beginning with slip knot on hook, partial dc in (last 2 dc of any corner shell, next sc, first 2 dc of next shell), yarnover and pull through all 6 loops on hook, ch 1 to close — *beginning cluster made,* *[ch 2, sc in next dc, ch 2, cluster] to corner st, ch 3, (sc, ch 1, sc) in corner dc, ch 3**, cluster over next 5 sts; rep from * around, ending last rep at **, join with slip st to first cluster.

Note: In Rnd 3, place each shell in the ch-1 space at the top of the clusters.

■ **Rnd 3:** Ch 3 (counts as dc), 2 dc in same st, *slip st in next sc, [shell in next cluster, slip st in next sc] to corner space, shell in corner ch-1 space; rep from * around, ending with slip st in next sc, 2 dc in same st as first dc, join with slip st to top of ch-3.

■ **Rnd 4:** Ch 1, sc in first st, *(2 dc, tr, 2 dc) in next slip st**, [sc in center dc of next shell, (2 dc, tr, 2 dc) in next slip st] to corner shell, (sc, hdc, sc) in center dc of corner shell; rep from * around, ending last rep at **, join with slip st to first sc.

■ **Rnd 5:** Ch 1, sc in same st and in next 2 dc, 2 sc in next tr, *[sc in next 5 sts, 2 sc in next tr] to 3 sts before corner st, sc in next 3 sts, 2 sc in corner hdc, sc in next 3 sts, 2 sc in next tr; rep from * around, ending with sc in last 2 dc, join with slip st to first sc. Fasten off.

Stitches & Notes

Stop at the end of Rnd 3 for a nice solid-yet-scalloped border.

Cluster: Partial dc in next 2 dc, partial dc in next sc, partial dc in next 2 dc, yarnover and pull through all 6 loops on hook, ch 1 to close.

Partial dc (partial double crochet): Yarnover, insert hook into st or space indicated and pull up a loop, yarnover and pull through 2 loops.

Shell: 5 dc in st or space indicated.

Reversible

Wide

Undulating

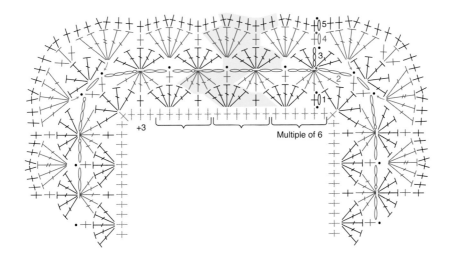

+3

Multiple of 6

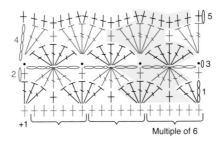

+1

Multiple of 6

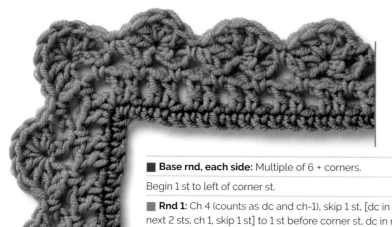

Base rnd, each side: Multiple of 6 + corners.

Begin 1 st to left of corner st.

■ **Rnd 1:** Ch 4 (counts as dc and ch-1), skip 1 st, [dc in next 2 sts, ch 1, skip 1 st] to 1 st before corner st, dc in next st, (dc, ch 3, dc) in corner st**, dc in next st, ch 1, skip 1 st; rep from * around, ending last rep at **, join with slip st to third ch of ch-4; slip st in next ch-1 space.

■ **Rnd 2:** Ch 1, sc in same space, ch 5, sc in next space, *ch 4, [sc in next space, ch 5, sc in next space, ch 4] to corner space, (sc, ch 5, sc) in corner space; rep from * around, ending ch 2, join with hdc to first sc.

■ **Rnd 3:** Ch 1, sc in space formed by joining hdc, [5 dc in center ch of next ch-5 loop, sc in next ch-4 space] to corner loop, 7 dc in center ch of next corner ch-5 loop; rep from * around, join with slip st to first sc. Fasten off.

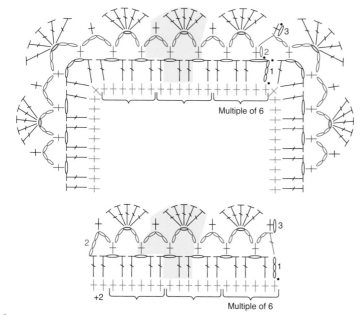

Medium

Undulating

#57

■ **Base rnd, each side:** Multiple of 2 + 1 + corners.

Begin 2 sts to left of corner st.

■ **Rnd 1:** Ch 4 (counts as dc, ch 1 here and through-out), *skip 1 st, [dc in next st, ch 1, skip 1 st] to corner st, (dc, ch 3, dc) in corner st**, ch 1; rep from * around, ending last rep at **, join with sc to third ch of ch-4.

■ **Rnd 2:** Ch 1, sc in space formed by joining sc, *ch 1, [sc in next space, ch 1] to corner, (sc, ch 1, sc) in corner space; rep from * around, join with sc to first sc.

■ **Rnd 3:** Ch 4, *[dc in next space, ch 1] to corner space, (dc, ch 3, dc) in corner space, ch 1; rep from * around, omitting last ch-1, join with sc to third ch of ch-4.

■ **Rnd 4:** Ch 1, sc in space formed by joining sc, ch 1, *[sc in next space, ch 1] to corner, (sc, ch 1) three times in corner space; rep from * around, join with slip st to first sc. Fasten off.

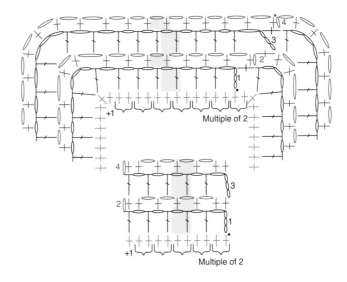

Reversible

Medium

Straight

Open/Lacy

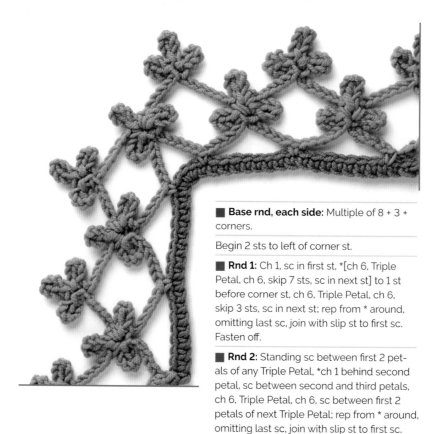

#58

■ **Base rnd, each side:** Multiple of 8 + 3 + corners.

Begin 2 sts to left of corner st.

■ **Rnd 1:** Ch 1, sc in first st, *[ch 6, Triple Petal, ch 6, skip 7 sts, sc in next st] to 1 st before corner st, ch 6, Triple Petal, ch 6, skip 3 sts, sc in next st; rep from * around, omitting last sc, join with slip st to first sc. Fasten off.

■ **Rnd 2:** Standing sc between first 2 petals of any Triple Petal, *ch 1 behind second petal, sc between second and third petals, ch 6, Triple Petal, ch 6, sc between first 2 petals of next Triple Petal; rep from * around, omitting last sc, join with slip st to first sc. Fasten off.

Stitches & Notes

Borrowing from traditional Irish crochet, this shamrock lace mesh gains new life as a border.

Triple Petal: (Ch 7, slip st in seventh ch from hook) three times, slip st in same st as first slip st.

Wide

Undulating

Open/Lacy

Fringy

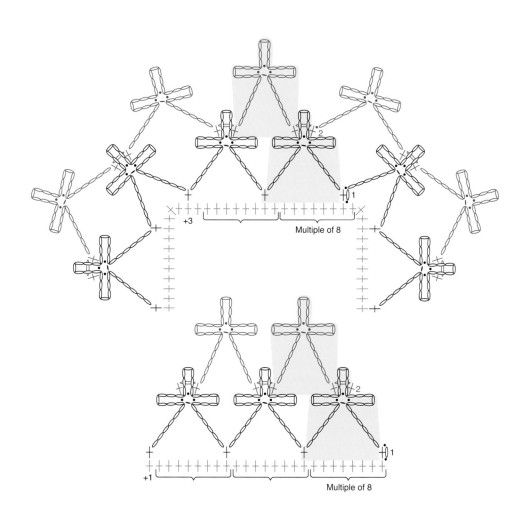

Multiple of 8

+3

+1

Multiple of 8

Base rnd, each side: Multiple of 4 + 3 + corners.

Begin 2 sts to left of corner st.

■ **Rnd 1:** Ch 1, sc in each st around, placing 3 sc in each corner st, join with slip st to first sc.

■ **Rnd 2:** Ch 5 (counts as tr and ch 1), hdc in same st, *[skip 3 sc, shell in next sc] to 2 sts before corner st, skip 2 sc, Corner Shell in corner st, skip 2 sc **, shell in next sc; rep from * around, ending last rep at **, hdc in same st as beginning ch, ch 1, join with slip st to fourth ch of ch-5.

■ **Rnd 3:** Ch 1, sc in same st, *ch 1, dc in space between 2 shells**, [ch 1, sc in tr of next shell, ch 1, dc in space between 2 shells] to Corner Shell, ch 1, skip 1 hdc, sc in next dc, ch 1, (sc, ch 1) two times in corner tr, sc in next dc; rep from * around, ending last rep at **, ch 1, join with slip st to first sc.

■ **Rnd 4:** Ch 1, sc in each st and ch-1 space around; join with slip st to first sc. Fasten off.

Stitches & Notes

Corner Shell: (Hdc, ch 1, dc, ch 1, tr, ch 1, dc, ch 1, hdc) in corner st.

Shell: (Hdc, ch 1, tr, ch 1, hdc) in st indicated.

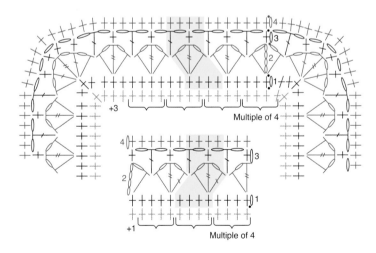

+3   Multiple of 4

+1   Multiple of 4

Reversible

Medium

Straight

#60

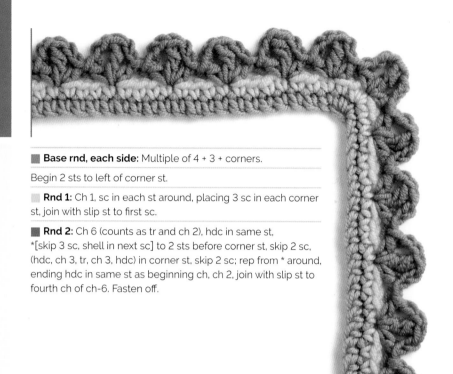

Stitches & Notes

This border is very similar to Border #59 (facing page). The difference comes from putting extra chains in the shell and leaving off after completing Rnd 2.

Shell: (Hdc, ch 2, tr, ch 2, hdc) in st indicated.

■ **Base rnd, each side:** Multiple of 4 + 3 + corners.

Begin 2 sts to left of corner st.

■ **Rnd 1:** Ch 1, sc in each st around, placing 3 sc in each corner st, join with slip st to first sc.

■ **Rnd 2:** Ch 6 (counts as tr and ch 2), hdc in same st, *[skip 3 sc, shell in next sc] to 2 sts before corner st, skip 2 sc, (hdc, ch 3, tr, ch 3, hdc) in corner st, skip 2 sc; rep from * around, ending hdc in same st as beginning ch, ch 2, join with slip st to fourth ch of ch-6. Fasten off.

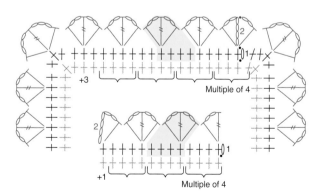

Reversible

Medium

Undulating

Base rnd, each side: Multiple of 2 + 1 + corners.

Begin 2 sts to left of corner st.

■ **Rnd 1:** Ch 4 (counts as dc and ch 1), *skip 1 st, [dc in next st, ch 1, skip 1 st] to corner st, [dc, (ch 1, dc) two times] in corner st, ch 1; rep from * around, join with slip st to third ch of ch-4. Fasten off.

Note: In Rnds 2, 4, and 6, keep the ch-1s from the previous rnd to the front when working all dcs.

■ **Rnd 2:** Standing sc in first dc, *[keeping ch-1 to the front, dc in next st 2 rnds below, sc in next dc] to space before corner st, dc in next corner st in rnd below, (sc, ch 1, sc) in corner dc, dc in same corner st in rnd below, sc in next dc; rep from * around, ending dc in next st in rnd below, join with slip st to first sc. Fasten off.

■ **Rnd 3:** Standing dc in first sc, *[ch 1, skip 1 dc, dc in next sc] to corner space, ch 1, (dc, ch 1, dc) in corner space, ch 1, dc in next sc; rep from * around, ending with ch 1, skip 1 dc, dc in next sc, ch 1, skip 1 dc, join with slip st to first sc. Fasten off.

■ **Rnd 4:** Standing sc in first dc, *[keeping ch-1 to the front, dc in next st 2 rnds below, sc in next dc] to space before corner space, dc in next corner space 2 rnds below, sc in next dc, (dc in same corner space 2 rnds below, sc in next dc) two times; rep from * around, ending with keeping ch-1 to the front, dc in next st 2 rnds below, sc in next dc, keeping ch-1 to the front, dc in next st 2 rnds below, join with slip st to first sc. Fasten off.

■ **Rnd 5:** Standing dc in first sc, ch 1, *skip 1 dc, [dc in next sc, ch 1, skip 1 dc] to sc before corner dc, (dc, ch 1, dc) in next sc, ch 1, skip corner dc, (dc, ch 1, dc) in next sc, ch 1; rep from * around, ending with skip 1 dc, [dc in next sc, ch 1, skip 1 dc] to end, join with slip st to first dc. Fasten off.

■ **Rnd 6:** Standing sc in first dc, *[keeping ch-1 to the front, dc in next st 2 rnds below, sc in next dc] to space before corner space, keeping ch-1 to the front, dc in next st 2 rnds below, sc in next dc, keeping ch-1 to the front, dc in next st 2 rnds below, sc in next dc, keeping ch-1 to the front, dc in next st 2 rnds below, sc in next dc; rep from * around, ending with [keeping ch-1 to the front, dc in next st 2 rnds below, sc in next dc] to end, omitting last sc, join with slip st to first sc. Fasten off.

Recognizing corners can be a bit tricky on this one, so use markers to help keep track of the corner stitches and spaces (see page 20).

Reversible

Wide

Straight

Layered

Textured

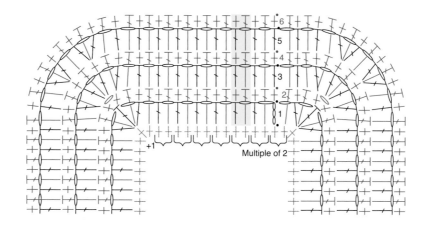

Multiple of 2

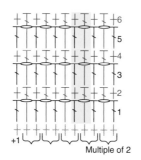

Multiple of 2

■ **Base rnd, each side:** Multiple of 2 + 1 + corners.

Begin 2 sts to left of corner st.

▨ **Rnd 1:** Ch 4 (counts as dc and ch 1), *skip 1 st, [dc in next st, ch 1, skip 1 st] to corner st, [dc, (ch 1, dc) two times] in corner st, ch 1; rep from * around, join with slip st to third ch of ch-4. Fasten off.

Note: In Rnd 2, keep the ch-1s from Rnd 1 to the front when working all dcs.

■ **Rnd 2:** Standing sc in first dc, *[keeping ch-1 to the front throughout, dc in next st 2 rnds below, sc in next dc] to space before corner st, dc in next corner st in rnd below, (sc, ch 1, sc) in corner dc, dc in same corner st in rnd below, sc in next dc; rep from * around, omitting last sc, join with slip st to first sc. Fasten off.

▨ **Rnd 3:** Standing dc in first sc, *[ch 1, skip 1 dc, dc in next sc] to corner space, ch 1, (dc, ch 1, dc) in corner space, ch 1, dc in next sc; rep from * around, ending with ch 1, skip 1 dc, dc in next sc, ch 1, skip 1 dc, join with slip st to first sc. Fasten off.

#62

Stitches & Notes

Here's an example of changing the character of the border in a simple way: leaving off Rnds 4–6 of Border #61 (page 114) changes the edging from wide and solid to more delicate and lacy.

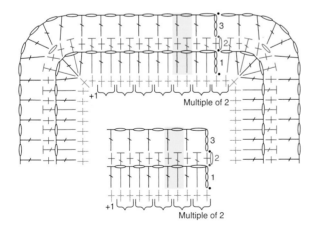

Multiple of 2

+1

Multiple of 2

Reversible

Medium

Straight

Layered

Textured

#63

Stitches & Notes

Large Open Shell: [(Dc, ch 1) four times, dc] in 1 st or space.

Open Shell: [(Dc, ch 1) two times, dc] in 1 st or space.

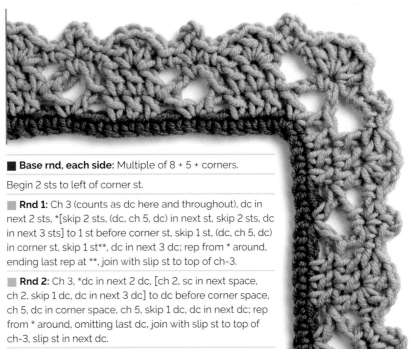

■ **Base rnd, each side:** Multiple of 8 + 5 + corners.

Begin 2 sts to left of corner st.

▨ **Rnd 1:** Ch 3 (counts as dc here and throughout), dc in next 2 sts, *[skip 2 sts, (dc, ch 5, dc) in next st, skip 2 sts, dc in next 3 sts] to 1 st before corner st, skip 1 st, (dc, ch 5, dc) in corner st, skip 1 st**, dc in next 3 dc; rep from * around, ending last rep at **, join with slip st to top of ch-3.

▨ **Rnd 2:** Ch 3, *dc in next 2 dc, [ch 2, sc in next space, ch 2, skip 1 dc, dc in next 3 dc] to dc before corner space, ch 5, dc in corner space, ch 5, skip 1 dc, dc in next dc; rep from * around, omitting last dc, join with slip st to top of ch-3, slip st in next dc.

▨ **Rnd 3:** Ch 4 (counts as dc, ch 1), (dc, ch 1, dc) in same st, *[skip 1 dc, sc in next space, (sc, ch 4, sc) in next sc, sc in next space, skip 1 dc, Open Shell in next dc] to space before corner st, (sc, ch 4, sc) in next space, Large Open Shell in corner st, (sc, ch 4, sc) in next space, skip 1 dc**, Open Shell in next dc; rep from * around, ending last rep at **, join with slip st to third ch of ch-4. Fasten off.

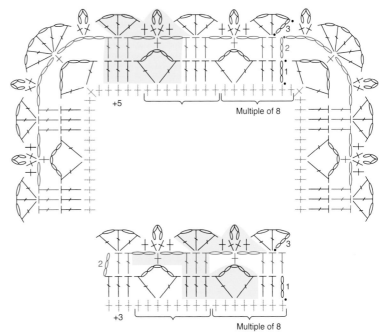

Reversible

Medium

Undulating

Open/Lacy

Base rnd, each side: Multiple of 4 + 1 + corners.

Begin 2 sts to left of corner st.

Rnd 1: Ch 4 (counts as dc and ch 1), skip 1 st, *[dc in next st, ch 1, skip 1 st] to corner, [(dc, ch 1) two times, dc] in corner st, ch 1, skip 1 st; rep from * around, join with slip st to third ch of ch-4. Fasten off.

Rnd 2: Standing sc in first dc, keeping Rnd-1 ch to the front, tr in next st 2 rnds below, sc in next dc, *keeping Rnd-1 ch to the back, tr in next st 2 rnds below**, sc in next dc, [keeping Rnd-1 ch to the front, tr in next st 2 rnds below, sc in next dc, keeping Rnd-1 ch to the back, tr in next st 2 rnds below, sc in next dc] to space before corner st, (sc in next space, sc in next dc) two times; rep from * around, ending last rep at **, join with slip st to first sc. Fasten off.

Rnd 3: Standing dc in first sc, ch 1, skip 1 st, *[dc in next sc, ch 1, skip 1 st**] to corner st, (dc, ch 1) three times in corner st, skip 1 st; rep from * around, ending last rep at **, join with slip st to first dc. Fasten off.

Rnd 4: Standing sc in first dc, *keeping Rnd-3 ch to the back, tr in next st 2 rnds below, sc in next dc, [keeping Rnd-3 ch to the front, tr in next st 2 rnds below**, sc in next dc, [keeping Rnd-3 ch to the back, tr in next st 2 rnds below] to space before corner st, sc in next dc, 2 sc in next (space, st, space), sc in next dc, keeping Rnd-1 ch to the back, tr in next st 2 rnds below, sc in next dc, keeping Rnd-3 ch to the front, tr in next st 2 rnds below**, sc in next dc; rep from * around, ending last rep at **, join with slip st to first sc. Fasten off.

Rnd 5: Standing sc in last st of Rnd 4, *ch 1, skip 1 st, sc in next st; rep from * around, omitting last sc, join with slip st to first sc. Fasten off.

Stitches & Notes

At first glance, this border may seem the same as Border #61 (see page 114). However, a change in placement of the long double crochet stitches in Rnds 2 and 4 does make a difference.

Reversible

Wide

Straight

Layered

Textured

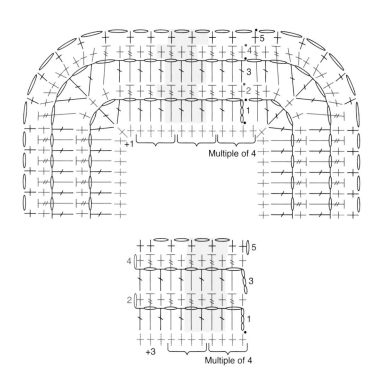

5

4

3

2

1

+1

Multiple of 4

5

4

3

2

1

+3

Multiple of 4

#65

■ **Base rnd, each side:** Multiple of 3 + 2 + corners.

Begin 3 sts to left of corner st.

▓ **Rnd 1:** Standing V-st in first st, *skip 2 sts, [V-st in next st, skip 2 sts] to corner st, (V-st, ch 1, V-st) in corner st — *corner group made*; rep from * around, ending skip 2 sts, join with slip st to first dc. Fasten off.

■ **Rnd 2:** Standing V-st in center of first V-st, *V-st in center of each V-st to corner, V-st in corner ch-1 space; rep from * around, ending V-st in last V-st, join with slip st to first dc. Fasten off.

Note: Rnd-3 sts are worked into Rnd 1, working over and enclosing the Rnd-2 sts.

▓ **Rnd 3:** Standing V-st in space between first 2 V-sts in Rnd 1, *V-st between each set of Rnd-1 V-sts to corner group, V-st in second dc of first V-st of corner group, V-st in corner ch-1 space, V-st in first dc of second V-st of corner group; rep from * around, ending V-st between next 2 Rnd-1 V-sts, join with slip st to first dc. Fasten off.

▓ **Rnd 4:** Standing V-st in center of first V-st, *V-st in center of each V-st to corner, ch 1, V-st in corner V-st, ch 1; rep from * around, ending V-st in each V-st to end of rnd, join with slip st to first dc. Fasten off.

Note: Rnd-5 sts are worked into Rnd 3, working over and enclosing the Rnd-4 sts.

▓ **Rnd 5:** Standing V-st in space between first 2 V-sts in Rnd 3, *V-st between each set of Rnd-3 V-sts to corner, ch 1, V-st in Rnd 4 corner V-st, ch 1; rep from * around, ending V-st between each set of Rnd-3 V-sts to end of rnd, join with slip st to first dc. Fasten off.

Stitches & Notes

Standing V-st (standing V-stitch): Beginning with slip knot on hook, work V-st.

V-st (V-stitch): (Dc, ch 1, dc) in st or space indicated.

Reversible

Wide

Straight

Layered

Textured

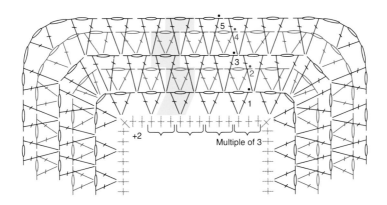

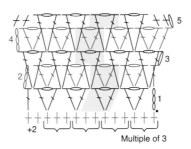

#66

Base rnd, each side: Multiple of 6 + 3 + corners.

Begin 5 sts to left of corner st.

Rnd 1: Ch 3 (counts as dc here and throughout), dc in next dc, *ch 4, skip 3 sts, [dc in next 3 dc, ch 4, skip 3 sts] to corner st, 3 dc in corner st; rep from * around, ending ch 4, skip 3 sts, dc in last st, join with slip st to top of ch-3.

Rnd 2: Ch 3, dc in next dc, *ch 4, [dc in next 3 dc, ch 4] to 1 st before corner st, 2 dc in next st, (dc, ch 1, dc) in corner st, 2 dc in next dc; rep from * around, ending ch 4, dc in last st, join with slip st to top of ch-3.

Rnd 3: Ch 3, Triple Picot, dc in same st, *[ch 3, skip 1 dc, working over Rnd 2 ch-space, sc in next ch-space 2 rnds below, ch 3, skip 1 dc**, (dc, Triple Picot, dc) in next dc] to 1 st before corner space, ch 3, sc in corner space, ch 3, skip 1 dc, (dc, Triple Picot, dc) in next dc; rep from * around, ending last rep at **, join with slip st to top of ch-3. Fasten off.

Stitches & Notes

Triple Picot: (Ch 3, slip st in third chain from hook) three times, slip st in base of first picot.

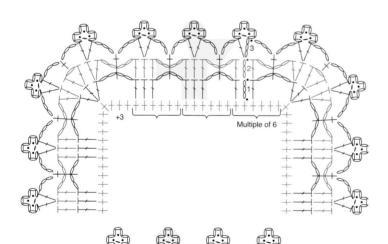

Reversible

Medium

Undulating

Open/Lacy

#67

Stitches & Notes

Cluster: Ch 3, (yarnover, insert hook into third ch from hook, yarnover and pull up a loop, yarnover and pull through 2 loops) two times, yarnover and pull through all 3 loops on hook.

Dtr (double treble crochet): Yarnover three times, insert hook into st or space indicated, yarnover and pull up a loop, (yarnover and pull through 2 loops) four times.

Large shell: [Dtr, (cluster, dc) three times] in 1 st.

V-st (V-stitch): (Dc, ch 1, dc) in st or space indicated.

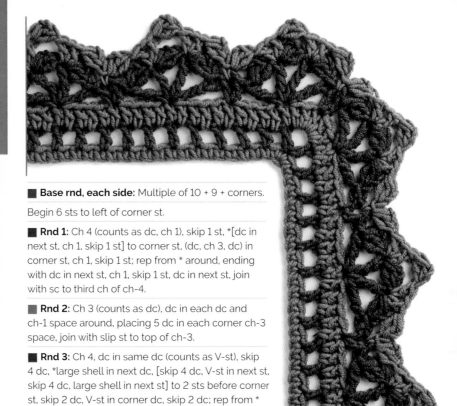

■ **Base rnd, each side:** Multiple of 10 + 9 + corners. Begin 6 sts to left of corner st.

■ **Rnd 1:** Ch 4 (counts as dc, ch 1), skip 1 st, *[dc in next st, ch 1, skip 1 st] to corner st, (dc, ch 3, dc) in corner st, ch 1, skip 1 st; rep from * around, ending with dc in next st, ch 1, skip 1 st, dc in next st, join with sc to third ch of ch-4.

■ **Rnd 2:** Ch 3 (counts as dc), dc in each dc and ch-1 space around, placing 5 dc in each corner ch-3 space, join with slip st to top of ch-3.

■ **Rnd 3:** Ch 4, dc in same dc (counts as V-st), skip 4 dc, *large shell in next dc, [skip 4 dc, V-st in next st, skip 4 dc, large shell in next st] to 2 sts before corner st, skip 2 dc, V-st in corner dc, skip 2 dc; rep from * around, ending with large shell in next dc, skip 4 dc, join with slip st to third ch of beginning ch-4.

■ **Rnd 4:** Ch 1, sc in first ch-1 space, *skip 1 dtr, (cluster, V-st in next dtr) two times, cluster, sc in center of next V-st; rep from * around, omitting last sc, join with slip st to first sc. Fasten off.

Reversible

Wide

Undulating

Open/Lacy

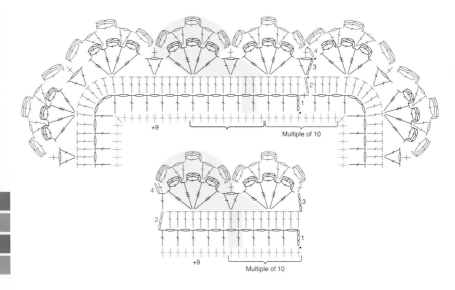

#68

Base rnd, each side: Multiple of 9 + 2 + corners.

Begin 6 sts to left of corner.

■ **Rnd 1:** Ch 4 (counts as tr), *dc in next st, hdc in next st, [sc in next 4 sts, hdc in next st, dc in next st, tr in next st, dc in next st, hdc in next st] to 3 sts before corner st, sc in next 3 sts, (hdc, dc, tr, dc, hdc) in corner st, sc in next 3 sts, hdc in next st, dc in next st, tr in next st; rep from * around, omitting last tr, join with slip st to top of ch-4.

■ **Rnd 2:** Ch 5 (counts as dc, ch 2), dc in same st — *beginning V-st made*, *dc in next 2 sts, [dc2tog over next 4 sc, dc in next 2 sts, V-st in next st, dc in next 2 sts] to 5 sts before corner st, dc2tog over next 3 sc, dc in next 2 sts, (V-st, ch 2, dc) in corner st, dc in next 2 sts, dc2tog over next 3 sc, dc in next 2 sts**, V-st in next st, rep from * around, ending last rep at **, join with slip st to third ch of ch-5.

▨ **Rnd 3:** Ch 3 (counts as dc), *V-st in next ch-space, [dc in next 2 dc, dc2tog over next 3 sts**, dc in next 2 dc, V-st in next ch-space] to corner st, V-st in corner dc; rep from * around, ending last rep at **, dc in last st, join with slip st to top of ch-3.

■ **Rnd 4:** Ch 1, *[sc in next 2 dc, (sc, ch 1, sc) in next ch-space, sc in next 2 dc, sc2tog over next 3 sts] to 1 st before first corner V-st, [sc in next 2 dc, (sc, ch 1, sc) in next ch-space] three times, sc in next 2 dc, sc2tog over next 3 sts; rep from * around, join with slip st to first sc. Fasten off.

Stitches & Notes

Dc2tog over 3 sts: Yarnover, insert hook into next st indicated, yarnover and pull up a loop, yarnover and pull through 2 loops, skip 1 st, yarnover, insert hook into next st, yarnover and pull up a loop, yarnover and pull through 2 loops, yarnover and pull through all 3 loops on hook.

Dc2tog over 4 sts: Yarnover, insert hook into next st indicated, yarnover and pull up a loop, yarnover and pull through 2 loops, skip 2 sts, yarnover, insert hook into next st and pull up a loop, yarnover and pull through 2 loops, yarnover and pull through all 3 loops on hook.

Sc2tog over 3 sts: Insert hook into next st and pull up a loop, skip 1 st, insert hook into next st and pull up a loop, yarnover and pull through all 3 loops on hook.

V-st (V-stitch): (Dc, ch 2, dc) in st or space indicated.

Reversible

Medium

Undulating

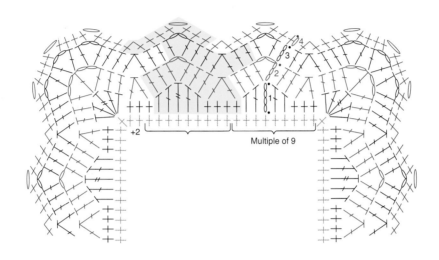

+2

Multiple of 9

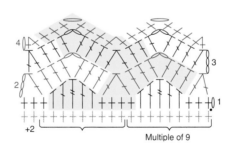

+2

Multiple of 9

#69

Base rnd, each side: Multiple of 9 + 2 + corners.

Begin 6 sts to left of corner.

Rnd 1: Ch 4 (counts as tr), *dc in next st, hdc in next st, [sc in next 4 sts, hdc in next st, dc in next st, tr in next st, dc in next st, hdc in next st] to 3 sts before corner st, sc in next 3 sts, (hdc, dc, tr, dc, hdc) in corner st, sc in next 3 sts, hdc in next st, dc in next st, tr in next st; rep from * around, omitting last tr, join with slip st to top of ch-4.

Rnd 2: Ch 5 (counts as dc, ch 2), dc in same st — *beginning V-st made*, *dc in next 2 sts, [dc2tog over next 4 sc, dc in next 2 sts, V-st in next st, dc in next 2 sts] to 5 sts before corner st, dc2tog over next 3 sc, dc in next 2 sts, (V-st, ch 2, dc) in corner st, dc in next 2 sts, dc2tog over next 3 sc, dc in next 2 sts**, V-st in next st, rep from * around, ending last rep at **, join with slip st to third ch of ch-5.

Rnd 3: Ch 1, sc in first st, slip st in next ch-2 space, sc in next st, hdc in next st, dc in next st, *tr in next st, dc in next st, [hdc in next st**, sc in next st, slip st in next ch-2 space, sc in next st, hdc in next st, dc in next st, tr in next st, dc in next st] to 2 sts before corner ch-2 space, dc in next st, hdc in next st, sc in next ch-2 space, 3 sc in corner dc, sc in next ch-2 space, hdc in next st, dc in next 2 dc; rep from * around, ending last rep at **, join with slip st to first sc.

Rnd 4: Ch 1, sc in each st around, placing 3 sc in each corner st, join with slip st to first sc. Fasten off.

Stitches & Notes

Instead of continuing with chevron stripes of color, Rnd 3 of this version of Border #68 (see page 124) flattens out the curves to make a straight final edge.

Dc2tog over 3 sts: Yarnover, insert hook into next st indicated, yarnover and pull up a loop, yarnover and pull through 2 loops, skip 1 st, yarnover, insert hook into next st, yarnover and pull up a loop, yarnover and pull through 2 loops, yarnover and pull through all 3 loops on hook.

Dc2tog over 4 sts: Yarnover, insert hook into next st indicated, yarnover and pull up a loop, yarnover and pull through 2 loops, skip 2 sts, yarnover, insert hook into next st and pull up a loop, yarnover and pull through 2 loops, yarnover and pull through all 3 loops on hook.

V-st (V-stitch): (Dc, ch 2, dc) in st or space indicated.

Reversible

Medium

Straight

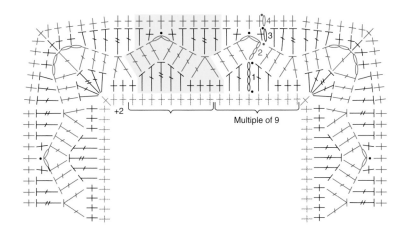

+2

Multiple of 9

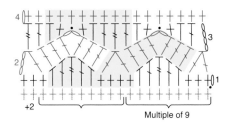

+2

Multiple of 9

#70

Base rnd, each side: Multiple of 6 + 3 + corners.

Begin in corner st.

■ **Rnd 1:** Ch 1, 2 sc in first st, *ch 5, skip 3 sts, [sc in next 3 sts, ch 5, skip 3 sts] to corner st, 3 sc in corner st; rep from * around, omitting last 3 sc, sc in same st as beginning sc, join with slip st to first sc.

■ **Rnd 2:** Ch 6 (counts as dc and ch 3), *sc in next sc, ch 3, sc in next space, ch 3, [skip 1 sc, sc in next sc, ch 3, sc in next space, ch 3] to 1 st before corner st, sc in next sc, ch 3**, dc in corner st, ch 3; rep from * around, ending last rep at **, join with slip st to third ch of ch-6.

■ **Rnd 3:** Ch 1, sc in first st, *ch 5, skip 1 space, sc in next (space, sc, space), [ch 5, sc in next (space, sc, space)] to space before corner st, ch 5, skip 1 space, sc in corner dc; rep from * around, omitting last sc, join with slip st to first sc.

■ **Rnd 4:** Ch 1, sc in first sc, *ch 3, sc in next space, ch 3, [skip 1 sc, sc in next sc, ch 3, sc in next space**, ch 3] to corner st, sc in corner sc; rep from * around, ending last rep at **, join with dc to first sc.

■ **Rnd 5:** Ch 1, sc in same st, sc in next space, *ch 7, skip corner sc, sc in next (space, sc, space), [ch 5**, sc in next (space, sc, space)] to corner, rep from * around, ending last rep at **, sc in last space, join with slip st to first sc.

■ **Rnd 6:** Ch 1, sc in first sc, *ch 3, (sc, ch 3) two times in corner space, skip 1 sc, sc in next sc, [ch 3, sc in next space, ch 3, skip 1 sc**, sc in next sc] to 1 st before corner space; rep from * around, ending last rep at **, join with slip st to first sc. Fasten off.

Reversible

Medium

Straight

Open/Lacy

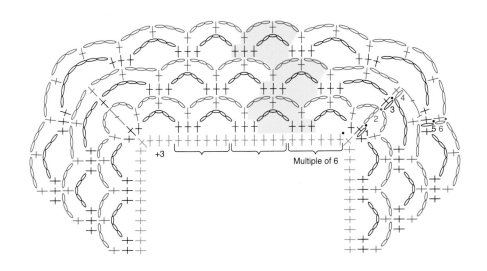

+3

Multiple of 6

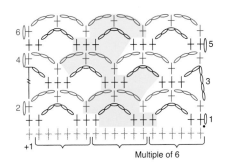

+1

Multiple of 6

Base rnd, each side: Multiple of 6 + 3 + corners.

Begin in corner st.

Rnd 1: Ch 1, 2 sc in first st, *ch 5, skip 3 sts, [sc in next 3 sts, ch 5, skip 3 sts] to corner st, 3 sc in corner st; rep from * around, omitting last 3 sc, sc in same st as beginning sc, join with slip st to first sc.

Rnd 2: Ch 6 (counts as dc and ch 3), *sc in next sc, ch 3, sc in next space, ch 3, [skip 1 sc, sc in next sc, ch 3, sc in next space, ch 3] to 1 st before corner st, sc in next sc, ch 3**, dc in corner st, ch 3; rep from * around, ending last rep at **, join with slip st to third ch of ch-6.

Rnd 3: Ch 1, sc in first st, *ch 5, skip 1 space, sc in next (space, sc, space) [ch 5, sc in next (space, sc, space)] to space before corner st, ch 5, skip 1 space, sc in corner dc; rep from * around, omitting last sc, join with slip st to first sc.

Rnd 4: Ch 1, sc in first sc, *ch 3, sc in next space, ch 3, [skip 1 sc, sc in next sc, ch 3, sc in next space, ch 3] to corner st**, sc in corner sc; rep from * around, ending last rep at **, join with slip st to first sc.

Rnd 5: Ch 1, sc in same st, *ch 3, sc in next sc, [ch 5, skip 1 sc, sc in next sc] to corner, ch 3**, (sc, ch 1, sc) in corner sc; rep from * around, ending last rep at **, sc in same st as first sc, join with sc to first sc.

Rnd 6: Ch 1, 2 sc in space formed by joining sc, sc in each sc, 3 sc in each ch-3 space, 5 sc in each ch-5 space and 2 sc in each ch-1 corner space around, join with slip st to first sc. Fasten off.

Stitches & Notes

Rnds 1–4 are exactly the same as Border #70 (see page 128), but a slight change in the last 2 rounds straightens up the edge.

Reversible

Medium

Straight

Open/Lacy

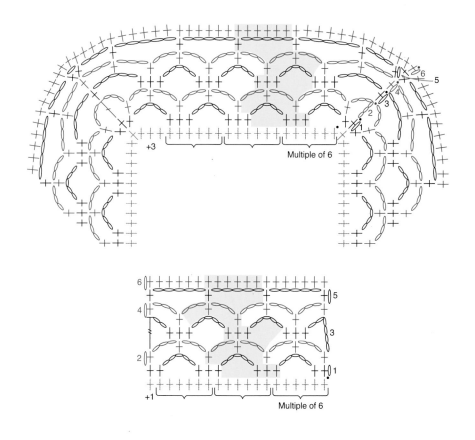

+3

Multiple of 6

6 5 4 3 2 1

+1

Multiple of 6

■ Base rnd, each side: Multiple of 10 + 3 + corners. Begin 2 sts to left of corner st.

■ Rnd 1: Ch 6 (counts as dc and ch 3), dc in same st, *[ch 1, skip 3 sts, dc in next 3 sts, ch 1, skip 3 sts, (dc, ch 3, dc) in next st] to 1 st before corner, ch 1, skip 1 st, 3 dc in corner st, ch 1, skip 1 st**, (dc, ch 3, dc) in next st; rep from * around, ending last rep at **, join with slip st to third ch of ch-6.

■ Rnd 2: Slip st in ch-3 space, ch 3 (counts as dc), 6 dc in same space, *ch 1, skip (dc, ch 1, dc), dc in next dc, ch 1, skip (dc, ch 1, dc)**, 7 dc in next space; rep from * around, ending last rep at **, join with slip st to top of ch-3, slip st in next 2 dc.

■ Rnd 3: Ch 3 (counts as dc), dc in next 2 dc, *[ch 1, skip 2 dc, (dc, ch 3, dc) in next dc, ch 1, skip 2 dc, dc in next 3 dc] to 3 sts before corner, ch 2, skip 2 dc, (dc, ch 3, dc) in corner dc, ch 2, skip 2 dc**, dc in next 3 dc; rep from * around, ending last rep at **, join with slip st to top of ch-3, slip st in next st.

■ Rnd 4: Ch 4 (counts as dc and ch 1), *[7 dc in next ch-3 space, ch 1, skip (dc, ch 1, dc), dc in next dc, ch 1] to ch-2 space before corner, 7 dc in next ch-2 space, ch 1, sc in corner ch-3 space, ch 1, 7 dc in next ch-2 space, ch 1, skip 1 dc**, dc in next dc, ch 1; rep from * around, ending last rep at **, join with slip st to third ch of ch-4.

■ Rnd 5: Ch 1, sc in same st, *ch 3, skip 2 dc, dc in next dc, (dc, tight picot-3, dc) in next dc, dc in next dc, ch 3, skip 2 dc**, [sc in next dc, ch 3, skip 2 dc, dc in next dc, (dc, tight picot-3, dc) in next dc, dc in next dc, ch 3] to corner st, sc in corner st; rep from * around, ending last rep at **, join with slip st to first sc. Fasten off.

#72

Stitches & Notes

Tight picot-3: Ch 3, slip st in third ch from hook and in st at bottom of ch together. (For an illustration of tight picot-3, see page 214.)

- Reversible
- Wide
- Undulating
- Open/Lacy

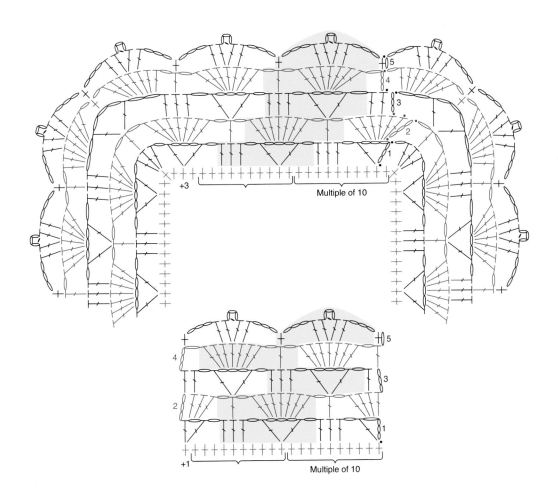

+3

Multiple of 10

Multiple of 10

+1

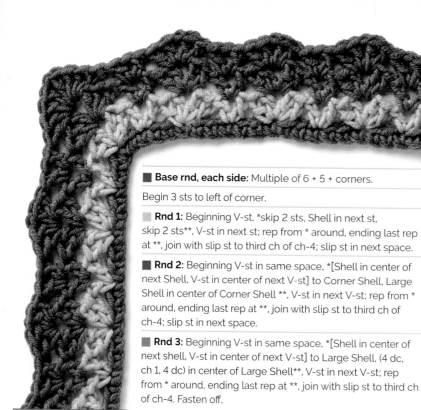

#73

Base rnd, each side: Multiple of 6 + 5 + corners.

Begin 3 sts to left of corner.

Rnd 1: Beginning V-st, *skip 2 sts, Shell in next st, skip 2 sts**, V-st in next st; rep from * around, ending last rep at **, join with slip st to third ch of ch-4; slip st in next space.

Rnd 2: Beginning V-st in same space, *[Shell in center of next Shell, V-st in center of next V-st] to Corner Shell, Large Shell in center of Corner Shell **, V-st in next V-st; rep from * around, ending last rep at **, join with slip st to third ch of ch-4; slip st in next space.

Rnd 3: Beginning V-st in same space, *[Shell in center of next shell, V-st in center of next V-st] to Large Shell, (4 dc, ch 1, 4 dc) in center of Large Shell**, V-st in next V-st; rep from * around, ending last rep at **, join with slip st to third ch of ch-4. Fasten off.

Stitches & Notes

Beginning V-st (beginning V-stitch): Ch 4, dc in same space.

Shell: (2 dc, ch 1, 2 dc) in st or space indicated.

Large Shell: (3 dc, ch 1, 3 dc) in space indicated.

V-stitch (V-st): (Dc, ch 1, dc) in st or space indicated.

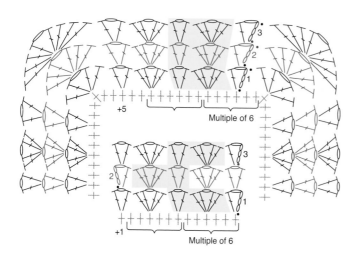

Reversible

Medium

Undulating

#74

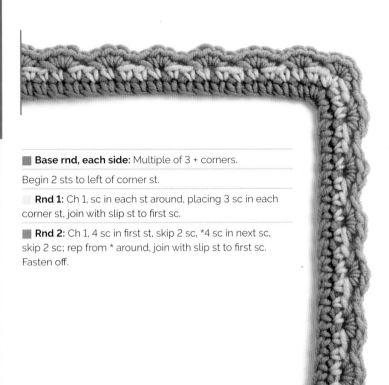

Base rnd, each side: Multiple of 3 + corners.

Begin 2 sts to left of corner st.

Rnd 1: Ch 1, sc in each st around, placing 3 sc in each corner st, join with slip st to first sc.

Rnd 2: Ch 1, 4 sc in first st, skip 2 sc, *4 sc in next sc, skip 2 sc; rep from * around, join with slip st to first sc. Fasten off.

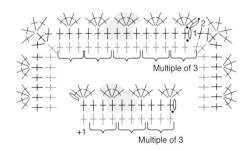

Reversible

Narrow

Undulating

#75

■ **Base rnd, each side:** Multiple of 16 + 11 + corners.

Begin in corner st.

■ **Rnd 1:** Ch 1, sc in first st, *ch 2, sc in next sc, ch 4, skip 2 sts, sc in next st, ch 5, skip 3 sts, sc in next st, ch 4, skip 2 sts, sc in next st, [(ch 2, skip 2 sts, sc in next st) two times, ch 4, skip 2 sts, sc in next st, ch 5, skip 3 sts, sc in next st, ch 4, skip 2 sts, sc in next st] to corner st, ch 2, sc in corner st; rep from * around, omitting last sc, join with slip st to first sc.

■ **Rnd 2:** Ch 3 (counts as dc here and throughout), 2 dc in same st, *ch 3, skip ch-2 space, sc in next ch-4 space, 9 dc in next space, sc in next space, ch 3, skip 1 sc, [3 dc in next sc, ch 3, skip ch-2 space, sc in next ch-4 space, 9 dc in next space, sc in next space, ch 3, skip 1 sc] to corner**, 5 dc in corner sc; rep from * around, ending last rep at **, 2 dc in same st as first dc, join with slip st to top of ch-3.

■ **Rnd 3:** Ch 1, 2 sc in same st, *sc in next 2 dc, ch 3, [(dc, ch 1) in next 8 dc, dc in next dc, [ch 1, sc in next 3 dc, ch 1, (dc, ch 1) in next 8 dc, dc in next dc] to sc before corner, ch 3, sc in next 2 dc**, 3 sc in corner dc; rep from * around, ending last rep at **, sc in same st as beginning sc, join with slip st to first sc.

■ **Rnd 4:** Ch 6 (counts as dc and ch 3), dc in same st, skip 1 sc, (dc, ch 3, dc) in next sc, *sc in next 2 spaces, (ch 3, sc in next space) seven times, sc in next space, [skip 1 sc, (dc, ch 3, dc) in next sc, sc in next 2 spaces, (ch 3, sc in next space) seven times, sc in next space] to 3 sts before corner st, [skip 1 sc, (dc, ch 3, dc) in next sc**] three times; rep from * around, ending last rep at **, join with slip st to third ch of ch-6. Fasten off.

Reversible

Wide

Undulating

Open/Lacy

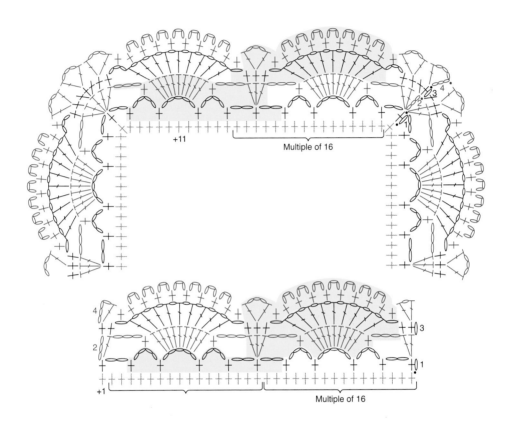

+11

Multiple of 16

4

2

3

1

+1

Multiple of 16

#76

Base rnd, each side: Multiple of 4 + 1 + corners.

Begin 2 sts to left of corner st.

Rnd 1: Ch 4 (counts as dc and ch 1 here and throughout), *skip 1 st, [dc in next 3 sts, ch 1, skip 1 st] to 2 sts before corner st, dc in next 2 sts, (dc, ch 3, dc) in corner st, dc in next 2 sts, ch 1; rep from * around, omitting last dc, join with slip st to third ch of ch-4.

Rnd 2: Ch 3 (counts as dc), working over Rnd-1 space, dc in next st 2 rnds below, *dc in next dc, [ch 1, skip 1 dc, dc in next dc, working over Rnd-1 space, dc in next st 2 rnds below, dc in next dc] to 2 sts before corner space, ch 1, skip 1 dc, dc in next dc, working over Rnd-1 space, tr in corner st 2 rnds below, (dc, ch 1, dc) in corner space of current row, tr in same corner st 2 rnds below; rep from * around, ending last rep dc in next dc, ch 1, skip 1 dc, join with slip st to top of ch-3.

Rnd 3: Ch 4, *skip 1 dc, [dc in next dc, working over Rnd-2 space, dc in next st 2 rnds below, dc in next dc, ch 1, skip 1 st] to 1 st before corner space, dc in next dc, (2 dc, ch 1, 2 dc) in corner space, dc in next dc, ch 1, skip 1 st, dc in next dc, working over Rnd-2 space, dc in next st 2 rnds below**, dc in next dc, ch 1; rep from * around, ending last rep at **; join with slip st to third ch of ch-4.

Rnd 4: Ch 3 (counts as dc), *working over Rnd-3 space, dc in next st 2 rnds below, dc in next dc, [ch 1, skip 1 dc**, dc in next dc; working over Rnd-3 space, dc in next st 2 rnds below, dc in next dc] to 2 sts before corner space, ch 1, skip 1 dc, dc in next dc; working over Rnd-3 space, tr in corner space 2 rnds below, (dc, ch 1, dc) in corner space of current rnd; working over Rnd-3 space, tr in same corner space 2 rnds below, dc in next dc, [ch 1, skip 1 dc, dc in next dc; rep from * around, ending last rep at **; join with slip st to top of ch-3. Fasten off.

Reversible

Medium

Straight

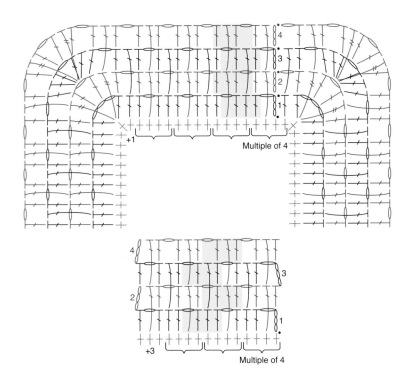

#77

Base rnd, each side: Multiple of 10 + corners. Begin in corner st.

Rnd 1: Ch 3 (counts as dc), 2 dc in same st, *dc in each st to corner, 5 dc in corner st; rep from * around, ending last rep with 2 dc in same st as first dc, join with slip st to first dc.

Rnd 2: Ch 1, sc in first st, ch 10, Chain Petal, *[slip st in next 5 ch, ch 5, make Chain Petal joining first petal to third petal of adjacent Chain Petal, slip st in next 5 ch, ch 5, skip 4 dc, sc in next dc**, ch 5, make Chain Petal joining second petal to third petal of previous Chain Petal, ch 5, skip 4 dc, sc in next dc, ch 10, Chain Petal joining first petal to 2 previous joined petals] across to corner ending at ** and placing last sc in corner st, ch 5***, make Chain Petal joining first petal to third petal of previous Chain Petal, slip st in next 5 ch, sc in same corner sc; ch 10, Chain Petal joining first petal to third petal of corner Chain Petal; rep from * around, ending last rep at ***, Chain Petal joining first petal to third petal of previous Chain Petal and joining third petal to first petal of beginning Chain Petal, slip st in next 5 ch, join with slip st to first sc. Fasten off.

While the instructions for Rnd 2 look daunting, the actual crocheting isn't difficult. Be sure to use the chart to help you understand what's happening.

When slip stitching in a chain, work in the back bump of each chain throughout. Refer to the stitch diagram to clarify joining points for petals. (For an illustration of working in the back bump, see page 210.)

Chain Petal: Ch 8, slip st in eighth ch from hook, (ch 7, slip st in same ch) two times.

Join Petal: Ch 4, slip st in previous petal indicated *(counts as a ch)*, ch 3, complete Chain Petal.

Reversible

Wide

Undulating

Open/Lacy

Fringy

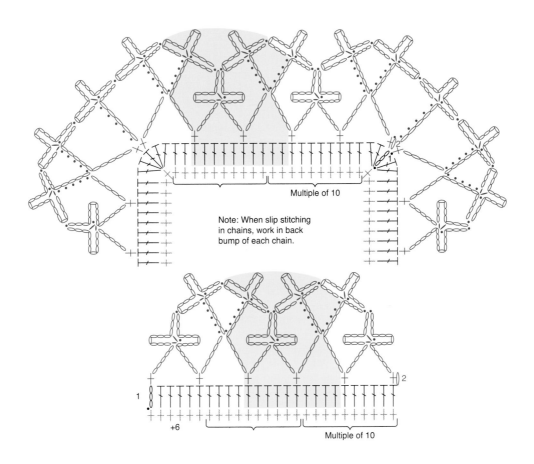

Multiple of 10

Note: When slip stitching
in chains, work in back
bump of each chain.

Multiple of 10

+6

Base rnd, each side: 11 + 5 + corners.

Begin in corner st.

Rnd 1: Ch 1, sc in first st, *make Shamrock, skip 5 sts, sc in next st, [(ch 1, picot-3) two times, ch 1, skip 4 sts, sc in next st, make Shamrock, skip 5 sts, sc in next st] to corner, placing last sc in corner st, picot-3, sc in same corner st; rep from * around, omitting last sc, join with slip st to first sc. Fasten off.

Rnd 2: Standing sc in center dc of second petal, ch 1, sc in same st, *[ch 8, partial sc in center dc of next petal, partial dtr in next picot-loop in ch-1 space between picots, partial sc in center dc of first petal of next Shamrock, yarnover and pull through all 4 loops on hook to join petals for cluster, ch 8, (sc, ch 1, sc) in center dc of next petal] to corner, ch 8, sc in center dc of next petal, ch 1, dtr in corner picot, ch 1, sc in center dc of first petal of next Shamrock, ch 8**, (sc, ch 1, sc) in center dc of next petal; rep from * around, ending last rep at **, join with slip st to first sc, slip st in next space.

Rnd 3: Ch 1, (sc, ch 1, sc) in same space, *[(ch 4, sc in next space) two times, ch 4, (sc, ch 1, sc) in next ch-1 space] to space before corner, ch 5, sc in next ch-8 space, ch 6, sc in next ch-8 space, ch 5**, (sc, ch 1, sc) in next ch-1 space; rep from * around, ending last rep at **, join with slip st to first sc. Fasten off.

#78

Stitches & Notes

This vintage Irish crochet edging gets a fresh new look worked with larger yarn and hook. Be careful not to twist the petals when you are working Rnd 2.

Shamrock: (Ch 1, picot-3) two times, ch 7, slip st in sixth ch from hook to form center ring, turn; (ch 5, sc in ring) three times, turn; (sc, 9 dc, sc) in each of next 3 ch-5 spaces, sc in center ring, ch 1, picot-3, slip st in ch-space between picots opposite picot-3, picot-3, ch 1.

Partial sc: Insert hook into st indicated and pull up a loop.

Partial dtr (partial double treble crochet): Yarnover three times, insert hook into st or space indicated, yarnover and pull up a loop, (yarnover and pull through 2 loops) three times.

Reversible

Wide

Undulating

Motifs

Open/Lacy

+5

Multiple of 11

+2

Multiple of 11

#79

Base rnd, each side: 11 + 5 + corners.

Begin in corner st.

Rnd 1: Ch 1, sc in first st, *make Shamrock, skip 5 sts, sc in next st, [(ch 1, picot-3) two times, ch 1, skip 4 sts, sc in next st, make Shamrock, skip 5 sts, sc in next st] to corner st, placing last sc in corner st, picot-3, sc in same corner st; rep from * around, omitting last sc, join with slip st to first sc. Fasten off.

Use stitch diagram for Border #78 on page 142, but omit Rnds 2 and 3.

Stitches & Notes

Form shamrock-y fringes (or is that fringy shamrocks?) by working only the first round of Border #78 (page 142).

Picot-3: Ch 3, slip st in third chain from hook.

Shamrock: (Ch 1, picot-3) two times, ch 7, slip st in sixth ch from hook to form center ring, turn; (ch 5, sc in ring) three times, turn; (sc, 9 dc, sc) in each of next 3 ch-5 spaces, sc in center ring, ch 1, picot-3, slip st in ch-space between picots opposite picot-3, picot-3, ch 1.

Reversible

Wide

Undulating

Motifs

Open/Lacy

Fringy

#80

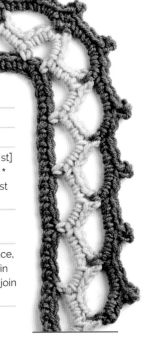

Stitches & Notes

Tight picot-3: Ch 3, slip st in third ch from hook and in st at bottom of ch together. (For an illustration of tight picot-3, see page 214.)

■ **Base rnd, each side:** Multiple of 4 + 1 + corners.

Begin 1 st to the left of corner st.

▨ **Rnd 1:** Ch 1, sc in first st, *[ch 5, skip 3 sts, sc in next st] to corner st, ch 5, skip corner st, sc in next st; rep from * around, omitting last sc, join with slip st to first sc, slip st in next ch-space.

▨ **Rnd 2:** Ch 1, (3 sc, ch 3, 3 sc) in each ch-5 space around, join with slip st to first sc. Fasten off.

■ **Rnd 3:** (Standing sc, ch 1, sc) in any corner ch-3 space, *ch 4, [sc in next space, ch 4] to corner**, (sc, ch 1, sc) in corner space; rep from * around, ending last rep at **, join with sc to first sc, slip st in corner ch-1 space.

■ **Rnd 4:** Ch 1, *(sc, tight picot-3, sc) in corner space, [3 sc, tight picot-3, 3 sc] in each space to corner; rep from * around, join with sc to first sc. Fasten off.

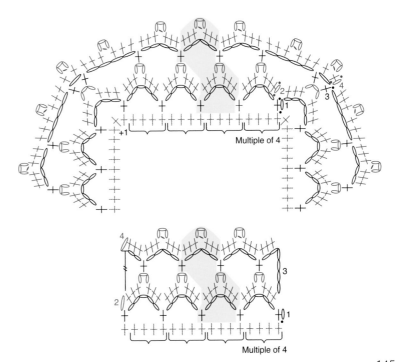

Reversible

Medium

Open/Lacy

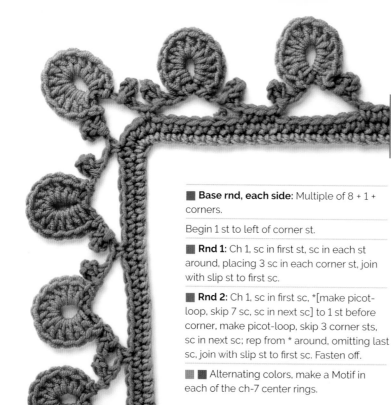

■ Base rnd, each side: Multiple of 8 + 1 + corners.

Begin 1 st to left of corner st.

■ Rnd 1: Ch 1, sc in first st, sc in each st around, placing 3 sc in each corner st, join with slip st to first sc.

■ Rnd 2: Ch 1, sc in first sc, *[make picot-loop, skip 7 sc, sc in next sc] to 1 st before corner, make picot-loop, skip 3 corner sts, sc in next sc; rep from * around, omitting last sc, join with slip st to first sc. Fasten off.

▨ ▨ Alternating colors, make a Motif in each of the ch-7 center rings.

#81

Stitches & Notes

Picot-loop: Ch 7, slip st in sixth ch from hook, ch 9, slip st in seventh ch from hook, ch 8, slip st in sixth ch from hook, ch 1 — *2 ch-6 small rings and 1 ch-7 center ring made.*

Motif: With RS facing, beginning with slip knot on hook, slip st in ch-2 space before ch-7 ring, 13 dc in ch-7 ring, slip st in next ch-2 space. Fasten off.

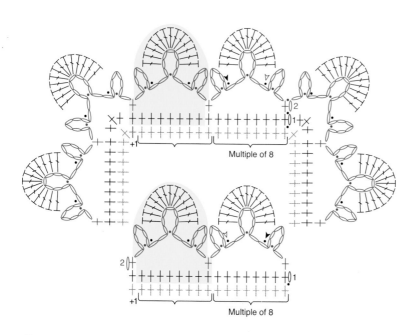

Multiple of 8

Multiple of 8

Reversible

Wide

Undulating

Motifs

Fringy

#82

Stitches & Notes

Picot-loop: Ch 7, slip st in sixth ch from hook, ch 9, slip st in seventh ch from hook, ch 8, slip st in sixth ch from hook, ch 1 — *2 ch-6 small rings and 1 ch-7 center ring made.*

Small Motif: With RS facing, beginning with a slip knot on hook, slip st in ch-space before ch-6 ring, 8 sc in ch-6 ring, slip st in ch-space after ch-6 ring. Fasten off.

Large Motif: With RS facing, beginning with slip knot on hook, slip st in ch-space before ch-7 ring, (6 dc, picot-3, 6 dc) in ring, slip stitch in next ch-space. Fasten off.

■ **Base rnd, each side:** Multiple of 10 + 9 + corners.
Begin 1 st to left of corner st.

■ **Rnd 1:** Ch 1, sc in first st, sc in each st around, placing 3 sc in each corner st, join with slip st to first sc.

■ **Rnd 2:** Ch 1, sc in first sc, *[make picot-loop, skip 7 sc, sc in next 3 sc] to 1 st before corner and omitting the last 2 sc, make picot-loop, skip 3 corner sts, sc in next sc; rep from * around, omitting last sc, join with slip st to first sc. Fasten off.

■ ■ Make a Small Motif in each of the ch-6 rings, and a Large Motif in each of the ch-7 rings.

Reversible
Wide
Undulating

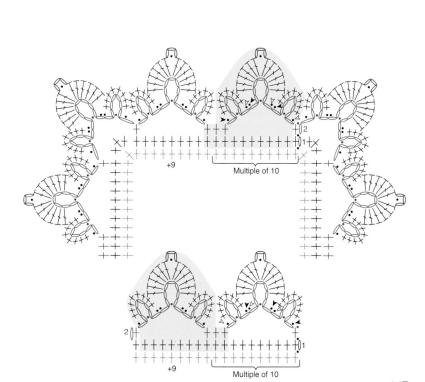

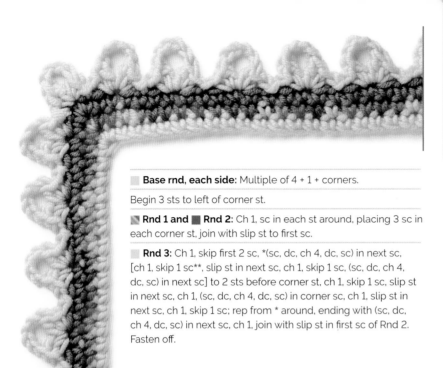

#83

Base rnd, each side: Multiple of 4 + 1 + corners.

Begin 3 sts to left of corner st.

Rnd 1 and Rnd 2: Ch 1, sc in each st around, placing 3 sc in each corner st, join with slip st to first sc.

Rnd 3: Ch 1, skip first 2 sc, *(sc, dc, ch 4, dc, sc) in next sc, [ch 1, skip 1 sc** slip st in next sc, ch 1, skip 1 sc, (sc, dc, ch 4, dc, sc) in next sc] to 2 sts before corner st, ch 1, skip 1 sc, slip st in next sc, ch 1, (sc, dc, ch 4, dc, sc) in corner sc, ch 1, slip st in next sc, ch 1, skip 1 sc; rep from * around, ending with (sc, dc, ch 4, dc, sc) in next sc, ch 1, join with slip st in first sc of Rnd 2. Fasten off.

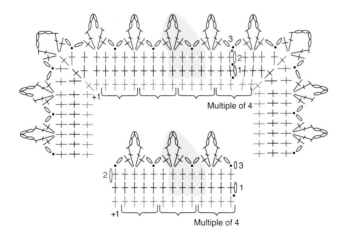

Reversible

Medium

Undulating

Motifs

#84

Stitches & Notes

Use markers to keep track of corners (see page 20).

Embossed Popcorn: Leaving a tail for weaving in, standing dc in 3rd hdc of Rnd 1, just to the right (left) of the Rnd-2 hdc, 2 more dc in same st, 3 dc in next hdc of Rnd 1, just to the left of the Rnd-2 hdc, drop loop from hook and insert hook from front to back into top of first dc, place loop back on hook and pull through, ch 1. Fasten off. Take both yarn tails to the wrong side at the level of Rnd 3 and weave in ends.

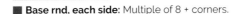

■ **Base rnd, each side:** Multiple of 8 + corners.

Begin 2 sts to left of corner st.

■ **Rnd 1:** Ch 2 (counts as hdc here and throughout), hdc in each st around, placing 3 hdc in each corner st, join with slip st to top of ch-2.

■ **Rnd 2:** Ch 2, hdc in each hdc around, placing 4 hdc in each corner st and placing a marker in the second of these 4 sts to mark corner st, join with slip st to top of ch-2.

■ **Rnd 3:** Ch 2, *[hdc in next 5 hdc, FPdc in next 2 sts 2 rnds below, hdc in next hdc] to marked st, 2 hdc in next 2 hdc and place marker in the first of these sts, hdc in next hdc, FPdc in next 2 sts 2 rnds below, hdc in next hdc; rep from * around, omitting last hdc, join with slip st to top of ch-2.

■ **Rnd 4:** Ch 2, *hdc in next hdc, dc in next 2 hdc, hdc in next 2 hdc, sc in next 2 FPdc, [hdc in next 2 hdc, dc in next 2 hdc, hdc in next 2 hdc, sc in next 2 FPdc] to 1 st before marked st, hdc in next hdc, 2 hdc in next hdc, removing marker; 2 dc in next 2 hdc, 2 hdc in next 2 hdc, hdc in next hdc, sc in next 2 FPdc, hdc in next hdc; rep from * around, omitting last hdc, join with slip st to top of ch-2. Fasten off.

■ ■ **Optional:** Place Embossed Popcorns in Rnd-1 stitches. Make the first popcorn as described; center additional popcorns between the FPdc "legs" of Rnd 3. Place corner popcorns in corner Rnd-1 hdc, either side of Rnd-2 hdcs.

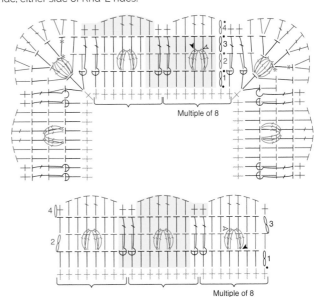

Multiple of 8

Multiple of 8

Medium

Undulating

Layered

Textured

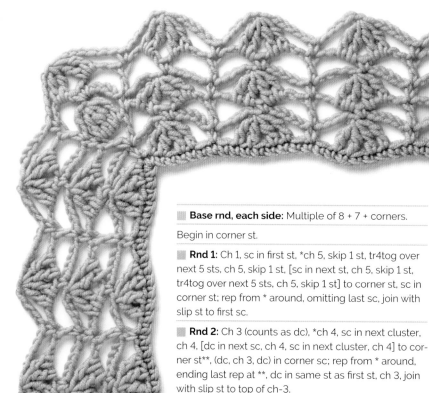

Base rnd, each side: Multiple of 8 + 7 + corners.

Begin in corner st.

Rnd 1: Ch 1, sc in first st, *ch 5, skip 1 st, tr4tog over next 5 sts, ch 5, skip 1 st, [sc in next st, ch 5, skip 1 st, tr4tog over next 5 sts, ch 5, skip 1 st] to corner st, sc in corner st; rep from * around, omitting last sc, join with slip st to first sc.

Rnd 2: Ch 3 (counts as dc), *ch 4, sc in next cluster, ch 4, [dc in next sc, ch 4, sc in next cluster, ch 4] to corner st**, (dc, ch 3, dc) in corner sc; rep from * around, ending last rep at **, dc in same st as first st, ch 3, join with slip st to top of ch-3.

Rnd 3: Ch 1, sc in same st, *[ch 5, 2 partial tr in next 2 spaces, yarnover and pull through all 5 loops on hook to complete tr4tog over 2 spaces, ch 5, sc in next dc] to corner space, ch 5, 4-tr Cluster in corner space, ch 5, sc in next dc; rep from * around, omitting last sc, join with slip st to first sc.

Rnd 4: Ch 7 (counts as dc and ch 4), *[sc in next cluster, ch 4, dc in next sc, ch 4] to corner, (sc, ch 1, sc) in corner cluster, ch 4**, dc in next sc, ch 4; rep from * around, ending last rep at **, join with slip st to third ch of ch-7.

Rnd 5: Ch 1, sc in same st, *[ch 5, 2 partial tr in next 2 spaces, yarnover and pull through all 5 loops on hook to complete tr4tog over 2 spaces, ch 4, sc in next dc] to space before corner space, ch 6, 2 partial tr in next space, skip corner space, 2 partial tr in next space, yarnover and pull through all 5 loops on hook, ch 6, sc in next dc; rep from * around, omitting last sc, join with slip st to first sc.

Stitches & Notes

4-tr Cluster (4 treble crochet cluster): Yarnover two times, insert hook into st or space indicated and pull up a loop, (yarnover and pull through 2 loops) two times, [yarnover two times, insert hook into same st or space and pull up a loop, (yarnover and pull through 2 loops) two times] three times, yarnover and pull through all 5 loops on hook.

Partial tr (partial treble crochet): Yarnover two times, insert hook into st or space indicated and pull up a loop, (yarnover and pull through 2 loops on hook) two times.

Tr4tog over 5 sts (treble crochet 4 together over 5 stitches): Partial tr in next 2 sts, skip 1 st, partial tr in next 2 sts, yarnover and pull through all 5 loops on hook.

Reversible

Wide

Undulating

Open/Lacy

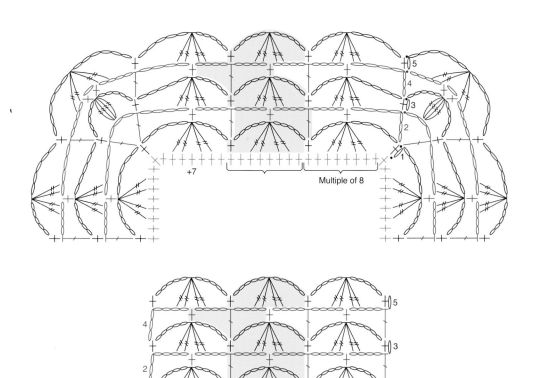

+7

Multiple of 8

+7

Multiple of 8

Base rnd, each side: Multiple of 8 + 7 + corners.

Begin 4 sts to left of corner st.

Rnd 1: Ch 1, sc in first st, *[ch 1, skip 3 sts, 5-dc shell in next st, ch 1, skip 3 sts, sc in next st; rep from * around, omitting last sc, join with slip st to first sc. Fasten off.

Rnd 2: Beginning with slip knot on hook, 3-dc cluster in first ch-1 space of first shell, ch 2, sc in next space, *[ch 1, sc in next space, ch 2, 3-dc cluster in next space, ch 1, 3-dc cluster in first ch-1 space of next shell, ch 2, sc in next space] to corner, ch 3, sc in next space, ch 2, 3-dc cluster in next space**, ch 1, 3-dc cluster in first ch-1 space of next shell, ch 2, sc in next space; rep from * around; ending last rep at **, join with sc to first cluster.

Rnd 3: Ch 4 (counts as dc and ch 1), [(dc, ch 1) three times, dc] in space formed by joining sc — *beginning shell made*, ch 1, *[skip ch-2 space, sc in next ch-1 space, ch 1, 5-dc shell in next ch-1 space between clusters, ch 1] across to ch-2 space before corner, sc in next space, ch 1, 3-dc shell in corner space, ch 1, sc in next space, ch 1**, 5-dc shell in next ch-1 space between clusters; rep from * around, ending last rep at **, join with slip st to third ch of ch-4. Fasten off.

Rnd 4: Beginning with slip knot on hook, 3-dc cluster in first ch-1 space of first shell, ch 2, sc in next space, ch 1, sc in next space, ch 2, 3-dc cluster in next space, ch 1, *[3-dc cluster in first ch-1 space of next shell, ch 2, sc in next space, ch 1, sc in next space, ch 2, 3-dc cluster in next space, ch 1] across to corner shell, 3-dc cluster in first ch-1 space of 3-dc shell, ch 1, V-st in corner dc, ch 1, 3-dc cluster in next ch-1 space**, ch 1; rep from * around, ending last rep at **, join with sc to first cluster.

Rnd 5: Ch 4 (counts as dc and ch 1), [(dc, ch 1) three times, dc] in space formed by joining sc — *beginning shell made*, ch 1, *[skip ch-2 space, sc in next ch-1 space, ch 1, 5-dc shell in next ch-1 space between clusters, ch 1] across to corner, skip 1 space, sc in center of corner V-st, ch 1, skip 1 space**, 5-dc shell in next ch-1 space between clusters, ch 1; rep from * around, ending last rep at **, join with slip st to third ch of ch-4. Fasten off.

3-dc Cluster (3 double crochet cluster): Yarnover, insert hook into st or space indicated and pull up a loop, yarnover and pull through 2 loops, (yarnover, insert hook into same st or space and pull up a loop, yarnover and pull through 2 loops) two times, yarnover and pull through all 4 loops on hook.

3-dc Shell (3 double crochet shell): [Dc, (ch 1, dc) two times] in st or space indicated.

5-dc Shell (5 double crochet shell): [Dc, (ch 1, dc) two times] in st or space indicated.

V-st (V-stitch): (Dc, ch 1, dc) in stitch or space indicated.

Reversible

Wide

Undulating

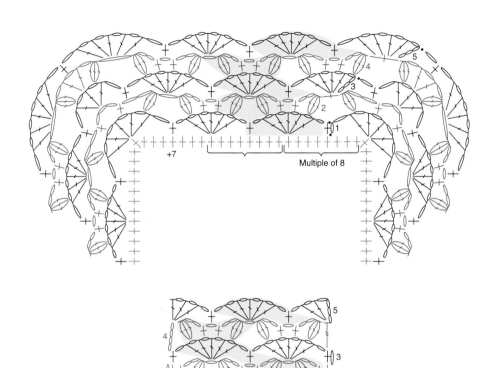

+7

Multiple of 8

+1

Multiple of 8

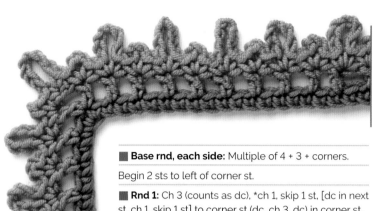

#87

Base rnd, each side: Multiple of 4 + 3 + corners.

Begin 2 sts to left of corner st.

Rnd 1: Ch 3 (counts as dc), *ch 1, skip 1 st, [dc in next st, ch 1, skip 1 st] to corner st (dc, ch 3, dc) in corner st, ch 1, skip 1 st, dc in next st; rep from * around, omitting last dc, join with slip st to first dc.

Rnd 2: Ch 1, (sc, ch 7, sc) in first st, *(sc, ch 3, sc) in next dc**, [(sc, ch 7, sc) in next dc, (sc, ch 3, sc) in next dc] to corner space, skip 1 ch, (sc, ch 7, sc) in next ch, (sc, ch 3, sc) in next dc**, (sc, ch 7, sc) in next dc; rep from * around, ending last rep at **, join with slip st to first sc. Fasten off.

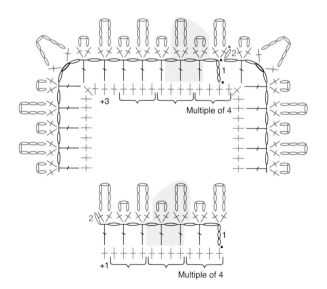

Reversible

Medium

Undulating

#88

Stitches & Notes

This border is written for separate colors on each row, but if you prefer to make it all in one color, simply use what you've learned about adapting the ends-of-rounds (page 26) to make the switch to one continuous yarn.

Puff st (puff stitch):
(Yarnover, insert hook and pull up a loop) three times in st or space indicated, yarnover and pull through all 7 loops on hook. (For an illustration of puff stitch, see page 214.)

Wide

Straight

Textured

■ **Base rnd, each side:** Multiple of 4 + 1 + corners.

Begin 3 sts to left of corner st.

■ **Rnd 1:** Ch 1, sc in first st, sc in each st around, placing 3 sc in corner st, join with slip st to first sc. Fasten off.

▨ **Rnd 2:** Standing sc in first st, *ch 2, skip 1 st, puff st in next st, ch 2, skip 1 st, sc in next st; rep from * around, omitting last sc, join with slip st to first sc. Fasten off.

■ **Rnd 3:** Standing sc in ch-2 space after last puff st, *ch 3, sc in next space, ch 1, sc in next space; rep from * around, omitting last sc, join with slip st to first sc. Fasten off.

▨ **Rnd 4:** Standing sc in last ch-1 space, *[ch 2, puff st in next ch-3 space, ch 2, sc in next space] to space before corner space, ch 3, puff st in corner space, ch 3, sc in next space; rep from * around, omitting last sc, join with slip st to first sc. Fasten off.

■ **Rnd 5:** Standing sc in first space, [ch 1, sc in next space, ch 3, sc in next space] to corner st, (ch 3, sc in next space) two times; rep from * around, omitting last sc, join with slip st to first sc.

■ **Rnd 6:** Ch 1, sc in each ch-1 space, 3 sc in each ch-3 space, and 5 sc in each corner space around, join with slip st to first sc. Fasten off.

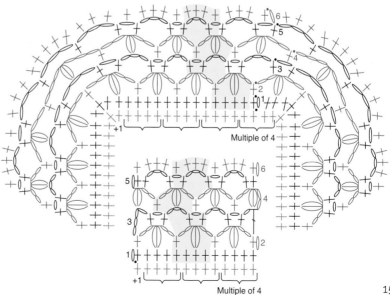

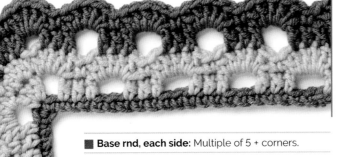

89

■ **Base rnd, each side:** Multiple of 5 + corners.

Begin 3 sts to left of corner st.

■ **Rnd 1:** Ch 3 (counts as dc), dc in next dc, *[ch 2, skip 2 sts, dc in next 3 sts] to 1 st before corner st, ch 2, skip 1 st, 3 dc in corner st, ch 2, skip 1 st, dc in next 3 sts; rep from * around, omitting last 2 dc, join with slip st to top of ch-3.

■ **Rnd 2:** Ch 1, sc in first st, *5 dc in next space, [skip 1 dc, sc in next dc, 5 dc in next ch-2 space] to 1 st before corner st, sc in next dc, 3 dc in corner dc, sc in next dc — *corner group made,* 5 dc in next space, skip next dc, sc in next dc; rep from * around, omitting last sc, join with slip st to first sc. Fasten off.

■ **Rnd 3:** Standing dc in center dc of last 5-dc group made, *dc in next dc, ch 2, [skip (dc, sc, dc), dc in next 3 dc, ch 2] across to corner group, skip (dc, sc), 2 dc in next dc, (dc, ch 2, dc) in corner dc, 2 dc in next dc, ch 2, skip (sc, dc), dc in next 2 dc; rep from * around, omitting last dc, join with slip st to first dc.

■ **Rnd 4:** Ch 1, sc in same st, *5 dc in next space, skip 1 dc, sc in next dc; rep from * around, omitting last sc, join with slip st to first sc. Fasten off.

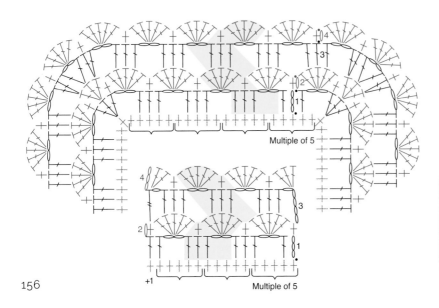

Multiple of 5

Multiple of 5

Reversible

Wide

Undulating

Open/Lacy

#90

Stitches & Notes

3-dc Cluster (3 double crochet cluster): Yarnover, insert hook into st or space indicated and pull up a loop, yarnover and pull through 2 loops, (yarnover, insert hook into same st or space and pull up a loop, yarnover and pull through 2 loops) two times, yarnover and pull through all 4 loops on hook.

Reversible

Medium

Undulating

Open/Lacy

■ **Base rnd, each side:** Multiple of 8 + 5 + corners.

Begin in corner st.

■ **Rnd 1:** Ch 1, 2 sc in first st, *ch 3, skip 1 st, sc in next st, ch 5, skip 1 st, sc in next st, ch 3, skip 1 st, [sc in next 3 sts, ch 3, skip 1 st, sc in next st, ch 5, skip 1 st, sc in next st, ch 3, skip 1 st] to corner st**, 3 sc in corner st; rep from * around, ending last rep at **, sc in same st as first sc, join with slip st to first sc.

■ **Rnd 2:** Ch 1, sc in same st, *sc in next space, ch 2, (3-dc cluster, ch 3, 3-dc cluster) in next space, ch 2, sc in next space, skip 1 sc, sc in next sc, skip 1 sc; rep from * around, omitting last sc, join with slip st to first sc.

■ **Rnd 3:** Ch 1, sc in same corner st, *2 sc in next space, sc in next cluster, (2 sc, ch 1, 2 sc) in next space, sc in next cluster, 2 sc in next space, skip 1 sc**, sc in next sc, skip 1 sc; rep from * around, ending last rep at **, join with slip st to first sc. Fasten off.

■ **Base rnd, each side:** Multiple of 8 + 5 + corners.

Begin in corner st.

▨ **Rnd 1:** Ch 1, 2 sc in first st, *ch 3, skip 1 st, sc in next st, ch 5, skip 1 st, sc in next st, ch 3, skip 1 st, [sc in next 3 sts, ch 3, skip 1 st, sc in next st, ch 5, skip 1 st, sc in next st, ch 3, skip 1 st] to corner st**, 3 sc in corner st; rep from * around, ending last rep at **, sc in same st as first sc, join with slip st to first sc.

▨ **Rnd 2:** Ch 1, sc in same st, *sc in next space, ch 2, (3-dc cluster, ch 3, 3-dc cluster) in next space, ch 2, sc in next space, skip 1 sc, sc in next sc, skip 1 sc; rep from * around, omitting last sc, join with slip st to first sc. Fasten off.

■ **Rnd 3:** Beginning with slip knot on hook, FPhdc in first cluster, *ch 2, sc in next space, ch 2, FPhdc in next cluster, ch 2, FPhdc2tog over next 3 sc, ch 2**, FPhdc in next cluster, rep from * around, ending last rep at **, join with slip st to first hdc, slip st in next space.

■ **Rnd 4:** Ch 2 (counts as partial dc), 2 partial dc in same space, yarnover and pull through all 3 loops on hook to dc3tog, *ch 3, 3-dc cluster in next space, [ch 2, skip next space, sc in next st, ch 2, skip next space, 3-dc cluster in next space, ch 3, 3-dc cluster in next space] across to space before corner, ch 3, (sc, ch 1, sc) in corner st, ch 3, skip next space, 3-dc cluster in next space; rep from * around, omitting last cluster, join with slip st to first cluster. Fasten off.

▨ **Rnd 5:** Beginning with slip knot on hook, FPhdc in first cluster, *ch 2, sc in next space, ch 2, FPhdc in next cluster, [ch 2, FPhdc in next sc, ch 2, FPhdc in next cluster, ch 2, sc in next space, ch 2, FPhdc in next cluster] to sc before corner space, (ch 3, FPhdc in next sc) two times, ch 3, FPhdc in next cluster; rep from * around, omitting last FPhdc, join with slip st to first hdc, slip st in next space.

▨ **Rnd 6:** Ch 1, 3 sc in each ch-2 space and 4 sc in each ch-3 space around, join with slip st to first sc. Fasten off.

Stitches & Notes

This border starts out with the first 2 rounds of Border #90 (see page 156), but goes on to look entirely different.

FPhdc (front post half double crochet): Yarnover, insert hook from front to back to front around post of st indicated, yarnover and pull up a loop, yarnover and pull through all 3 loops on hook.

FPhdc2tog over 3 sts (front post half double crochet 2 together over 3 stitches): Yarnover, insert hook from front to back to front around post of next st, yarnover and pull up a loop, skip 1 st, yarnover, insert hook from front to back to front around post of next st, yarnover and pull up a loop, yarnover and pull through all 5 loops on hook.

Partial dc (partial double crochet): Yarnover, insert hook into st or space indicated and pull up a loop, yarnover and pull through 2 loops on hook.

Wide

Undulating

Textured

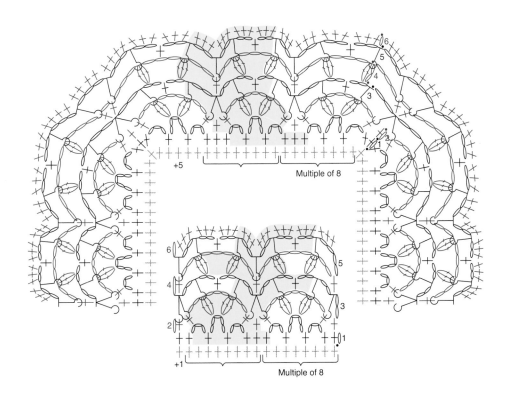

+5

Multiple of 8

+1

Multiple of 8

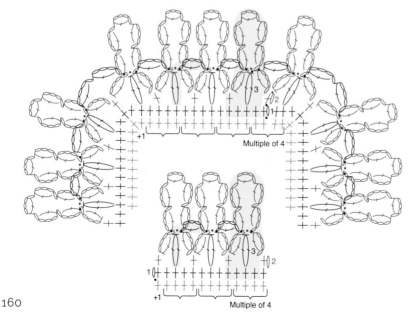

#92

- **Base rnd, each side:** 4 + 1 + corners.

Begin 3 sts to left of corner st.

Rnd 1: Ch 1, sc in each st around, placing 3 sc in each corner st, join with slip st to first sc.

Rnd 2: Ch 1, sc in same st; work Large Loop, skip 3 sts, sc in next st; rep from * around, omitting last sc. Fasten off.

Note: Rnd-3 sts are worked into Rnd-1 sts. Hold yarn behind Rnd-2 sts and keep hook in front of Rnd-2 sts at all times during this round.

Rnd 3: Beginning with slip knot on hook, 2-dc cluster in center sc of any 3 skipped sc on Rnd 1, *slip st between sixth and seventh scallop, [scallop, slip st between first and second scallop of next Large Loop, 2-dc cluster in center sc of next 3 skipped scs, slip st between sixth and seventh scallops of same Large Loop] to corner, 2 scallops at corner, slip st in same space as next slip st of previous rnd, 2-dc cluster in center sc of next 3 skipped scs; rep from * around, omitting last cluster, join with slip st to top of first cluster. Fasten off.

Stitches & Notes

2-dc Cluster: Yarnover, insert hook into st or space indicated and pull up a loop, yarnover and pull through 2 loops, yarnover, insert hook into same st or space and pull up a loop, yarnover and pull through 2 loops, yarnover and pull through all 3 loops on hook.

Large Loop: (Ch 4, dc in fourth ch from hook — *scallop made*) six times, slip st in space between fifth and sixth scallop from hook, make 1 scallop.

Wide

Fringy

Layered

160

#93

Stitches & Notes

Ring: Ch 10, insert tail of chain in hole formed by ch-1 space and join with slip st to form a ring; ch 2, 18 hdc in ring, join with slip st to top of ch-2.

Note: *Depending on your yarn, you may need to put additional hdcs in each ring to fill ring.*

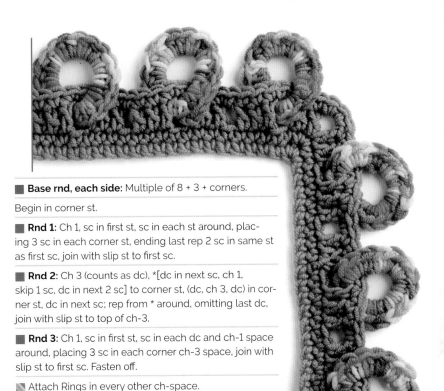

■ **Base rnd, each side:** Multiple of 8 + 3 + corners.

Begin in corner st.

■ **Rnd 1:** Ch 1, sc in first st, sc in each st around, placing 3 sc in each corner st, ending last rep 2 sc in same st as first sc, join with slip st to first sc.

■ **Rnd 2:** Ch 3 (counts as dc), *[dc in next sc, ch 1, skip 1 sc, dc in next 2 sc] to corner st, (dc, ch 3, dc) in corner st, dc in next sc; rep from * around, omitting last dc, join with slip st to top of ch-3.

■ **Rnd 3:** Ch 1, sc in first st, sc in each dc and ch-1 space around, placing 3 sc in each corner ch-3 space, join with slip st to first sc. Fasten off.

◥ Attach Rings in every other ch-space.

Reversible

Wide

Motifs

Textured

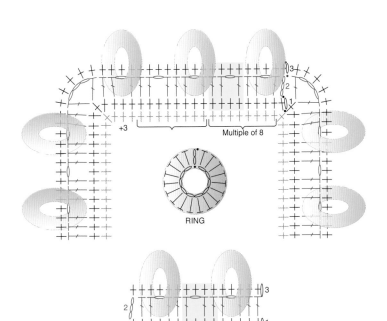

RING

+3

Multiple of 8

+7

Multiple of 8

161

#94

Base rnd, each side: Multiple of 2 + 1 + corners.

Begin 2 sts to left of corner st.

Rnd 1: Ch 3 (counts as dc), dc in each st around, placing 3 dc in each corner st, join with slip st to first dc. Fasten off.

Rnd 2: Standing FPdtr in first st, *[BPdtr in next dc, FPdtr in next st] to corner st, (BPdtr, ch 1, FPdtr) in corner st, FPdtr in next st; rep from * around, ending BPdtr in last st, join with slip st to first st.

Rnd 3: Ch 1, hdc in space between trs around, placing 3 hdc in each corner ch-1 space. Fasten off.

Stitches & Notes

Front post double treble crochet stitches provide a lacy texture to this straight-edged border. For a more delicate look, leave off Rnd 3. For a less open look, use front post double crochet stitches instead of front post trebles.

BPdtr: Yarnover three times, insert hook from back to front to back around post of st, yarnover and pull up a loop, (yarnover and pull through 2 loops) four times.

FPdtr: Yarnover three times, insert hook from front to back to front around post of st indicated, yarnover and pull up a loop, (yarnover and pull through 2 loops) four times.

Standing FPdtr (standing front post double treble crochet): Beginning with slip knot on hook, work FPdtr.

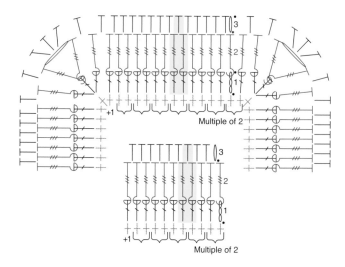

Multiple of 2

Multiple of 2

Reversible

Medium

Straight

Layered

Textured

#95

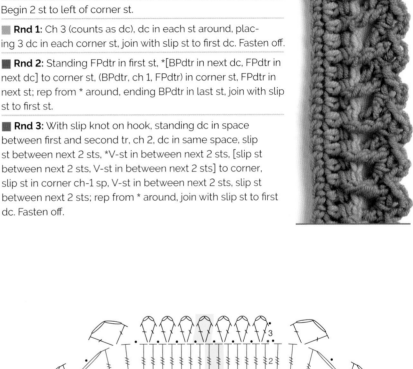

Stitches & Notes

Create a gentle ruffle by replacing Rnd 3 in Border #94 (facing page) with V-sts and slip stitches worked between the post stitches.

BPdtr (back post double treble crochet): Yarnover three times, insert hook from back to front to back around post of st, yarnover and pull up a loop, (yarnover and pull through 2 loops) four times.

FPdtr (front post double treble crochet): Yarnover three times, insert hook from front to back to front around post of st indicated, yarnover and pull up a loop, (yarnover and pull through 2 loops) four times.

Standing FPdtr (standing front post double treble crochet): Beginning with slip knot on hook, work FPdtr.

V-st (V-stitch): (Dc, ch 2, dc) in st or space indicated.

Reversible

Medium

Undulating

Layered

Textured

■ **Base rnd, each side:** Multiple of 2 + 1 + corners.

Begin 2 st to left of corner st.

■ **Rnd 1:** Ch 3 (counts as dc), dc in each st around, placing 3 dc in each corner st, join with slip st to first dc. Fasten off.

■ **Rnd 2:** Standing FPdtr in first st, *[BPdtr in next dc, FPdtr in next dc] to corner st, (BPdtr, ch 1, FPdtr) in corner st, FPdtr in next st; rep from * around, ending BPdtr in last st, join with slip st to first st.

■ **Rnd 3:** With slip knot on hook, standing dc in space between first and second tr, ch 2, dc in same space, slip st between next 2 sts, *V-st in between next 2 sts, [slip st between next 2 sts, V-st in between next 2 sts] to corner, slip st in corner ch-1 sp, V-st in between next 2 sts, slip st between next 2 sts; rep from * around, join with slip st to first dc. Fasten off.

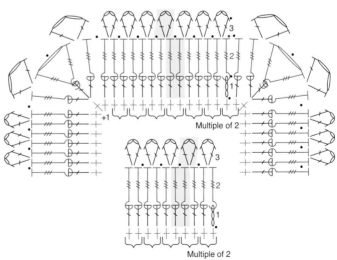

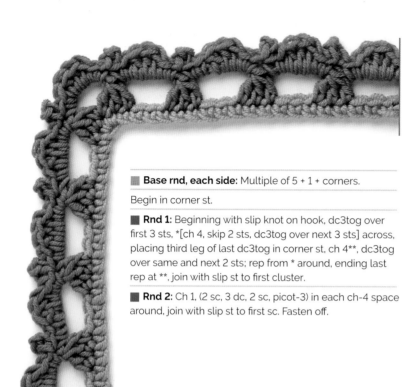

96

▓ **Base rnd, each side:** Multiple of 5 + 1 + corners.

Begin in corner st.

▓ **Rnd 1:** Beginning with slip knot on hook, dc3tog over first 3 sts, *[ch 4, skip 2 sts, dc3tog over next 3 sts] across, placing third leg of last dc3tog in corner st, ch 4**, dc3tog over same and next 2 sts; rep from * around, ending last rep at **, join with slip st to first cluster.

▓ **Rnd 2:** Ch 1, (2 sc, 3 dc, 2 sc, picot-3) in each ch-4 space around, join with slip st to first sc. Fasten off.

Stitches & Notes

Dc3tog (double crochet 3 together): (Yarnover, insert hook into next st or space indicated, yarnover and pull up a loop, yarnover and pull through 2 loops) three times, yarnover and pull through all 4 loops on hook.

Picot-3: Ch 3, slip st in third chain from hook.

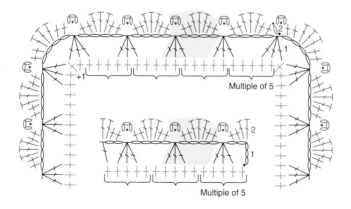

Multiple of 5

Multiple of 5

Reversible

Narrow

Undulating

Open/Lacy

#97

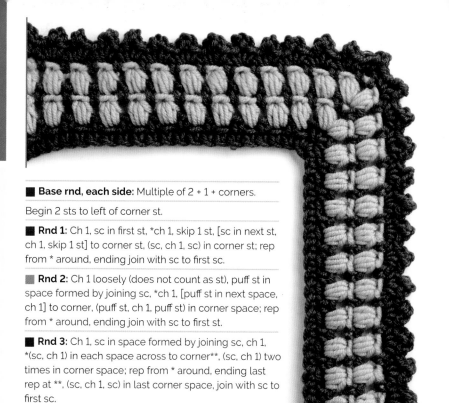

Stitches & Notes

Puff st (puff stitch): (Yarnover, insert hook and pull up a loop) three times in st or space indicated, yarnover and pull through all 7 loops on hook. (For an illustration of puff stitch, see page 214.)

Base rnd, each side: Multiple of 2 + 1 + corners.

Begin 2 sts to left of corner st.

Rnd 1: Ch 1, sc in first st, *ch 1, skip 1 st, [sc in next st, ch 1, skip 1 st] to corner st, (sc, ch 1, sc) in corner st; rep from * around, ending join with sc to first sc.

Rnd 2: Ch 1 loosely (does not count as st), puff st in space formed by joining sc, *ch 1, [puff st in next space, ch 1] to corner, (puff st, ch 1, puff st) in corner space; rep from * around, ending join with sc to first st.

Rnd 3: Ch 1, sc in space formed by joining sc, ch 1, *(sc, ch 1) in each space across to corner**, (sc, ch 1) two times in corner space; rep from * around, ending last rep at **, (sc, ch 1, sc) in last corner space, join with sc to first sc.

Rnd 4: Rep Rnd 2.

Rnd 5: Ch 1, (sc, ch 3, sc) in space formed by joining sc, (sc, ch 3, sc) in each space around, join with slip st to first sc. Fasten off.

Reversible

Medium

Undulating

Layered

Textured

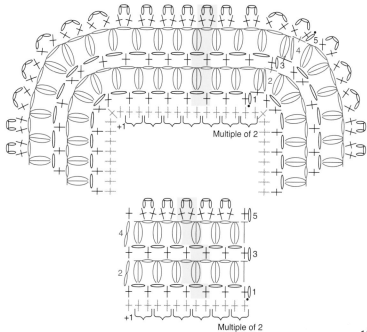

Base rnd, each side: Multiple of 4 + 3 + corners.

Begin 4 sts to left of corner st.

Rnd 1: Beginning with slip knot on hook, (3-dc cluster, ch 3, 3-dc cluster) in first st, skip 3 sts, *(3-dc cluster, ch 3, 3-dc cluster) in next st, skip 3 sts; rep from * around, join with slip st to first cluster, slip st in next space.

Rnd 2: Ch 2 (counts as partial dc), partial dc in same space, yarnover and pull through all 3 loops on hook, ch 3, 2-dc cluster in same space, *ch 2, [(2-dc cluster, ch 3, 2-dc cluster) in next space, ch 2] to corner space, [(2-dc cluster, ch 3) two times, 2-dc cluster] in corner space — *corner group made*; rep from * around, ending with ch 2, join with slip st to first cluster, slip st in next space.

Rnd 3: Ch 2 (counts as partial dc), partial dc in same space, yarnover and pull through all 3 loops on hook, ch 1, 2-dc cluster in same space, *ch 2, sc in next space, ch 2**, [(2-dc cluster, ch 1, 2-dc cluster) in next space, ch 2, sc in next space, ch 2] to corner group, (2-dc cluster, ch 1, 2-dc cluster) in next space, ch 2, sc in next cluster, ch 2, (2-dc cluster, ch 1, 2-dc cluster) in next space; rep from * around, ending last rep at **, join with slip st to first cluster. Fasten off.

#98

Stitches & Notes

The third round creates a gentle ruffle in this versatile edging.

2-dc Cluster (2 double crochet cluster): (Yarnover, insert hook into st or space indicated and pull up a loop, yarnover and pull through 2 loops, yarnover, insert hook into same st or space and pull up a loop, yarnover and pull through 2 loops, yarnover and pull through all 3 loops on hook.

3-dc Cluster (3 double crochet cluster): Yarnover, insert hook into st or space indicated and pull up a loop, yarnover and pull through 2 loops, (yarnover, insert hook into same st or space and pull up a loop, yarnover and pull through 2 loops) two times, yarnover and pull through all 4 loops on hook.

Partial dc (partial double crochet): Yarnover, insert hook into st or space indicated and pull up a loop, yarnover and pull through 2 loops.

Reversible

Medium

Undulating

Open/Lacy

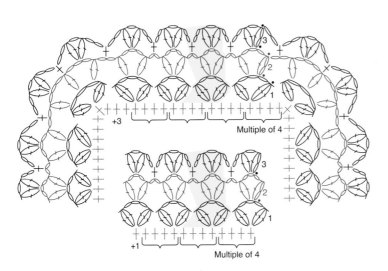

#99

Stitches & Notes

The length of the elongated loop in this Solomon's Knot border can vary based on the size of the yarn you are using. Generally speaking, it should be about the same length as 2 single crochet stitches, but try out different lengths to see what looks best.

Knot st (Knot stitch): Draw up loop on hook from ¼" to ¾"/6 mm to 2 cm (see above). Ch 1, insert hook into leftmost (rightmost for lefties) strand of the 3 vertical strands, yarnover and pull up a loop, yarnover and pull through 2 loops on hook to complete a single crochet. (For an illustration of Knot stitch, see page 213.)

Picot-3: Ch 3, slip st in third chain from hook.

Picot-4: Ch 4, slip st in third chain from hook.

Triple picot: Picot-3, picot-4, picot-3, slip st in same ch as first picot.

Reversible

Wide

Undulating

Open/Lacy

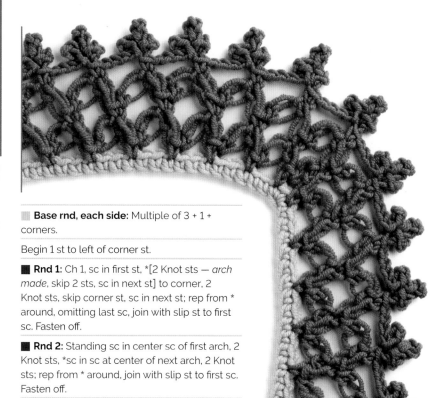

Base rnd, each side: Multiple of 3 + 1 + corners.

Begin 1 st to left of corner st.

Rnd 1: Ch 1, sc in first st, *[2 Knot sts — *arch made*, skip 2 sts, sc in next st] to corner, 2 Knot sts, skip corner st, sc in next st; rep from * around, omitting last sc, join with slip st to first sc. Fasten off.

Rnd 2: Standing sc in center sc of first arch, 2 Knot sts, *sc in sc at center of next arch, 2 Knot sts; rep from * around, join with slip st to first sc. Fasten off.

Rnd 3: Beginning with slip knot on hook, (sc, triple picot, sc) in center sc of any arch, ch 4, *(sc, triple picot, sc) in center sc of next loop, ch 4; rep from * around, join with slip st to first sc. Fasten off.

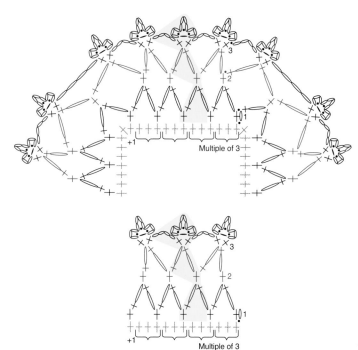

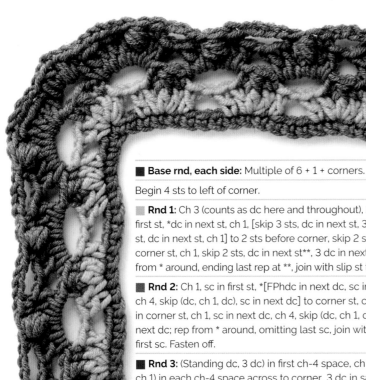

#100

Base rnd, each side: Multiple of 6 + 1 + corners.

Begin 4 sts to left of corner.

Rnd 1: Ch 3 (counts as dc here and throughout), 2 dc in first st, *dc in next st, ch 1, [skip 3 sts, dc in next st, 3 dc in next st, dc in next st, ch 1] to 2 sts before corner, skip 2 sts, 5 dc in corner st, ch 1, skip 2 sts, dc in next st**, 3 dc in next st; rep from * around, ending last rep at **, join with slip st to first dc.

Rnd 2: Ch 1, sc in first st, *[FPhdc in next dc, sc in next dc, ch 4, skip (dc, ch 1, dc), sc in next dc] to corner st, ch 1, FPhdc in corner st, ch 1, sc in next dc, ch 4, skip (dc, ch 1, dc), sc in next dc; rep from * around, omitting last sc, join with slip st to first sc. Fasten off.

Rnd 3: (Standing dc, 3 dc) in first ch-4 space, ch 1, *(5 dc, ch 1) in each ch-4 space across to corner, 3 dc in same ch-space, ch 1, skip 2 ch-1 spaces, (3 dc, ch 1, 5 dc, ch 1) in next ch-4 space; rep from * around, ending dc in same space as first 4 dc, join with slip st to first dc.

Rnd 4: Ch 1, sc in same st, *FP puff st in next dc, sc in next dc, [ch 4, skip (dc, ch 1, dc)**, sc in next dc, FP puff st in next dc, sc in next dc] across, ending in last 5-dc group of side, ch 4, skip (dc, ch 1, 2 dc), sc in next dc, (puff st, ch 2, puff st) in corner ch-1 space, sc in next dc, ch 4, skip (2 dc, ch 1, dc), sc in next dc; rep from * around, ending last rep at **, join with slip st to first sc. Fasten off.

Stitches & Notes

FPhdc (Front post half double crochet): Yarnover, insert hook from front to back to front around post of st indicated, yarnover and pull up a loop, yarnover and pull through 3 loops on hook.

FP puff st (Front post puff stitch): Yarnover, insert hook from front to back to front around post of st indicated and pull up a loop, (yarnover, insert hook from front to back to front around post of same st, yarnover and pull up a loop) two times, yarnover and pull through all 7 loops on hook.

Puff st (puff stitch): (Yarnover, insert hook and pull up a loop) three times in st or space indicated, yarnover and pull through all 7 loops on hook. (For an illustration of puff stitch, see page 214.)

Medium

Straight

Open/Lacy

Textured

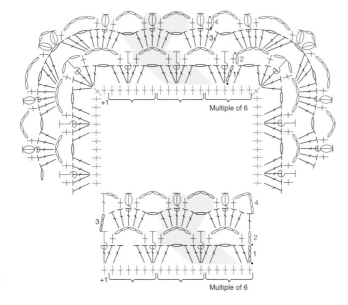

Multiple of 6

Multiple of 6

#101

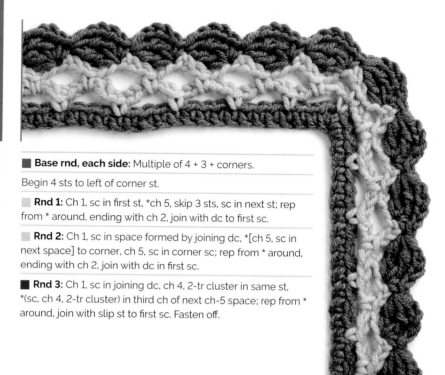

Stitches & Notes

2-tr cluster (2 treble crochet cluster):
*Yarnover two times, insert hook into st or space indicated and pull up a loop, (yarnover and pull through 2 loops) two times; rep from * once, yarnover and pull through all 3 loops on hook.

■ Base rnd, each side: Multiple of 4 + 3 + corners.

Begin 4 sts to left of corner st.

■ Rnd 1: Ch 1, sc in first st, *ch 5, skip 3 sts, sc in next st; rep from * around, ending with ch 2, join with dc to first sc.

■ Rnd 2: Ch 1, sc in space formed by joining dc, *[ch 5, sc in next space] to corner, ch 5, sc in corner sc; rep from * around, ending with ch 2, join with dc in first sc.

■ Rnd 3: Ch 1, sc in joining dc, ch 4, 2-tr cluster in same st, *(sc, ch 4, 2-tr cluster) in third ch of next ch-5 space; rep from * around, join with slip st to first sc. Fasten off.

Medium

Undulating

Open/Lacy

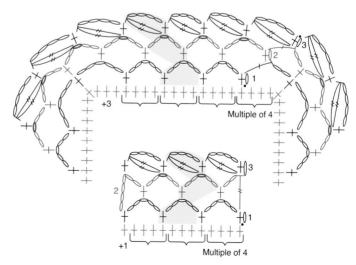

169

#102

■ Base rnd, each side: Multiple of 2 + 1 + corners.

Begin 2 sts to left of corner st.

■ Rnd 1: Standing tr in first st, ch 1, skip 1 st, *[tr in next st, ch 1, skip 1 st] to corner, (tr, ch 3, tr) in corner st, ch 1, skip 1 st; rep from * around, join with slip st to first tr.

■ Rnd 2: Ch 1, sc in same st, sc in each tr and ch-1 space around, placing 3 sc in each corner space, join with slip st to first sc. Fasten off.

■ Rnd 3: *Holding yarn on wrong side of fabric throughout,* insert hook in space before first tr, place slip knot on hook, surface chain around post of first tr, *[ch 1, surface chain around post of next tr] to corner space, ch 2, surface chain around post of next tr; rep from * around, ending ch 1, join with slip st to first ch. Fasten off.

Stitches & Notes

Surface chain: Holding yarn on wrong side of fabric, insert hook from front to back into next st or around post of st as indicated, pull up a loop through fabric and through loop on hook.

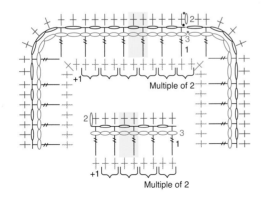

Multiple of 2

Multiple of 2

Narrow

Straight

Open/Lacy

Layered

#103

Stitches & Notes

Here's another border that looks great with fewer rounds, too. Stop after Rnd 3 for a narrower, scalloped border.

■ **Base rnd, each side:** Multiple of 6 + 3 + corners.

Begin 5 sts to left of corner st.

■ **Rnd 1:** Ch 1, sc in first st, sc in next st, *ch 5, skip 3 sts, [sc in next 3 sts, ch 5, skip 3 sts] to corner st, 3 sc in corner st; rep from * around, ending last rep ch 5, skip 3 sts, sc in next st, join with slip st to first sc.

■ **Rnd 2:** Ch 1, sc in same st, *ch 3, sc in next space, ch 3, [skip 1 sc, sc in next sc, ch 3, sc in next space, ch 3] to sc before corner st, sc in next sc, ch 3, skip corner st, sc in next sc; rep from * around, ending with ch 3, sc in next space, ch 3, skip 1 sc, join with slip st to first sc.

■ **Rnd 3:** Ch 3 (counts as dc), 2 dc in same st, *[sc in next sc, 5 dc in next sc] to corner, sc in corner space, 5 dc in next sc, sc in next sc; rep from * around, ending last rep 2 dc in same st as first dc, join with slip st to top of ch-3. Fasten off.

■ **Rnd 4:** Ch 1, sc in first st, *ch 3, skip 2 dc, sc in next sc, ch 3, skip 2 dc, sc in next dc; rep from * around, omitting last sc, join with slip st to first sc.

■ **Rnd 5:** Ch 1, sc in same st, *ch 3, sc in next sc; rep from * around, omitting last sc, join with slip st to first sc. Fasten off.

Medium

Undulating

Open/Lacy

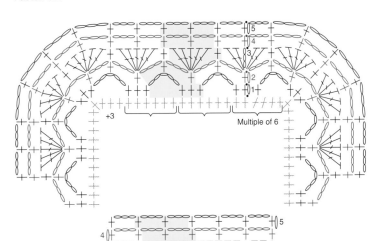

#104

■ Base rnd, each side: Multiple of 4 + 3 + corners.
Begin 2 sts to left of corner st.

■ Rnd 1: Ch 1, sc in each st around, placing 3 sc in each corner st, join with slip st to first sc. Fasten off.

Note: On Rnds 2 and 3, work in back bump of each chain throughout. (For an illustration of working in the back bump, see page 210.)

■ Rnd 2: Beginning with slip knot on hook, ch 3, slip st in first sc, turn; sc in each of first 3 chs, *[ch 6, turn; skip 3 sc in Rnd 1, slip st in next sc, turn; sc in each of first 3 chs] to 2 sts before corner st, (ch 6, skip 2 sc, slip st in next sc, turn; sc in each of first 3 chs**) two times; rep from * around, ending last rep at **, ch 3, join with slip st to first ch.

■ Rnd 3: Ch 1, sc in same ch, *sc in next 3 (free) ch, [sc in same ch as sc from Rnd 2, sc in next 3 ch] to corner, 3 sc in same ch as sc in corner; rep from * around, ending last rep sc in last 3 ch, join with slip st to first sc.

■ Rnd 4: Ch 1, sc in each st around, placing 3 sc in each corner st, join with slip st to first sc. Fasten off.

Stitches & Notes

Unique construction gives this border its unusual look. Don't over-block, or you'll lose the slight forward bend of each of the upright elements.

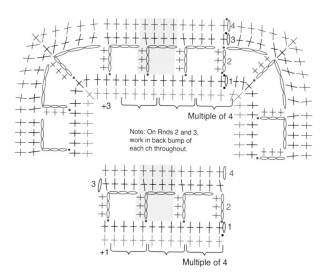

Note: On Rnds 2 and 3, work in back bump of each ch throughout.

Multiple of 4

Multiple of 4

Reversible

Medium

Straight

Open/Lacy

#105

Stitches & Notes

Beg Flat X-st (Beginning Flat X-stitch): *Worked over 3 sts and counts as 3 sts.* Ch 2, skip 1 st or space, dc in next st or space, ch 3, dc in space where ch-2 and dc meet.

Flat X-st (Flat X-stitch): *Worked over 3 sts and counts as 3 sts.* Yarnover two times, insert hook into next st or space indicated and pull up a loop, yarnover and pull through 2 loops, yarnover, skip 1 st, insert hook into next st or space, yarnover and pull up a loop, (yarnover and pull through 2 loops on hook) four times, ch 1, dc under 2 loops where 2 legs of this st join. (For an illustration of Flat X-stitch, see page 211.)

■ **Base rnd, each side:** Multiple of 3 + 2 + corners.

Begin 2 sts to left of corner st.

■ **Rnd 1:** Ch 1, sc in each st around, placing 3 sc in each corner st, join with slip st to first sc.

■ **Rnd 2:** Beg Flat X-st, *Flat X-st across to corner placing last leg of st in corner st, ch 1, (tr, ch 1) two times in corner st, Flat X-st placing first leg of st in same corner st; rep from * around, join with slip st to ch-1 space of Beg Flat X-st.

■ **Rnd 3:** Ch 1, sc in same space, *[sc in next space between 2 Flat X-sts, sc in next ch-1 space] to ch-1 space before corner, 2 sc in next ch-1 space, 3 sc in corner space, 2 sc in next ch-1 space, sc in next ch-1 space; rep from * around, ending sc in next space between 2 X-sts, join with slip st to first sc. Fasten off.

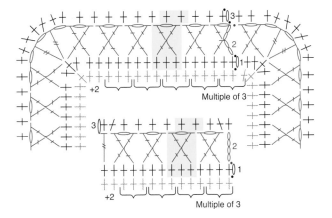

Reversible

Medium

Straight

Open/Lacy

Stitches & Notes

Work into the back bump of each chain throughout. (For an illustration of working in the back bump, see page 210.)

◼ **Base rnd, each side:** Multiple of 4 + 1 + corners.

Begin 3 sts to left of corner st.

◻ **Rnd 1:** Ch 1, sc in each st around, placing 3 sc in each corner st, join with slip st to first sc.

◻ **Rnd 2:** Ch 1, sc in same st, *ch 4, sc in second ch from hook, hdc in next ch, dc in next ch — *point made,* skip 3 sc of Rnd 1, sc in next sc; rep from * around, omitting last sc, join with slip st to first sc. Fasten off.

◼ **Rnd 3:** Standing sc in sc at tip of first point after any corner, *hdc in next hdc, dc in next dc, [tr in next sc, sc in sc at tip of next point, hdc in next hdc, dc in next dc] to corner sc, 4 tr in corner st, place marker in the second of these 4 tr, sc in sc at tip of next point; rep from * around, omitting last st, join with slip st to first sc.

◼ **Rnd 4:** Ch 1, sc in same st, *[make point, skip (hdc, dc, tr), sc in next sc] to 3 sts before marked st, make point, skip (hdc, dc, tr), sc in next tr, make point, skip next 2 tr, sc in next sc; rep from * around, omitting last sc, join with slip st to first sc. Fasten off.

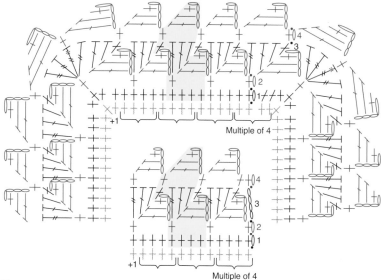

Reversible

Wide

Undulating

#107

Stitches & Notes

Picot-3: Ch 3, slip st in third chain from hook.

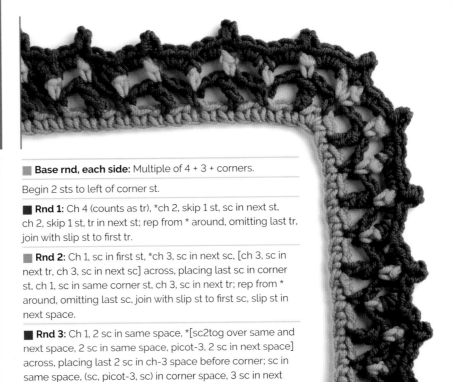

Base rnd, each side: Multiple of 4 + 3 + corners.

Begin 2 sts to left of corner st.

Rnd 1: Ch 4 (counts as tr), *ch 2, skip 1 st, sc in next st, ch 2, skip 1 st, tr in next st; rep from * around, omitting last tr, join with slip st to first tr.

Rnd 2: Ch 1, sc in first st, *ch 3, sc in next sc, [ch 3, sc in next tr, ch 3, sc in next sc] across, placing last sc in corner st, ch 1, sc in same corner st, ch 3, sc in next tr; rep from * around, omitting last sc, join with slip st to first sc, slip st in next space.

Rnd 3: Ch 1, 2 sc in same space, *[sc2tog over same and next space, 2 sc in same space, picot-3, 2 sc in next space] across, placing last 2 sc in ch-3 space before corner; sc in same space, (sc, picot-3, sc) in corner space, 3 sc in next space, picot-3, 2 sc in next space; rep from * around, omitting last 2 sc, join with slip st to first sc. Fasten off.

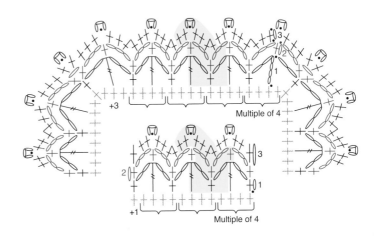

#108

Stitches & Notes

Base rnd, each side: Multiple of 2 + 1 + corners. Begin 2 sts to left of corner st.

Rnd 1: Ch 3 (counts as dc), *ch 1, skip 1 st, [dc in next st, ch 1, skip 1 st] to corner st, (dc, ch 3, dc) in corner st; rep from * around, ending join with sc to top of ch-3.

Rnd 2: Ch 1 loosely (does not count as a st), puff st in space formed by joining sc, *ch 1, [puff st in next space, ch 1] to corner space, (puff st, ch 3, puff st) in corner space; rep from * around, ending join with sc to first puff st.

Rnd 3: Ch 4 (counts as dc, ch 1), *[dc in next space, ch 1] to corner space, (dc, ch 3, dc) in corner space**, ch 1; rep from * around, ending last rep at **, join with sc to third ch of beg ch-4.

Rnd 4: Rep Rnd 2.

Rnd 5: Ch 4 (counts as dc, ch 1), *[dc in next space, ch 1] to space before corner space, (dc, ch 1) two times in next space, (dc, ch 3, dc) in corner space, ch 1, (dc, ch 1) two times in next space; rep from * around, ending last rep at **, dc in same space as beginning ch, join with sc to third ch of beg ch-4.

Rnd 6: Rep Rnd 2. Fasten off.

Puff st (puff stitch): (Yarnover, insert hook and pull up a loop) three times in st or space indicated, yarnover and pull through all 7 loops on hook. (For an illustration of puff stitch, see page 214.)

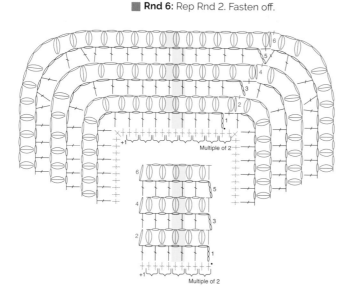

Multiple of 2

Multiple of 2

Reversible

Wide

Straight

Open/Lacy

Textured

#109

Stitches & Notes

Puff st (puff stitch):
(Yarnover, insert hook and pull up a loop) three times in st or space indicated, yarnover and pull through all 7 loops on hook. (For an illustration of puff stitch, see page 214.)

Reverse sc (reverse single crochet): Single crochet from left-to-right (right-to-left for lefties), as follows: with RS facing and keeping hook pointing to the left (to the right for lefties), insert hook into st indicated and pull up a loop, yarnover and pull through 2 loops. (For an illustration of reverse single crochet, see page 214.)

Base rnd, each side: Multiple of 2 + 1 + corners.

Begin 2 sts to left of corner st.

Rnd 1: Ch 3 (counts as dc), *ch 1, skip 1 st, [dc in next st, ch 1, skip 1 st] to corner st, (dc, ch 3, dc) in corner st; rep from * around, ending join with sc to top of ch-3.

Rnd 2: Ch 1 loosely (does not count as a st), puff st in space formed by joining sc, *ch 1, [puff st in next space, ch 1] to corner space, (puff st, ch 3, puff st) in corner space; rep from * around, ending join with sc to first puff st.

Rnd 3: Ch 4 (counts as dc, ch 1), *[dc in next space, ch 1] to corner space, (dc, ch 3, dc) in corner space**, ch 1; rep from * around, ending last rep at **, join with sc to third ch of beg ch-4.

Rnd 4: Ch 1, reverse sc in each dc and ch-1 space around, placing 3 reverse sc in each corner ch-3 space, join with slip st to first sc. Fasten off.

Reversible

Medium

Straight

Open/Lacy

Textured

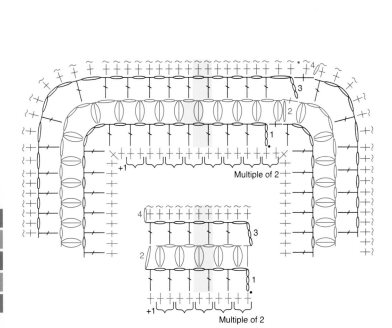

177

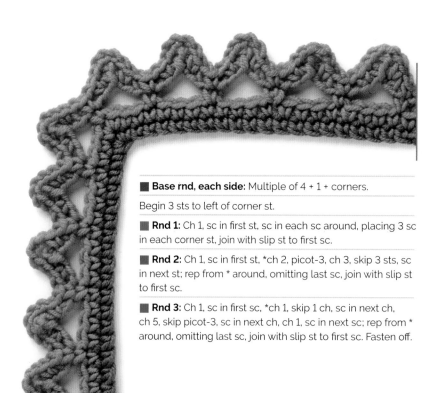

#110

Base rnd, each side: Multiple of 4 + 1 + corners.

Begin 3 sts to left of corner st.

■ **Rnd 1:** Ch 1, sc in first st, sc in each sc around, placing 3 sc in each corner st, join with slip st to first sc.

■ **Rnd 2:** Ch 1, sc in first st, *ch 2, picot-3, ch 3, skip 3 sts, sc in next st; rep from * around, omitting last sc, join with slip st to first sc.

■ **Rnd 3:** Ch 1, sc in first sc, *ch 1, skip 1 ch, sc in next ch, ch 5, skip picot-3, sc in next ch, ch 1, sc in next sc; rep from * around, omitting last sc, join with slip st to first sc. Fasten off.

Stitches & Notes

Picot-3: Ch 3, slip st in third chain from hook.

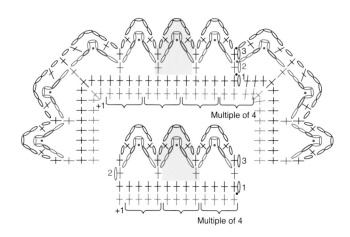

Reversible

Medium

Undulating

Open/Lacy

#111

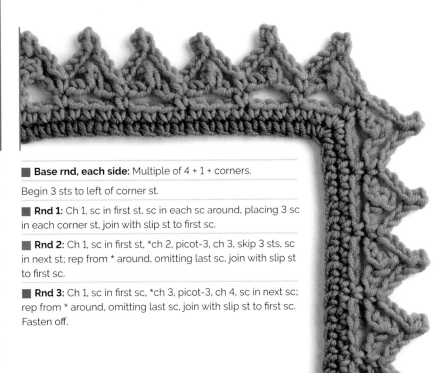

Stitches & Notes

Picot-3: Ch 3, slip st in third chain from hook.

Base rnd, each side: Multiple of 4 + 1 + corners.

Begin 3 sts to left of corner st.

Rnd 1: Ch 1, sc in first st, sc in each sc around, placing 3 sc in each corner st, join with slip st to first sc.

Rnd 2: Ch 1, sc in first st, *ch 2, picot-3, ch 3, skip 3 sts, sc in next st; rep from * around, omitting last sc, join with slip st to first sc.

Rnd 3: Ch 1, sc in first sc, *ch 3, picot-3, ch 4, sc in next sc; rep from * around, omitting last sc, join with slip st to first sc. Fasten off.

Reversible

Medium

Undulating

Open/Lacy

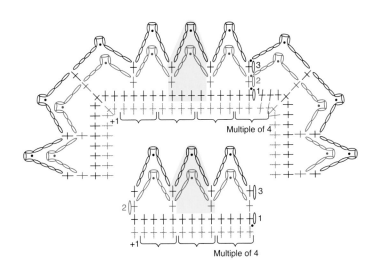

#112

■ **Base rnd, each side:** Multiple of 4 + 1 + corners.

Begin 2 sts to left of corner st.

■ **Rnd 1:** Ch 4 (counts as dc, and ch 1), *skip 1 st, [dc in next st, ch 1, skip 1 st] to corner st, (dc, ch 1) three times in corner st; rep from * around, skip 1 st, join with sc to third ch of ch-4.

■ **Rnd 2:** Ch 1, sc in space formed by joining sc, sc in each space and dc around, placing 3 sc in each corner dc, join with slip st to first sc.

■ **Rnd 3:** Ch 3, *skip 3 sts, [V-st in next st, skip 3 sts] to corner st, (V-st, ch 1, V-st) in corner st; rep from * around, ending dc in same st as beginning ch 3, ch 1 to complete beginning V-st, join with slip st to top of ch-3.

■ **Rnd 4:** Ch 1, sc in space between beginning V-st and next V-st, *ch 2, puff st in center of next V-st, ch 2**, [sc in next space between 2 V-sts, ch 2, puff st in center of next V-st, ch 2] to corner space, sc in ch-1 corner space, ch 2, puff st in center of next V-st, ch 2, sc in next space between 2 V-sts; rep from * around, ending last rep at **, join with slip st to first sc. Fasten off.

Puff st (puff stitch): (Yarnover, insert hook and pull up a loop) three times in st or space indicated, yarnover and pull through all 7 loops on hook. (For an illustration of puff stitch, see page 214.)

V-st (V-stitch): (Dc, ch 1, dc) in st or space indicated.

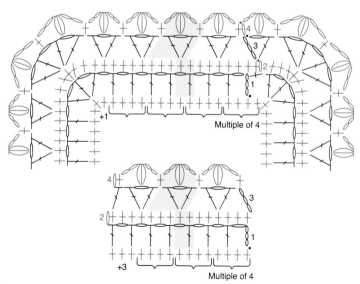

Multiple of 4 +

Multiple of 4

Reversible

Medium

Undulating

Textured

#113

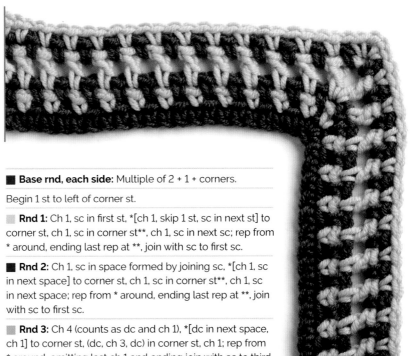

■ **Base rnd, each side:** Multiple of 2 + 1 + corners.

Begin 1 st to left of corner st.

▨ **Rnd 1:** Ch 1, sc in first st, *[ch 1, skip 1 st, sc in next st] to corner st, ch 1, sc in corner st**, ch 1, sc in next sc; rep from * around, ending last rep at **, join with sc to first sc.

■ **Rnd 2:** Ch 1, sc in space formed by joining sc, *[ch 1, sc in next space] to corner st, ch 1, sc in corner st**, ch 1, sc in next space; rep from * around, ending last rep at **, join with sc to first sc.

▨ **Rnd 3:** Ch 4 (counts as dc and ch 1), *[dc in next space, ch 1] to corner st, (dc, ch 3, dc) in corner st, ch 1; rep from * around, omitting last ch 1 and ending join with sc to third ch of ch-4.

■ **Rnd 4:** Ch 1, sc in space formed by joining sc, ch 1, *[sc in next space, ch 1] to corner space, (sc, ch 3, sc) in corner space, ch 1; rep from * around, omitting last ch 1 and ending join with sc to first sc.

▨ **Rnd 5:** Ch 1, sc in space formed by joining sc, ch 1, *[sc in next space, ch 1] to corner space, (sc, ch 2, sc) in corner space, ch 1; rep from * around, join with slip st to first sc. Fasten off.

Reversible

Medium

Straight

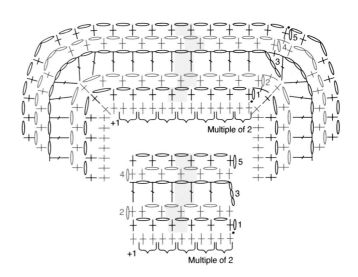

Base rnd, each side: Multiple of 3 + 1 + corners.

Begin 3 sts to left of corner st.

Rnd 1: Beg Flat X-st, *Flat X-st across to corner placing last leg of st in corner st, ch 1, (tr, ch 1) two times in corner st, Flat X-st placing first leg in same corner st; rep from * around, join with slip st in ch-1 space.

Rnd 2: Ch 2, 2-dc cluster in first ch-1 space, ch 2, (3-dc cluster, ch 2) in each ch-1 space around, join with slip st to top of first cluster, slip st in next space.

Note: Rnd 3 is worked into the ch-2 spaces throughout.

Rnd 3: Beg Flat X-st, *[Flat X-st over same and next space] to corner st, Flat Y-st in same space, Flat X-st over same and next space skipping corner cluster, Flat Y-st in same space; rep from * around, join with slip st to first st.

Rnd 4: Ch 1, 2 sc in each ch-1 space and 1 sc in space between each X-st and Y-st around, join with slip st to first sc. Fasten off.

Stitches & Notes

Beg Flat X-st (Beginning Flat X-stitch): *Worked over 3 sts and counts as 3 sts.* Ch 2, skip 1 st or space, dc in next st or space, ch 3, dc in space where ch-2 and dc meet.

Flat X-st (Flat X-stitch): *Worked over 3 sts and counts as 3 sts.* Yarnover two times, insert hook into next st or space indicated and pull up a loop, yarnover and pull through 2 loops, yarnover, skip 1 st, insert hook into next st or space, yarnover and pull up a loop, (yarnover and pull through 2 loops on hook) four times, ch 1, dc under 2 loops where 2 legs of this st join. (For an illustration of Flat X-stitch, see page 211.)

Flat Y-st (Flat Y-stitch): Tr, ch 1, dc in post of treble just made, inserting hook between the 2 horizontal loops of the post. (For an illustration of Flat Y-st, see page 212.)

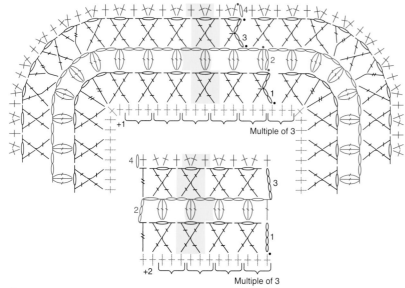

Reversible

Wide

Straight

Open/Lacy

#115

Stitches & Notes

3-dc Cluster (3 double crochet cluster): Yarnover, insert hook into st or space indicated and pull up a loop, yarnover and pull through 2 loops, (yarnover, insert hook into same st or space and pull up a loop, yarnover and pull through 2 loops) two times, yarnover and pull through all 4 loops on hook.

Sc2tog (single crochet 2 together): Insert hook into next st or space and pull up a loop, insert hook into next st or space indicated and pull up a loop, yarnover and pull through all 3 loops on hook.

■ **Base rnd, each side:** Multiple of 6 + 5 + corners. Begin 6 sts to left of corner st.

▥ **Rnd 1:** Ch 1, sc in first st, *ch 1, skip 2 sts, 5 dc in next st, ch 1, skip 2 sts**, [sc in next st, ch 1, skip 2 sts, 5 dc in next st, ch 1, skip 2 sts] to corner, (sc, ch 1, sc) in corner st; rep from * around, ending last rep at **, join with slip st to first sc.

▥ **Rnd 2:** Ch 1, sc in same st, *[ch 3, skip 2 dc, 3 dc in next dc, ch 3**, sc in next sc] to corner space, ch 2, 3 dc in corner space, ch 2, sc in next sc; rep from * around, ending last rep at **, join with slip st to first sc.

▥ **Rnd 3:** Ch 1, sc in same sc, *ch 5, skip 1 dc, 3-dc cluster in next dc**, ch 5, sc in next sc; rep from * around, ending last rep at **, ch 4, join with sc to first sc.

■ **Rnd 4:** Ch 1, sc2tog in space formed by joining sc and in next space, *4 sc in same space, (sc, ch 3, sc) in next cluster, 4 sc in next space**, sc2tog over same and next space; rep from * around, ending last rep at **, join with slip st to first sc. Fasten off.

Reversible

Wide

Undulating

Open/Lacy

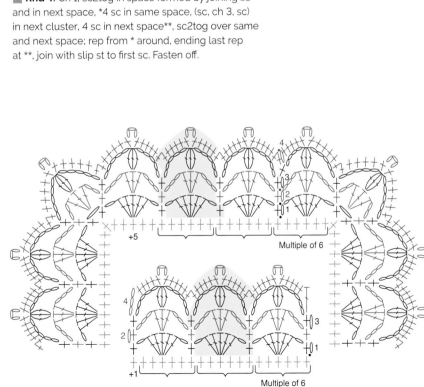

Stitches & Notes

Picot-3: Ch 3, slip st in third chain from hook.

■ **Base rnd, each side:** Multiple of 4 + 3 + corners.

Begin 1 st to left of corner st.

■ **Rnd 1:** Ch 1, sc in each st around, placing 3 sc in each corner st, join with slip st to first sc.

■ **Rnd 2:** Ch 4 (counts as dc and ch 1 here and throughout), skip 1 sc, *[dc in next sc, ch 1, skip 1 sc] to corner st, (dc, ch 3, dc) in corner st, ch 1, skip 1 sc; rep from * around, join with slip st to third ch of ch-4.

■ **Rnd 3:** Ch 4, *dc in next dc, [ch 1, dc in next dc] to corner space, ch 1, (dc, ch 3, dc) in corner space, ch 1; rep from * around, ending dc in next dc, ch 1, join with slip st to third ch of ch-4.

■ **Rnd 4:** Rep Rnd 3. Fasten off.

Note: Rnd 5 is worked in the skipped scs of Rnd 1 and in the ch-1 spaces of Rnd 2.

■ **Rnd 5:** Working into Rnd-1 sts, standing sc in any skipped sc just to left (right for lefties) of corner st, *ch 3, [working into Rnd-2 ch-spaces, skip 1 dc, sc in next ch-space, ch 3, skip 1 dc; working into Rnd-1 sts, skip 1 skipped sc, sc in next skipped sc, ch 3] to corner, sc in Rnd-2 corner space between two Rnd-3 dcs, ch 3, sc in next free Rnd-1 sc; rep from * around, omitting last sc, join with slip st to first sc. Fasten off.

Note: Rnd 6 is worked into the skipped ch-1 spaces of Rnd 2 and in ch-spaces of Rnd 3.

■ **Rnd 6:** Working into Rnd-2 spaces, standing sc in ch-1 space just above first st of Rnd 5, *[ch 3, working into Rnd-3 ch-spaces, sc in next ch-space, ch 3; working into Rnd-2 spaces, sc in next free ch-space] to space before Rnd-3 corner, ch 5, skip one Rnd-3 space, sc in Rnd-3 corner space between two Rnd-4 dcs, ch 5, skip one Rnd-3 space, sc in next Rnd-2 space; rep from * around, omitting last sc, join with slip st to first sc. Fasten off.

Medium

Undulating

Layered

Textured

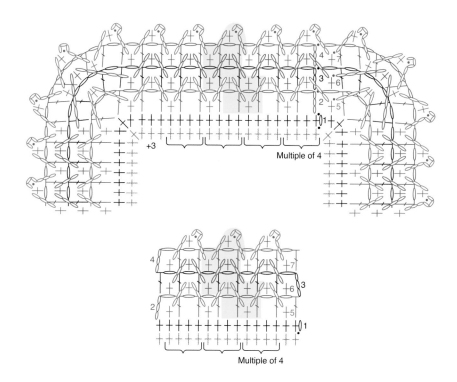

Note: Rnd 7 is worked into the skipped ch-spaces of Rnd 3 and in ch-spaces of Rnd 4. Refer to diagram to help understanding of stitch placement.

Rnd 7: Working into Rnd-3 spaces, standing sc in ch-1 space just above first st of Rnd 6, *[ch 3, picot-3; working into Rnd-4 ch-spaces, sc in next ch-space, ch 3; working into Rnd-3 spaces, sc in next free ch-space] to 2 spaces before Rnd-4 corner, ch 3, picot-3, sc in next Rnd-4 space, ch 3, sc in next Rnd-3 corner ch-3 space just to the right (left) of Rnd-4 dc, ch 3, picot-3; sc in Rnd-4 corner ch-3 space; ch 3, sc in same Rnd-3 corner space just to the left (right) of Rnd-4 dc; ch 3, picot-3, sc in next Rnd-4 space; rep from * around, ending ch 3, join with slip st to first sc. Fasten off.

Stitches & Notes

Each round motif is worked separately and joined to the existing border on the final round of the motif. When counting spaces in Rnd 1 of the border, count in a clockwise direction (counterclockwise for lefties).

Count ch-4 spaces in Rnd 2 of the motif in the ordinary counterclockwise (clockwise) manner. You may find it helpful to place a marker in the first ch-4 space of Rnd 2 to aid in counting. Refer to the diagram to help understand placement of joining sts.

■ **Base rnd, each side:** Multiple of 10 + 3 + corners.

Begin 2 sts to left of corner st.

■ **Rnd 1:** Ch 3 (counts as hdc and ch 1), skip 1 st, *[hdc in next st, ch 1, skip 1 st] to corner st, (hdc, ch 1, hdc) in corner st, ch 1, skip 1 st; rep from * around, join with slip st to second ch of ch-3. Fasten off.

Motif A

Ch 6, join with slip st to form a ring.

Rnd 1: Ch 4 (counts as dc and ch 1), dc in ring, (ch 1, dc) ten times in ring, join with sc to third ch of ch-4 — *12 dc and 12-ch-1 spaces.*

Rnd 2: Ch 1, sc in space formed by joining sc, (ch 4, sc in next space) eight times, ch 2, join motif to border with slip st in first space to right (left) of any corner space, ch 1, sc in next space of current motif, ch 2, slip st in next ch-1 space of border, ch 1, sc in next space of current motif, ch 4, sc in next space of current motif, ch 4, join with slip st to first sc. Fasten off.

Motif B

Work as for Motif A through Rnd 1 (above).

Rnd 2: Ch 1, sc in space formed by joining sc, (ch 4, sc in next space) five times, ch 2, slip st in first ch-4 space of previous motif, ch 1, sc in next space of current motif, ch 2, slip st in next ch-4 space of previous motif, ch 1, sc in next space of current motif, ch 4, sc in next space of current motif, ch 2, skip three ch-1 spaces in border, slip st in next space, ch 1, sc in next space of current motif, ch 2, slip st in next space of border, ch 1, sc in next space of current motif, ch 4, sc in next space of current motif, ch 4, join with slip st to first sc. Fasten off.

Repeat Motif B across, ending with last motif of side joined to last two spaces before corner space.

Wide

Motifs

Fringy

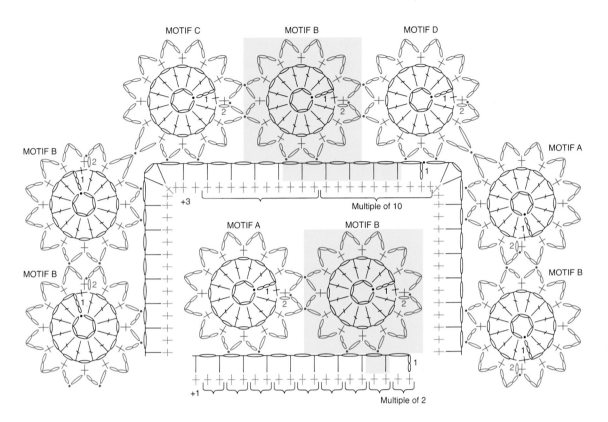

Motif C

Work as for Motif A through Rnd 1 (facing page).

Rnd 2: Ch 1, sc in space formed by joining sc, (ch 4, sc in next space) seven times, ch 2, slip st in eleventh ch-4 space of previous motif, ch 1, sc in next space of current motif, ch 2, skip corner space in border, slip st in next space, ch 1, sc in next space of current motif, ch 2, slip st in next space of border, ch 1, sc in next space of current motif, ch 4, sc in next space of current motif, ch 4, join with slip st to first sc. Fasten off.

Continue working Motif B across and Motif C at the beginning of each remaining side, ending with a final motif, as follows:

Motif D

Work as for Motif A through Rnd 1 (facing page).

Rnd 2: Ch 1, sc in space formed by joining sc, (ch 4, sc in next space) five times, ch 2, slip st in first ch-4 space of previous motif, ch 1, sc in next space of current motif, ch 2, slip st in next ch-4 space of previous motif, ch 1, sc in next space of current motif, ch 4, sc in next space of current motif, ch 2, skip three ch-1 spaces in border, slip st in next space, ch 1, sc in next space of current motif, ch 2, slip st in next space of border, ch 1, sc in next space of current motif, ch 2, slip st in eighth ch-4 space of Motif A, ch 1, sc in next space of current motif, ch 4, join with slip st to first sc. Fasten off.

Base rnd, each side: Multiple of 12 + 3 + corners.

Begin 4 sts to left of corner st.

Border Rnd 1: Ch 3 (counts as dc), 2 dc in same st, *ch 1, [skip 3 sts, 3 dc in next st, ch 1] to 3 sts before corner st, skip 3 sts, (3 dc, ch 2, 3 dc) in corner st, skip 3 sts, ch 1**, 3 dc in next st; rep from * around, ending last rep at **, join with slip st to top of ch-3. Fasten off.

First Granny Square

Ch 4, join with slip st to form a ring.

Rnd 1: Ch 3 (counts as dc), 2 dc in ring, ch 2, (3 dc, ch 2) three times in ring, join with slip st to top of ch-3. Fasten off.

Note: When counting spaces in Border Rnd 1, count in a clockwise direction (counterclockwise for lefties). Refer to the diagram (at right) to aid in understanding placement of joins.

Rnd 2 (Joining Rnd): (Standing dc, 2 dc, ch 2, 3 dc) in any ch-2 corner space, ch 1, (3 dc, ch 2, 3 dc, ch 1) in next space, 3 dc in next space, ch 1, slip st in any corner space of border Rnd 1, 3 dc in same space of granny square, slip st in next space of border rnd, 3 dc in next space of granny square, slip st in next space of border rnd, ch 1, 3 dc in same corner space of granny square, ch 1, join with slip st to first dc. Fasten off.

Subsequent Granny Squares

Work as for first granny square, placing first join of each square in next free space of border round. The last join of one side and the first join of the next side share a corner space in the Border Rnd 1.

Border Rnd 2: Standing sc in rightmost (leftmost) ch-1 space of first granny square on any side, *[sc in each dc and ch-1 space and 2 sc in each corner space around granny square to joined corner of granny**, sc2tog over granny corner space and adjacent ch-1 border space, sc in next 3 dc of border Rnd 1, sc2tog over next border space and granny corner space] to border corner, ending at **; sc2tog over next granny corner space and border corner space, sc2tog over same border corner space and next granny corner space; rep from * around, ending sc in each dc and ch-1 space to beginning, join with slip st to first sc. Fasten off.

Stitches & Notes

Use up your yarn scraps with this fun granny square border. Each granny square motif is worked separately and joined to the existing border on the second round of the motif. Mix and match colors at will!

Sc2tog (single crochet 2 together): Insert hook into next st or space and pull up a loop, insert hook into next st or space indicated and pull up a loop, yarnover and pull through all three loops on hook.

Reversible

Wide

Straight

Motifs

Fringy

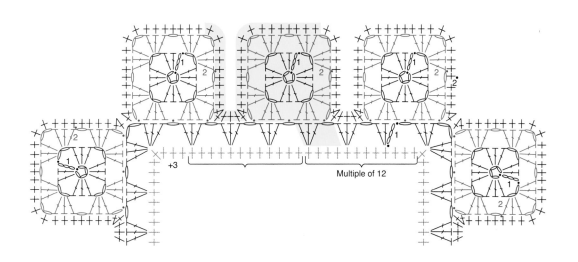

+3

Multiple of 12

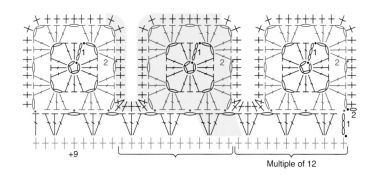

+9

Multiple of 12

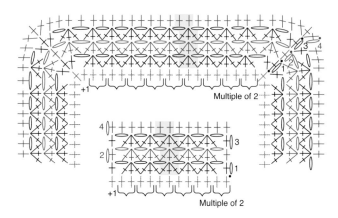

#119

Base rnd, each side: Multiple of 2 + 1 + corners.

Begin in corner st.

Rnd 1: Ch 1, 2 sc in first st, *ch 1, sc3tog over next 3 sts, ch 1, [sc3tog over same st as last sc and next 2 sts, ch 1] to corner st**, 3 sc in corner st; rep from * around, ending last rep at **, ch 1, sc in same st as first sc, join with slip st to first sc.

Note: Rnds 2–4 sts are worked into ch-1 spaces and tops of sc3togs in previous rnd.

Rnd 2: Ch 1, sc in same corner st, *ch 1, [sc3tog over same and next 2 sts, ch 1] across, placing last leg of last sc3tog in corner st, ch 1, sc in corner st; rep from * around, omitting last sc, join with slip st to first sc.

Rnd 3: Rep Rnd 1.

Rnd 4: Ch 1, 3 sc in same corner st, sc in each st and ch-1 space around, placing 3 sc in each corner st, join with slip st to first sc. Fasten off.

Stitches & Notes

Sc3tog (single crochet 3 together): (Insert hook into next st or space and pull up a loop) three times, yarnover and pull through all 3 loops on hook.

Multiple of 2

Multiple of 2

Medium

Straight

Textured

#120

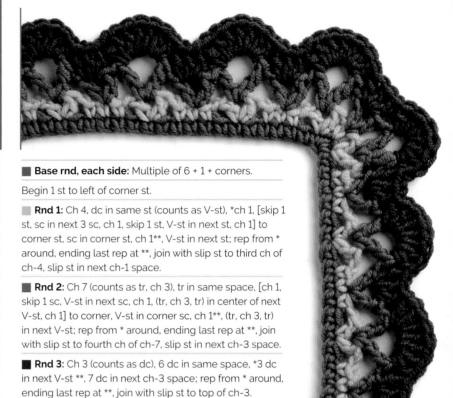

Stitches & Notes

The final round of this border creates a gentle ruffle — more like a three-dimensional edging than a true ruffle.

V-st (V-stitch): (Dc, ch 1, dc) in st or space indicated.

■ **Base rnd, each side:** Multiple of 6 + 1 + corners.

Begin 1 st to left of corner st.

■ **Rnd 1:** Ch 4, dc in same st (counts as V-st), *ch 1, [skip 1 st, sc in next 3 sc, ch 1, skip 1 st, V-st in next st, ch 1] to corner st, sc in corner st, ch 1**, V-st in next st; rep from * around, ending last rep at **, join with slip st to third ch of ch-4, slip st in next ch-1 space.

■ **Rnd 2:** Ch 7 (counts as tr, ch 3), tr in same space, [ch 1, skip 1 sc, V-st in next sc, ch 1, (tr, ch 3, tr) in center of next V-st, ch 1] to corner, V-st in corner sc, ch 1**, (tr, ch 3, tr) in next V-st; rep from * around, ending last rep at **, join with slip st to fourth ch of ch-7, slip st in next ch-3 space.

■ **Rnd 3:** Ch 3 (counts as dc), 6 dc in same space, *3 dc in next V-st **, 7 dc in next ch-3 space; rep from * around, ending last rep at **, join with slip st to top of ch-3. Fasten off.

Reversible

Wide

Undulating

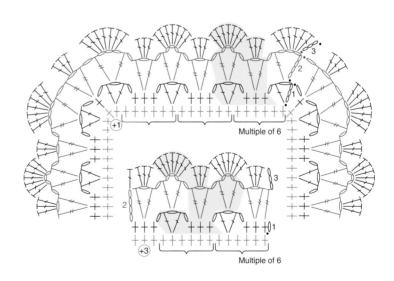

#121

Base rnd, each side: Multiple of 4 + 1 + corners.

Begin 3 sts to left of corner st.

Rnd 1: Ch 1, sc in first st, *[ch 4, skip 3 sts, sc in next st] to 2 sts before corner st, ch 4, skip 2 sts, sc in corner st, ch 4, skip 2 sts, sc in next st; rep from * around, omitting last sc, join with slip st to first sc.

Rnd 2: Ch 4, partial tr in same st, 2 partial tr in next sc, yarnover and pull through all 4 loops on hook to tr4tog, *[ch 4, tr4tog over same and next sc**] across, placing last 2 partial tr in corner st, ch 4, 2-tr cluster in same corner sc; rep from * around, ending last rep at **, ch 3, join with sc to first cluster.

Rnd 3: Ch 1, *sc2tog over same and next space, [sc, (ch 3, sc) three times] in same space; rep from * around, join with slip st to first sc. Fasten off.

Stitches & Notes

2-tr Cluster (2 treble crochet cluster): *(Yarnover) two times, insert hook into st or space indicated and pull up a loop, (yarnover and pull through 2 loops) two times; rep from * once, yarnover and pull through all 3 loops on hook.

Partial tr (partial treble crochet): (Yarnover) two times, insert hook into st or space indicated and pull up a loop, (yarnover and pull through 2 loops) two times.

Sc2tog (single crochet 2 together): Insert hook into next st or space and pull up a loop, insert hook into next st or space indicated and pull up a loop, yarnover and pull through all 3 loops on hook.

Tr4tog over same and next sc (treble crochet 4 together over same and next single crochet): 2 partial tr in same sc, 2 partial tr in next sc, yarnover and pull through all 5 loops on hook.

Reversible

Medium

Undulating

Open/Lacy

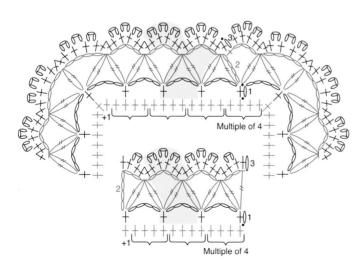

Multiple of 4

Multiple of 4

#122

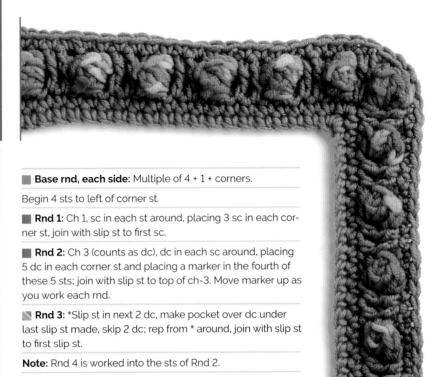

Stitches & Notes

FPdc (front post double crochet): Yarnover, insert hook from front to back to front around post of st indicated, yarnover and pull up a loop, (yarnover and pull through 2 loops) two times.

Pocket: (Sc, hdc, 3 dc) around post of dc indicated.

■ **Base rnd, each side:** Multiple of 4 + 1 + corners.

Begin 4 sts to left of corner st.

■ **Rnd 1:** Ch 1, sc in each st around, placing 3 sc in each corner st, join with slip st to first sc.

■ **Rnd 2:** Ch 3 (counts as dc), dc in each sc around, placing 5 dc in each corner st and placing a marker in the fourth of these 5 sts; join with slip st to top of ch-3. Move marker up as you work each rnd.

◥ **Rnd 3:** *Slip st in next 2 dc, make pocket over dc under last slip st made, skip 2 dc; rep from * around, join with slip st to first slip st.

Note: Rnd 4 is worked into the sts of Rnd 2.

■ **Rnd 4:** Ch 1, *FPdc in next 2 dc 2 rnds below, sc in next 2 dc behind pocket; rep from * around, join with slip st to first FPdc.

■ **Rnd 5:** Ch 1, sc in each st around, placing 3 sc in each marked st, join with slip st to first sc. Fasten off.

Medium

Straight

Textured

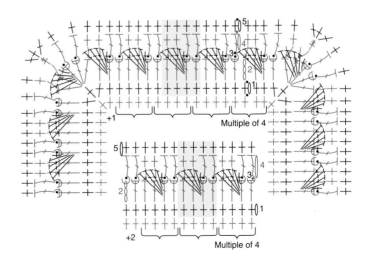

■ **Base rnd, each side:** Multiple of 4 + 3 + corners.

Begin 2 sts to left of corner st.

▮ **Rnd 1:** Ch 2 (counts as partial dc), skip 1 st, partial dc in next st, yarnover and pull through 2 loops on hook to complete beginning dc2tog, *[ch 1, dc2tog over 3 sts placing first leg of st in same st as previous st**] to corner placing last leg of dc2tog in corner st, ch 1, V-st in corner st; rep from * around, ending last rep at **, ch 1, join with slip st to top of first dc2tog.

Note: On Rnd 2, skip all ch-spaces around.

▮ **Rnd 2:** Ch 3 (counts as partial tr), partial tr in next st, yarnover and pull through 2 loops on hook to complete beginning tr2tog, *[ch 1, tr2tog over same and next st] to corner V-st placing last leg of tr2tog in first dc of corner V-st, ch 3, tr2tog over same and next dc, ch 3, tr2tog over same and next st; rep from * around, ending last repeat ch 1, tr2tog over same st and same st as beginning ch-3, ch 1, join with slip st to top of first st.

▮ **Rnd 3:** Ch 1, sc in same st, sc in each st and ch-1 space around, placing 3 sc in each ch-3 space and 2 sc in each corner st, join with slip st to first sc. Fasten off.

Note: Rnd 4 sts are worked around the posts of the tr2togs of Rnd 2 and into the ch-1 spaces of Rnd 1.

▮ **Rnd 4:** Beginning with slip knot on hook, modified crocodile st in any corner tr2tog, *slip st in next ch-1 space in Rnd 1, skip next tr2tog in Rnd 2, modified crocodile st in next tr2tog; rep from * around, ending last rep slip st in last ch-1 space in Rnd 1, join with slip st to first dc. Fasten off.

Stitches & Notes

Modified crocodile stitches add texture, without becoming as heavy as standard crocodile stitches.

Modified Crocodile St: (Dc, ch 1) two times around first post of tr2tog indicated, dc around same post, tight picot-3, (dc, ch 1) two times around next post of same tr2tog, dc around same post.

Tight picot-3: Ch 3, slip st in third ch from hook and in st at bottom of ch together. (For an illustration of tight picot-3, see page 214.)

Tr2tog (treble crochet 2 together): Yarnover two times, insert hook into stitch or space indicated and pull up a loop, (yarnover and pull through 2 loops) two times, yarnover two times, insert hook into next st or space indicated and pull up a loop, (yarnover and pull through 2 loops) two times, yarnover and pull through all 3 loops on hook.

V-st (V-stitch): (Dc, ch 1, dc) in st or space indicated.

Medium

Undulating

Layered

Textured

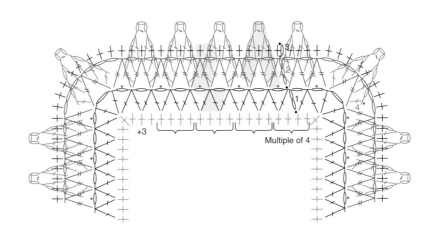

+3

Multiple of 4

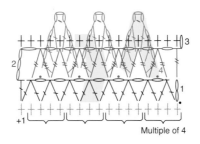

+1

Multiple of 4

#124

Base rnd, each side: Multiple of 4 + 3 + corners.

Begin 4 sts to left of corner st..

Rnd 1: Ch 3 (counts as dc here and throughout), dc in same st, *[make point, skip 3 sts**, 3 dc in next st] to 3 sts before corner st, skip 3 sts, (3 dc, make point, 3 dc) in corner st; rep from * around, ending last rep at **, dc in same st as first dc, join with slip st to top of ch-3.

Rnd 2: Ch 3, dc in same st, *[make point, skip (point, dc), 2 dc in next dc] to corner, ch 1, make point, ch 1, skip (point, dc), 2 dc in next dc, rep from * around, ending make point, skip (point, dc); join with slip st to top of ch-3.

Rnd 3: Ch 3, dc in next dc, *[make point, skip point, dc in next 2 dc] to corner, (make point) two times, skip point, dc in next 2 dc; rep from * around, ending make point, join with slip st to top of ch-3. Fasten off.

Stitches & Notes

Make point: Ch 4, 2 dc in fourth ch from hook.

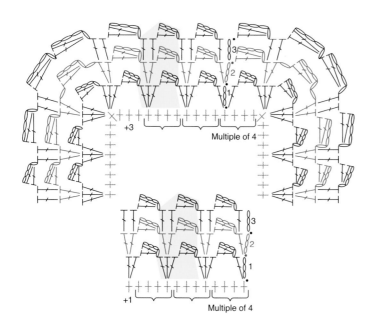

Wide

Undulating

Textured

#125

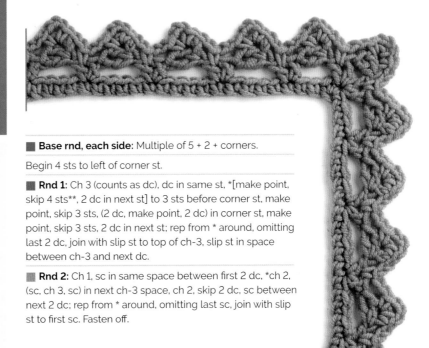

Stitches & Notes

Stop after Rnd 1 of #124 (facing page), and add a round of gentle chains and single crochets to create this simple edging.

Make point: Ch 4, 2 dc in fourth ch from hook.

Base rnd, each side: Multiple of 5 + 2 + corners.

Begin 4 sts to left of corner st.

Rnd 1: Ch 3 (counts as dc), dc in same st, *[make point, skip 4 sts**, 2 dc in next st] to 3 sts before corner st, make point, skip 3 sts, (2 dc, make point, 2 dc) in corner st, make point, skip 3 sts, 2 dc in next st; rep from * around, omitting last 2 dc, join with slip st to top of ch-3, slip st in space between ch-3 and next dc.

Rnd 2: Ch 1, sc in same space between first 2 dc, *ch 2, (sc, ch 3, sc) in next ch-3 space, ch 2, skip 2 dc, sc between next 2 dc; rep from * around, omitting last sc, join with slip st to first sc. Fasten off.

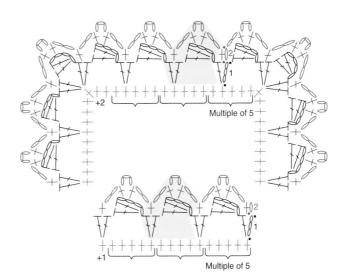

Reversible

Medium

Undulating

APPENDIX

Reading Crochet Patterns

Although crochet instructions may at first look like a foreign language, they can be interpreted once you understand how they are written and you become familiar with abbreviations in a new context. Crochet punctuation is explained below; crochet terms are defined and abbreviations are listed on page 202. Most special stitches used in a particular pattern are defined right next to the pattern where they are used; if you don't find them with the pattern, check the Glossary on page 210.

While I've attempted to make it clear where to put your hook for each stitch, you may find it helpful to refer to the stitch diagram to figure out the relationship of stitches to each other; diagrams help with that visualization. I encourage you to take time to examine the fabric you are creating and learn how each new stitch fits in with its neighbors. Crochet is so much easier when you learn to "read" your stitches in this way.

Crochet Punctuation

*ASTERISKS

Indicate a point of repeat. Here are some examples:

EXAMPLE | *Sc in next st, ch 1, skip 1 st; rep from * four more times.

Work a single crochet into every other stitch, with a chain-1 between each single crochet stitch. The last stitch worked is a ch-1, and you'll be skipping a stitch before you move on to the next instruction. Note that you work from the asterisk to the semicolon once, then you repeat it four more times, so that the group of stitches is worked a total of five times.

EXAMPLE | *Dc in next dc, ch 3; rep from * around, join with slip stitch.

Continue repeating the instructions between the asterisk and the semicolon until you reach the end of the round. Because the joining stitch comes directly after the word "around," you know that the entire series of actions (in this case: dc, ch 3) will be completed on the final repeat.

EXAMPLE | *Dc in next space, ch 5, dc in next dc**, tr in next dc; rep from * around, ending last rep at **, join with slip stitch to first dc.

Double asterisks may be used to indicate a final incomplete repeat. In this example, a series consisting of "dc, ch 5, dc, tr" is worked all the way around the edge. On the final repeat, only a portion of that series is worked ("dc, ch 5, dc") before joining.

EXAMPLE | *3 sc in ch-3 space, dc in next stitch, 3 sc in ch-3 space, sc in next 2 stitches; rep from * around, ending last rep sc in next stitch, join with slip stitch to first sc.

Sometimes a series of actions is repeated several times, but on the final repeat only the first portion of the series is worked. Here, you work the series of actions between the asterisk and the semicolon as many times as necessary to get almost all the way around the motif. The words "ending last repeat . . ." indicate that final repeat is not to be a complete one, so you end as follows: "3 sc in ch-3 space, dc in next stitch, 3 sc in ch-3 space, sc in next stitch, join with slip stitch to first sc." The final "missing" stitch is probably the stitch that started the round. It will be clear to you when you have the work in your hands.

( ) PARENTHESES

Set off stitches that are worked as a group; may be used for explanatory text.

EXAMPLE | (Sc, 3 dc, sc) in next dc

Put all 5 stitches into the next double crochet stitch.

EXAMPLE | (Dc in next dc, ch 2) five times, dc in next dc

Work a double crochet stitch into the next 6 double crochet stitches, putting 2 chain stitches between each double crochet stitch.

[ ] BRACKETS

Set off stitches that are worked as a group; sometimes used with parentheses when there are two groups of instructions nested within each other.

EXAMPLE | [Sc in next st, ch 4, skip 3 sts] to corner st

Follow the instructions within the brackets as many times as needed, all the way across the edge to the corner stitch. The last 3 skipped stitches will be the last 3 stitches before the corner stitch.

EXAMPLE | [(Dc3tog, ch 3) two times, dc3tog] in next ch-3 space

Follow the instructions between the brackets once, working all stitches into the same ch-3 space. To be specific: "in the next ch-3 space work (dc3tog, ch 3, dc3tog, ch 3, dc3tog)."

CROCHET SHORTHAND

Used occasionally when the meaning is quite clear.

EXAMPLE | Sc in each st around, placing 3 sc in each corner st

As you come to each stitch, work a single crochet into it, and as you come to each corner stitch, work 3 single crochet stitches into it.

Reading Charts

We use symbols in our daily life without even realizing it. Each time we see an icon on our phones or on public signs, we understand their meaning immediately without the use of words.

Symbol crochet takes this idea and applies it to crochet instructions. Each symbol is a graphic representation of a stitch and makes a certain kind of sense all by itself. Symbol charts offer a number of advantages over text alone. A quick look at a symbol chart tells you several things:

- The overall shape of the finished item
- The types of stitches used
- The relationship of stitches to each other
- The right side of the fabric

In this book, we have presented each chart in two or more colors to make it easy for you to track the rounds visually as you stitch. The yellow-shaded sections are the stitches that are repeated across the round to the corner (see page 24). If you find yourself distracted by viewing the entire chart, use a piece of paper (or a couple of pieces of paper) to mask the portion of the chart that you are not currently stitching. This makes it easier to focus only on the section immediately before you.

A few borders may be represented by layers of stitches worked on top of each other or into an unexpected spot. In those instances, you may find it easier to refer to the written text to help you decipher a chart. You may find charts easier to read if you use your scanner or copier to enlarge them. Don't worry if you see a symbol you don't recognize; you'll find a Stitch Key on page 202. You'll soon find that you understand new symbols without the help of a key.

Crochet Symbols

Chain stitch. When the symbol for a single chain stitch (⬮) is linked with other chain stitches, they represent several chains worked one after another.

linked chains

Slip stitch. A slip-stitch symbol is very short and tight, mimicking an actual slip stitch.

Single, half double, double, and treble crochet. Note how the symbols are related to one another, with each one gaining height (and crosshatches) as its corresponding stitch gets taller.

| tr | dc | hdc | sc | slip st |

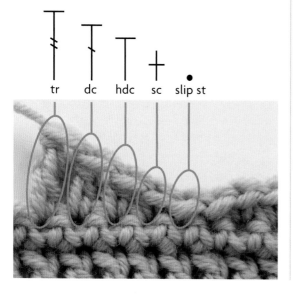

Stitch placement. Each chart indicates where to put each stitch. You may see several stitches made in the same base stitch (**A**), or several stitches made in the same base stitch and worked together (**B**).

A  3 sc in one stitch

B  4-dc cluster

Working into a chain. In most cases, a stitch shown on top of a chain is worked in the chain space created by that chain. If the stitch above the chain is meant to be worked into the chain itself rather than into the chain space, the chain will be bold.

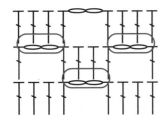

Working into a chain space

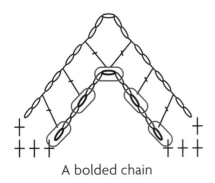

A bolded chain

Variations. While the symbols may be stretched or skewed to imitate the shape of the crocheted piece, they retain their unique recognizable markings to enable you to identify the stitch. For instance, a double crochet always has a bar at the top of the stem and a small crosshatch on the stem (**A**). In addition, different publishers may use slightly different symbols to represent the same thing. For instance, these symbols (**B**) are alternate versions of single crochet (sc).

A Double crochet symbols

B Single crochet symbols

STITCH KEY

◯ = chain (ch)

⬭ = worked in chain

◯ = surface chain

• = slip stitch (slip st)

+ = single crochet (sc)

T = half double crochet (hdc)

⊤ = double crochet (dc)

⧨ = treble crochet (tr)

⧩ = double treble crochet (dtr)

⧩ = triple treble crochet (trtr)

+⬭ = knot stitch (knot st)

⧨ = reverse single crochet (reverse sc)

⊥ = foundation single crochet (fsc)

⧩ = Linked treble crochet (Ltr)

⌡ = front post hdc (FPhdc)

⌡ = front post dc (FPdc)

⌡ = back post dc (BPdc)

⌡ = front post dtr (FPdtr)

⌡ = back post dtr (BPdtr)

Y Y = V-stitch (V-st)

Ж = X-stitch (X-st)

Ж = Beginning Flat X-stitch (Beg Flat X-st)

Ж = Flat X-stitch (Flat X-st)

⋀ = Corner Flat X-stitch (Corner Flat X-st)

Y = Y-stitch (Y-st)

⋏ = single crochet 2 together (sc2tog)

⋏⋏ = single crochet 3 together (sc3tog)

⋀ = front post hdc 2 together (FPhdc2tog)

⋀ = double crochet 2 together (dc2tog)

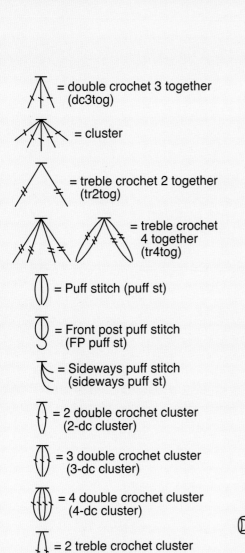

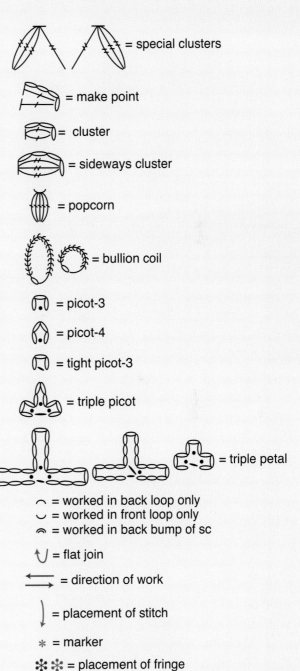

= double crochet 3 together (dc3tog)

= cluster

= treble crochet 2 together (tr2tog)

= treble crochet 4 together (tr4tog)

= Puff stitch (puff st)

= Front post puff stitch (FP puff st)

= Sideways puff stitch (sideways puff st)

= 2 double crochet cluster (2-dc cluster)

= 3 double crochet cluster (3-dc cluster)

= 4 double crochet cluster (4-dc cluster)

= 2 treble crochet cluster (2-tr cluster)

= 3 treble crochet cluster (3-tr cluster)

= 4 treble crochet cluster (4-tr cluster)

= triple cluster

= special clusters

= make point

= cluster

= sideways cluster

= popcorn

= bullion coil

= picot-3

= picot-4

= tight picot-3

= triple picot

= triple petal

⌒ = worked in back loop only

⌣ = worked in front loop only

⌢ = worked in back bump of sc

= flat join

= direction of work

= placement of stitch

∗ = marker

❈ ❈ = placement of fringe

▷ = join yarn/begin

➤ = fasten off

Table of Attributes

Use these descriptive tags to search for the just-right border for your project. Assigning attributes is not an exact science, however, so feel free to mark up these pages to classify the borders in any way that makes sense to you.

	Reversible	Wide	Medium	Narrow	Undulating	Straight	Motifs	Open/Lacy	Layered	Fringy	Textured
A				•		•					
B				•		•					
C				•	•						
D				•	•						
E				•	•						
F				•							
G				•							
H				•		•					
I				•		•					
J				•	•						
K				•	•						
L				•							
M				•		•		•			
N				•		•					
1	•	•			•			•		•	
2	•	•						•			
3	•		•			•					
4	•			•	•						
5	•			•		•		•			•
6	•			•	•				•		
7	•			•				•			
8	•				•						
9			•			•					•
10			•			•					
11	•		•								
12	•		•	•				•			
13	•		•							•	
14	•		•							•	•
15	•	•						•			
16			•	•	•				•		
17	•		•					•			
18	•			•	•						
19	•		•								
20			•								•
21				•							•
22	•	•				•					

	Reversible	Wide	Medium	Narrow	Undulating	Straight	Motifs	Open/Lacy	Layered	Fringy	Textured
23		•					•			•	•
24	•	•				•	•			•	
25	•			•	•						
26	•		•			•			•		
27	•	•					•				
28			•	•							•
29	•		•			•			•		
30	•	•				•			•		
31	•		•			•			•		
32	•		•			•			•		
33	•	•				•					
34	•					•					
35	•		•					•		•	
36			•		•	•					•
37	•	•							•	•	
38	•			•				•	•		
39	•			•	•		•			•	
40	•		•		•						
41	•	•				•					•
42	•		•				•		•		
43	•		•							•	
44				•	•						
45				•	•						•
46	•	•			•						
47	•		•								•
48	•	•						•	•		
49	•			•						•	
50	•			•					•		•
51		•									
52	•		•								
53	•		•						•		
54		•				•				•	•
55	•	•		•							
56		•									
57	•		•							•	
58		•		•				•		•	

	Reversible	Wide	Medium	Narrow	Undulating	Straight	Motifs	Open/Lacy	Layered	Fringy	Textured
59	●		●			●					
60	●		●		●						
61	●	●				●			●		●
62	●		●			●			●		●
63	●		●		●			●			
64	●	●				●			●		●
65	●	●			●						●
66	●		●		●			●			
67	●	●			●			●			
68	●		●		●						
69	●		●			●					
70	●		●			●		●			
71	●		●			●		●			
72	●	●			●			●			
73	●		●		●						
74	●			●	●						
75	●	●			●			●			
76	●		●			●					
77	●	●			●			●		●	
78	●	●			●		●	●			
79	●	●			●				●		
80	●		●					●			
81	●	●			●			●		●	
82	●	●			●		●				
83	●		●		●						
84			●		●				●		●
85	●	●			●			●			
86	●		●		●						
87	●		●		●						
88		●				●					●
89	●	●			●			●			
90	●		●		●			●			
91		●			●						●
92		●							●	●	
93	●						●				●
94	●		●			●			●		●

	Reversible	Wide	Medium	Narrow	Undulating	Straight	Motifs	Open/Lacy	Layered	Fringy	Textured
95	●		●		●				●		●
96	●			●				●			
97	●		●		●				●		●
98	●		●		●			●			
99	●	●			●			●			
100			●			●		●			●
101			●		●			●			
102				●		●		●	●		
103			●		●			●			
104	●		●			●		●			
105	●		●			●		●			
106	●	●			●						
107			●		●						
108	●	●				●					●
109	●		●		●						●
110			●					●			
111			●		●			●			
112	●		●			●					●
113	●		●			●					
114	●		●			●		●			
115	●		●					●			
116			●						●		●
117		●					●			●	
118		●				●	●			●	
119			●			●					●
120	●	●			●						
121	●		●					●			
122			●			●					
123			●			●			●		●
124		●			●						●
125	●		●		●						

Border Directory

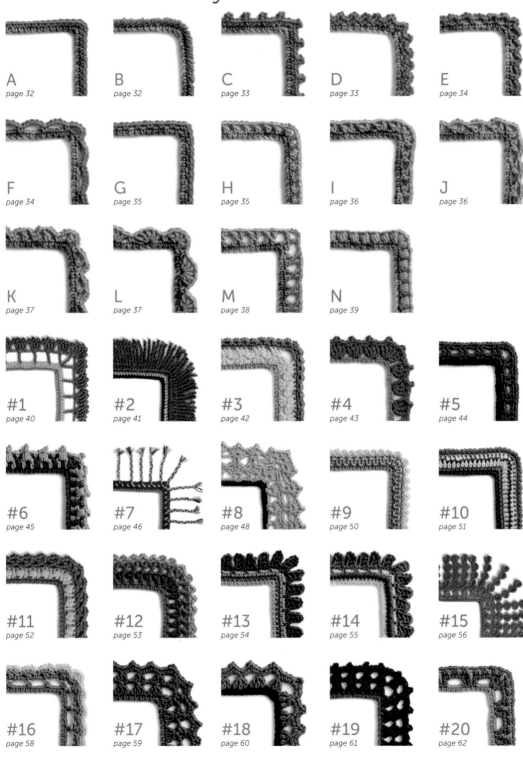

A
page 32

B
page 32

C
page 33

D
page 33

E
page 34

F
page 34

G
page 35

H
page 35

I
page 36

J
page 36

K
page 37

L
page 37

M
page 38

N
page 39

#1
page 40

#2
page 41

#3
page 42

#4
page 43

#5
page 44

#6
page 45

#7
page 46

#8
page 48

#9
page 50

#10
page 51

#11
page 52

#12
page 53

#13
page 54

#14
page 55

#15
page 56

#16
page 58

#17
page 59

#18
page 60

#19
page 61

#20
page 62

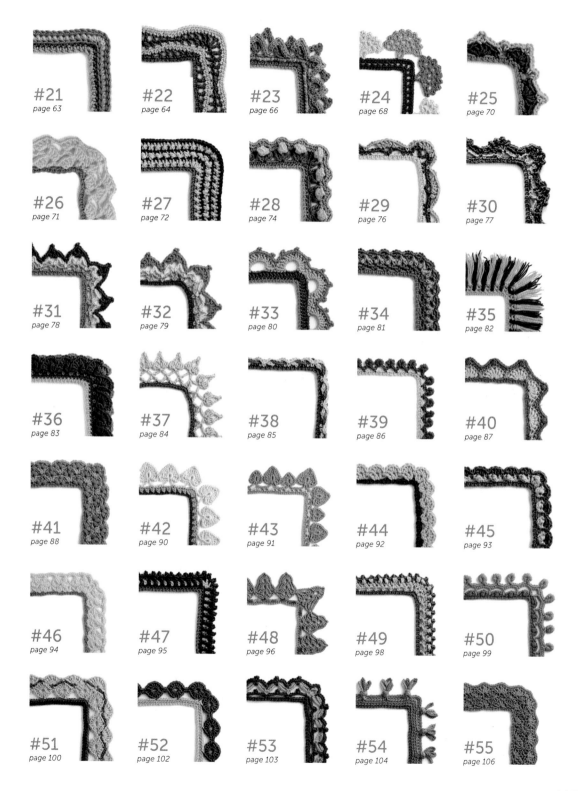

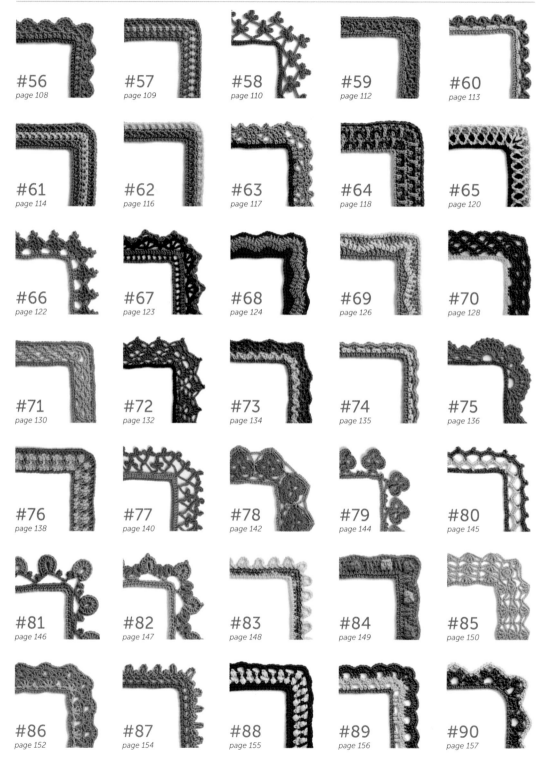

#56
page 108

#57
page 109

#58
page 110

#59
page 112

#60
page 113

#61
page 114

#62
page 116

#63
page 117

#64
page 118

#65
page 120

#66
page 122

#67
page 123

#68
page 124

#69
page 126

#70
page 128

#71
page 130

#72
page 132

#73
page 134

#74
page 135

#75
page 136

#76
page 138

#77
page 140

#78
page 142

#79
page 144

#80
page 145

#81
page 146

#82
page 147

#83
page 148

#84
page 149

#85
page 150

#86
page 152

#87
page 154

#88
page 155

#89
page 156

#90
page 157

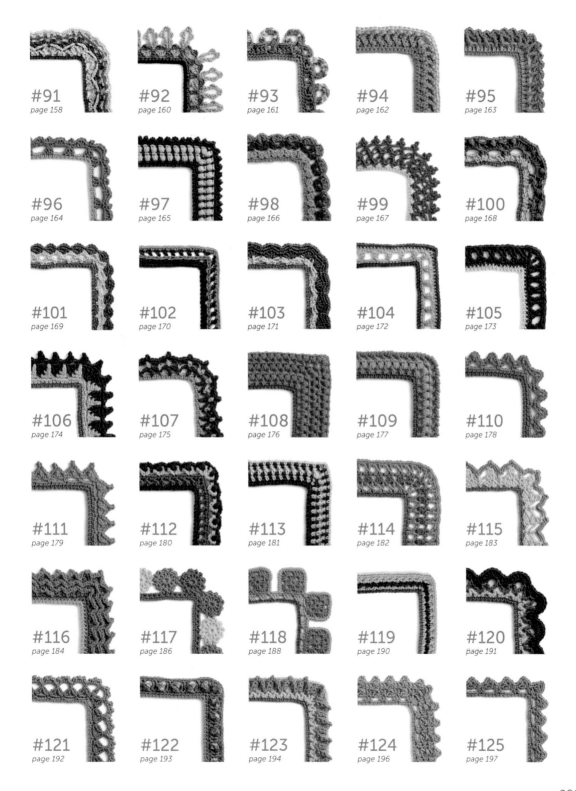

#91
page 158

#92
page 160

#93
page 161

#94
page 162

#95
page 163

#96
page 164

#97
page 165

#98
page 166

#99
page 167

#100
page 168

#101
page 169

#102
page 170

#103
page 171

#104
page 172

#105
page 173

#106
page 174

#107
page 175

#108
page 176

#109
page 177

#110
page 178

#111
page 179

#112
page 180

#113
page 181

#114
page 182

#115
page 183

#116
page 184

#117
page 186

#118
page 188

#119
page 190

#120
page 191

#121
page 192

#122
page 193

#123
page 194

#124
page 196

#125
page 197

Glossary

2-dc Cluster. Yarnover, insert hook into st or space indicated and pull up a loop, yarnover and pull through 2 loops, yarnover, insert hook into same st or space and pull up a loop, yarnover and pull through 2 loops, yarnover and pull through all 3 loops on hook.

2-tr Cluster. *Yarnover two times, insert hook into st or space indicated and pull up a loop, (yarnover and pull through 2 loops) two times; rep from * once, yarnover and pull through all 3 loops on hook.

3-dc Cluster. Yarnover, insert hook into st or space indicated and pull up a loop, yarnover and pull through 2 loops, (yarnover, insert hook into same st or space and pull up a loop, yarnover and pull through 2 loops) two times, yarnover and pull through all 4 loops on hook.

3-tr Cluster. Yarnover two times, insert hook into st or space indicated and pull up a loop, (yarnover and pull through 2 loops) two times, [yarnover two times, insert hook into same st or space and pull up a loop, (yarnover and pull through 2 loops) two times] two times, yarnover and pull through all 4 loops on hook.

4-dc Cluster. Yarnover, insert hook into st or space indicated and pull up a loop, yarnover and pull through 2 loops, (yarnover, insert hook into same st or space and pull up a loop, yarnover and pull through 2 loops) three times, yarnover and pull through all 5 loops on hook.

4-tr Cluster. Yarnover two times, insert hook into st or space indicated and pull up a loop, (yarnover and pull through 2 loops) two times, [yarnover two times, insert hook into same st or space and pull up a loop, (yarnover and pull through 2 loops) two times] three times, yarnover and pull through all 5 loops on hook.

Back bump, working in. When working into chain, insert hook into back bump of chain and work stitch as indicated (A). When working into single crochet, insert hook from top to bottom into the horizontal bar lying just behind the top V of the single crochet (B).

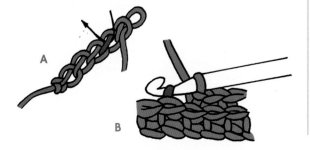

Beg Flat X-st (beginning Flat X-stitch). *Worked over 3 sts and counts as 3 sts.* Ch 2, skip 1 st or space, dc in next st or space, ch 3, dc in space where ch-2 and dc meet.

BLsc (back loop single crochet). Single crochet into the back loop only.

Blanket Stitch. Thread a yarn needle with thread or yarn. Secure your thread on the WS near the edge where you will add your crochet border and draw your yarn through to the right side, at the edge (A). *Insert the needle from RS to WS about ⅛" to ¼" (3 to 6 mm) from the edge and that same distance to the right of the starting point (B). Draw the needle through, looping the thread under the needle so that it covers the edge. Keep spaces from edge and between stitches consistent. Repeat from *. Take 3 stitches at each corner: one over the straight edge, one over the corner, and the last over the other straight edge (C).

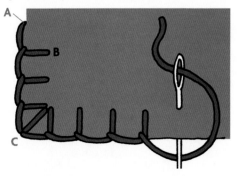

BPdc (back post double crochet). Yarnover, insert hook from back to front to back around post of st, yarnover and pull up a loop, (yarnover and pull through 2 loops on hook) two times.

BPdtr (back post double treble crochet). Yarnover three times, insert hook from back to front to back around post of st, yarnover and pull up a loop, (yarnover and pull through 2 loops on hook) four times.

Bullion Coil. Yarnover the number of times indicated, yarnover and pull through all loops on hook (A), ch 1 to close (B), pulling chain tightly to fold coil.

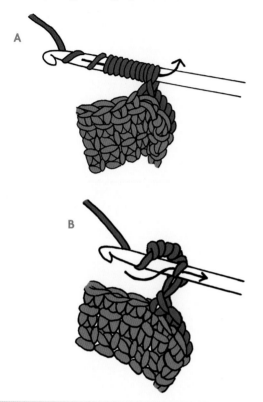

Ch (chain). Yarnover and pull through loop on hook.

Cluster. A group of stitches finished off together and usually counting as one stitch; refer to Stitches & Notes for specific definitions.

Crossed dcs (crossed double crochets). Skip 1 st, dc in next st, dc in skipped st working behind dc just made.

Dc (double crochet). Yarnover, insert hook into st or space indicated, yarnover and pull up a loop, (yarnover and pull through 2 loops on hook) two times.

Dc2tog (double crochet 2 together). (Yarnover, insert hook into next st or space indicated, yarnover and pull up a loop, yarnover and pull through 2 loops) two times, yarnover and pull through all 3 loops on hook.

Dc2tog over 3 sts. Yarnover, insert hook into next st indicated, yarnover and pull up a loop, yarnover and pull through 2 loops, skip 1 st, yarnover, insert hook into next st, yarnover and pull up a loop, yarnover and pull through 2 loops, yarnover and pull through all 3 loops on hook.

Dc2tog over 4 sts. Yarnover, insert hook into next st indicated, yarnover and pull up a loop, yarnover and pull through 2 loops, skip 2 sts, yarnover, insert hook into next st and pull up a loop, yarnover and pull through 2 loops, yarnover and pull through all 3 loops on hook.

Dc3tog (double crochet 3 together). (Yarnover, insert hook into next st or space indicated, yarnover and pull up a loop, yarnover and pull through 2 loops) three times, yarnover and pull through all 4 loops on hook.

Dtr (double treble crochet). (Yarnover) three times, insert hook into st or space indicated, yarnover and pull up a loop, (yarnover and pull through 2 loops) four times.

Embroidered Chain Stitch. Secure yarn on WS; insert threaded needle from WS to RS at point A and pull through. *Insert needle from RS to WS at point A and from WS to RS at point B, pull yarn through, looping the yarn under the needle; rep from *, keeping sts evenly spaced.

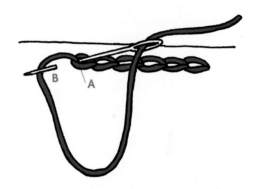

Flat X-st (Flat X-stitch). *Worked over 3 sts and counts as 3 sts.* (Yarnover) two times, insert hook into next st or space indicated and pull up a loop, yarnover and pull through 2 loops, yarnover, skip 1 st, insert hook into next st or space, yarnover and pull up a loop, (yarnover and pull through 2 loops) four times, ch 1, dc under 2 loops where two legs of this st join.

Flat Y-st (Flat Y-stitch). Tr, ch 1, dc in post of treble just made, inserting hook between the 2 horizontal loops of the post.

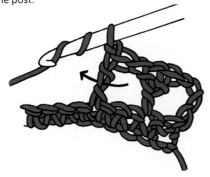

Fsc Arch (foundation single crochet arch). (Note that in the illustrations below one arch is already complete.) Insert hook into same st (A), yarnover and pull up a loop, yarnover and pull through 1 loop — 1 chain made. Yarnover and pull through 2 loops — 1 fsc made. *Insert hook under 2 loops of ch at base of previous fsc (B), yarnover and pull up a loop, yarnover and pull through 1 loop, yarnover and pull through 2 loops; rep from * four times, ch 3, fsc in ch at base of previous fsc (C), fsc 4.

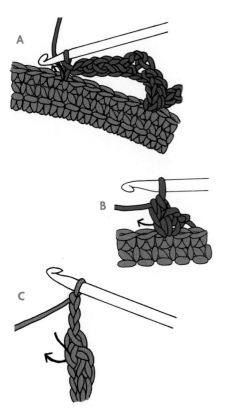

FPdc (front post double crochet). Yarnover, insert hook from front to back to front around post of st indicated, yarnover and pull up a loop, (yarnover and pull through 2 loops on hook) two times.

FPdtr (front post double treble crochet). Yarnover three times, insert hook from front to back to front around post of stitch indicated, yarnover and pull up a loop, (yarnover and pull through 2 loops on hook) four times.

FPhdc (front post half double crochet). Yarnover, insert hook from front to back to front around post of stitch indicated, yarnover and pull up a loop, yarnover and pull through 3 loops on hook.

FPhdc2tog over 3 sts (front post half double crochet 2 together over 3 stitches). Yarnover, insert hook from front to back to front around post of next st, yarnover and pull up a loop, skip 1 st, yarnover, insert hook from front to back to front around post of next st, yarnover and pull up a loop, yarnover and pull through 5 loops on hook.

Fringe, twisted. Pull up loop on hook to two-and-a-half times the desired length of fringe, rotate hook counterclockwise (or clockwise, but be consistent) 15 to 30 times (or more or less, depending on the length of your loop and the attributes of your yarn) (A), bring

hook back toward the border and allow loop to twist back upon itself, slip st in same st, slip st in next st (B). *Note:* To keep the loops a consistent size, cut a template out of cardboard and use it to help size the original long loop; twist that loop the same number of times for each fringe. You may find it easier to twist the loop with your forefinger: remove the hook from the loop and use your forefinger to make the twists, then replace the loop on the hook and continue.

Fringe, braided. Cut three strands, each approximately four times the desired finished length of fringe. Holding three strands together, insert hook through designated stitch or space, hook the strands and bring one end of the yarns through; bring ends of yarn together to fold fringe in half. Divide strands into three sets of two strands each (holding same colors together, if desired) and braid them; secure ends with an overhand knot. Trim ends. *Tip:* Wrap a piece of paper around the fringe, exactly the length you want it to be. Use the paper as a guide to trim the ends.

Hdc (half double crochet). Yarnover, insert hook into st or space indicated, yarnover and pull up a loop, yarnover and pull through all 3 loops on hook.

Knot st (knot stitch). Draw up loop on hook from ¼" to ¾"/6 mm–2 cm. Ch 1, insert hook into leftmost (rightmost for lefties) strand of the 3 vertical strands (A), yarnover and pull up a loop, yarnover and pull through 2 loops on hook to complete a single crochet (B).

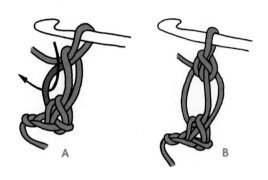

Partial dc (partial double crochet). Yarnover, insert hook into stitch or space indicated and pull up a loop, yarnover and pull through 2 loops.

Partial dtr (partial double treble crochet). Yarnover three times, insert hook into st or space indicated, yarnover and pull up a loop, (yarnover and pull through 2 loops) three times.

Partial sc (partial single crochet). Insert hook into st indicated and pull up a loop.

Partial tr (partial treble crochet). (Yarnover) two times, insert hook into st or space indicated and pull up a loop, (yarnover and pull through 2 loops) two times.

Picot-3. Ch 3, slip st in third chain from hook.

Picot-4. Ch 4, slip st in third chain from hook.

Popcorn. 5 dc in st or space indicated, drop loop from hook, insert hook from front to back through top of first of these 5 dc, place loop on hook, and pull through st, ch 1 to close.

Puff stitch (puff st). (Yarnover, insert hook, yarnover and pull up a loop) three times in st or space indicated, yarnover and pull through all 7 loops on hook.

Reverse sc (reverse single crochet). Single crochet from left-to-right (right-to-left for lefties), as follows: with RS facing and keeping hook pointing to the left (to the right for lefties), insert hook into st indicated and pull up a loop (A), yarnover and pull through 2 loops (B).

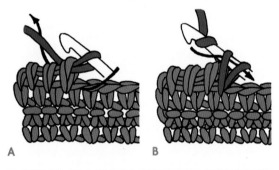

A   B

Sc (single crochet). Insert hook into st or space indicated, yarnover and pull up a loop, yarnover and pull through 2 loops on hook.

Sc2tog (single crochet 2 together). Insert hook into next st or space and pull up a loop, insert hook into next st or space indicated and pull up a loop, yarnover and pull through all 3 loops on hook.

Sc2tog over 3 sts (single crochet 2 together over 3 stitches). Insert hook into next st and pull up a loop, skip 1 st, insert hook into next st and pull up a loop, yarnover and pull through all 3 loops on hook.

Sc3tog (single crochet 3 together). (Insert hook into next st or space and pull up a loop) three times, yarnover and pull through all 3 loops on hook.

Shell. Stitches or stitch/chain combinations worked into one stitch or space; refer to Stitches & Notes for specific definitions.

Sideways Cluster. Ch 4, 2 partial tr in fourth ch from hook, yarnover and pull through all 3 loops on hook.

Sideways puff st (sideways puff stitch). (Yarnover, insert hook around post of dc just made, yarnover and pull up a loop) three times, yarnover and pull through all 7 loops on hook.

Standing stitch (slip st, sc, dc, tr, V-st, etc.). Beginning with slip knot on hook, work the designated st. (For more information, see page 25.)

Surface chain. Holding yarn on WS of fabric, insert hook from front to back into next st or around post of stitch as indicated, pull up a loop through fabric and through loop on hook.

Tight picot-3. Ch 3, slip st in third ch from hook and in st at bottom of ch together.

Triple treble crochet (trtr). Yarnover four times, insert hook into st or space indicated, yarnover and pull up a loop, (yarnover and pull through 2 loops) five times.

Tr2tog (treble crochet 2 together). Partial tr in next 2 sts, yarnover and pull through all 3 loops on hook.

Tr4tog over 5 sts. Partial tr in next 2 sts, skip 1 st, partial tr in next 2 sts, yarnover and pull through all 5 loops on hook.

Triple Cluster. Ch 4, 2 partial tr in fourth ch from hook, 3 partial tr in same base-rnd st, skip 3 sts, 3 partial tr in next st, yarnover and pull through all 9 loops on hook, ch 1.

Triple Petal. (Ch 7, slip st in seventh ch from hook) three times, slip st in same st as first slip st.

Triple picot. Picot-3, picot-3 (or -4), picot-3, slip st in same ch as first picot.

V-st (V-stitch). (Dc, ch 2, dc) or (dc, ch 1, dc) in st or space indicated; refer to Stitches & Notes for specific definitions.

X-st (X-stitch). *Worked over 2 sts and counts as 2 sts.* Skip 1 st, dc in next st, working over dc just made, dc in last skipped st.

INDEX

Page numbers in *italic* represent photos and illustrations.

Acknowledgments

Several intrepid crocheters volunteered to help test the early stages of these borders to ensure that they really do lie flat around corners. Thanks to Ruth Allen, Sara Doherty, Ronni Fogle, Phyllis Glaz, Susan Heyn, Susan Leibowitz, Kristy Lucas, Robin Paone, Angie Nash, Valarie Rogers, Andrea Rudkin, Jenny Snedeker, and Claudia Wittmann. In particular, Andrea and Phyllis logged uncountable hours on the project; without their help I would have been lost.

Barry Klein at Trendsetter Yarns cheerfully provided the beautiful Lana Grossa Cool Wool yarn for the samples. Universal Yarn provided Universe yarn for the necklace on page 2. Karen Manthey is the Mistress of Crochet Diagrams and Instructions; any errors you find are my fault. Michal Lumsden has much better-looking hands than mine, for which we are all thankful. Photographers John Polak and Mars Vilaubi make my work look its best, and the Storey staff of Jessica Armstrong, Liseann Karandisecky, and Ilona Sherratt, as well as freelancers Valerie Shrader and Kathy Brock, continue to produce books I'm proud of, all while being truly nice people to work with.

Love and thanks to Bill Eckman, whose mad skills at placing hang tags on hundreds of tiny crocheted pieces serves him well.

Finally, thanks to the unflappable Gwen Steege, who called me out of the blue in 2004 and convinced me I could write a crochet book. *The Crochet Answer Book* was the result of that call, and apparently she was correct: I can write a crochet book. Thank you, Gwen, for your friendship and for all you have done to make me look good for more than a decade.

ALSO BY EDIE ECKMAN

Whether you want lacy or simple, elegant or bold, search no further for the perfect finishing touch for your handmade project! This colorful collection of 150 crochet borders includes clear instructions, charts, and color photos.

Stretch yourself with these 144 unique designs for circles, stars, triangles, hexagons, and more. Experiment with sizes and color combinations, then work the motifs into wearables, accessories, and home goods with the help of 60 clever project ideas.

This dazzling array of 101 innovative motif designs includes easy-to-follow directions on how to combine multiples of a motif to create new patterns and stunning fabrics.

Unsnarl any crocheting conundrum with this essential reference. Its accessible question-and-answer format highlights unusual techniques such as Tunisian crochet and seemingly complex stitch patterns like broomstick lace, with detailed illustrations for both right-handed and left-handed crocheters.

Keep Crocheting with More Books from Storey

edited by Judith Durant & Edie Eckman

Turn your orphan skeins into charming treasures with these 101 designs for bags, scarves, gloves, toys, hats, and more. Crocheters of every skill level will find the perfect gift or personal indulgence to stitch with a single skein.

edited by Judith Durant & Edie Eckman

Show the little ones in your life lots of love with crocheted gifts! Each of these 101 adorable projects — including blankets, booties, and beanies — use just one skein of yarn.

by Dora Ohrenstein

Introducing a surprising range of stitch patterns and shapes achievable with a crochet hook, this detailed guide features 75 stitch-along swatches and a wide variety of ways they can be used to create elegant wearables and accessories.

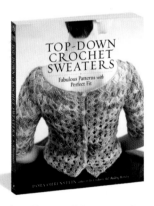

by Dora Ohrenstein

Adapt this favorite knitting technique to make sure your crocheted sweaters look great and drape beautifully. These 14 patterns flatter bodies of all shapes and sizes, and instructions on how and why to adjust the patterns ensure an exquisite customized fit.